Life
CEO

Take charge and start
doing your Life's Work
not your busy work

DR. BEN CARVOSSO

Published by Dr. Ben Carvosso 2018

Disclaimer
Every effort has been made to ensure that this book is free from error or omissions. Information provided is of general nature only and should not be considered legal or financial advice. The intent is to offer a variety of information to the reader. However, the author, publisher, editor or their agents or representatives shall not accept responsibility for any loss or inconvenience caused to a person or organisation relying on this information.

Book cover design and formatting services by BookCoverCafe.com

www.LifeCEO.com

ISBN:
978-0-6482167-0-4 (pbk)
978-0-6482167-1-1 (e-bk)

*Dedicated to my champion, lover and best
friend, my chairman of the board:
my wife, **Michelle***

*In memory of **Mum**, my coach:
"Sweet dreams."*

Contents

Foreword

Much of what matters in life is parked in our rush to join the traffic jam of an increasingly busy existence. And we a pay a heavy personal price for neglecting many things that provide joy and enable a richer life.

Materialism, status and corporate endeavour sap your energy and provide little spiritual or emotional nourishment if pursued with singularity. I fell foul to this ailment and wanted to bring greater meaning and contentment in my life. As a 'successful' corporate CEO I felt that I was in charge of my personal journey but indeed this was but an illusion and stemmed from bravado rather than reality. I realised that I had to take myself away from my comfortable corporate mindset and expose myself to different ways of seeing and doing.

I reached out to Ben and he provided me with a safe and powerful way of recalibrating my personal purpose and approach to life. I thank him. This book gives the reader a wonderful insight and sense of approaching our personal lives in a way that starts with what matters and builds a program that guides and challenges you in your life journey. I commend it to you.

Andrew Grant – Company Chairman, CEO, Entrepreneur and now a human with a much deeper sense of day to day purpose.

Preface

I was on a tropical island in Fiji, the sun was setting, and I was finishing my afternoon Piña colada as I walked along the beach with my wife, Michelle. We'd had two weeks relaxing with the kids, my team back in Australia was looking after the practice, and everything in life was just great.

For two weeks I had been admiring a magnificent palm tree on the beach. It stretched horizontally across the sand and across the water at high tide, before curving up towards the sky and ending with an impressive clump of fronds—and coconuts, ready for the taking.

On this particular night the tree had a beautiful sunset as a backdrop. I turned to Michelle and told her what a great photo I thought it would make if I sat on the trunk above the water. She didn't agree. She thought it was a stupid and dangerous idea, and that I shouldn't spoil our last night by breaking my neck. So of course I handed her the camera and started to climb.

Now, palm trees are incredibly flexible. The trunk is designed like a bundle of cables, which gives it strength and flexibility. This I found out as my eighty kilograms got further up the trunk and it started to sway from side to side. I looked down at the shallow water and sand below, trying to remember exactly how high the trunk was from the surface of the water. I found out soon enough, when I fell in feet first.

I vividly remember the splash as I hit the water, and the solid whack that jolted right through my body as my feet hit what had looked like sand, but was in fact a giant flat rock covered by a thin layer of sand. I lay in the water, both feet throbbing with intense pain. Over the next few minutes, with Michelle yelling from the shore, "I told you not to", the right foot started to feel better while the left got worse.

So began my journey to getting stuck.

I was taken to the hospital, where an x-ray revealed that I'd smashed the heel of my left foot beyond recognition. After my foot was put in a makeshift plaster cast, we were on a plane home. Within three days I had had surgery to reconstruct the foot, and was sent home to let my body do its repair work.

At this point in my journey to getting stuck, I was all good. I figured I would make the most of the next three months. I would build a model plane (I'd always wanted the time to do that), read some books, and stroll around the house like Hugh Heffner in my dressing gown. It was going to be great.

And so it was for the first eight weeks.

Then I started to get bored. I told myself I just had to hang in there for four more weeks, and I would be back to getting on with stuff.

The day came to have the cast removed, and it did not go to plan. The foot was seriously injured. It looked like something out of *The Walking Dead*. Worse than that, due to the foot being immobilized so the bones could heal, the joints had completely seized up. My expectations of getting back to work were not about to be met. It would be another three months before I finally set foot (feet) in practice.

The afternoon after the cast was removed, Michelle and I drove to Wangaratta to stay with some friends for a long weekend. I have another vivid memory: I'm sitting on the edge of the bath, washing away three months of dead flesh, and crying.

Over the next forty-eight hours, I felt myself sinking into a dark place. On the trip home, I told Michelle not to go home. "Let's just keep driving," I said. This was a defining moment for me.

Over the next three months, I merely went through the motions of living. Every day I felt empty and trapped, and kept asking myself why this had happened to me. I became seriously stuck.

Now, I get that a busted-up foot is nothing compared to the injuries and trauma that others have faced, but as you'll find out in the following chapters, it's not what happens to you but the meaning you give to those events that counts.

I felt like I had lost direction. I started questioning my purpose, what I was doing, where I was going. I lost my confidence; my mojo had gone, and I found myself performing the magic trick of self-sabotage. Crucially, I had lost my willpower. I struggled to focus and follow through on my intentions—not that I had many.

I felt uncertain about my life and where I was going, so I kept trying to create more certainty to make my life safer and more predictable. I was retreating from a growth-thinking mindset to a small and rapidly shrinking mindset. I was well and truly stuck.

Have you ever felt like that? Have you ever experienced any of these feelings:

- Anger
- Exhaustion
- Frustration
- Tiredness
- Lack of fulfillment
- Boredom

- Misunderstood
- Busyness
- Overwhelm
- Overthinking things
- Depression

Have you ever found yourself doing any of these things:

- Procrastinating
- Thinking negative thoughts
- Becoming stressed at work
- Overthinking
- Blaming others
- Making excuses
- Aiming for perfection
- Being distracted

Do you ever compensate by doing any of these things:

- Spending too much time on social media
- Eating
- Drinking
- Surfing the Internet
- Watching YouTube videos
- Watching too much TV
- Taking drugs
- Shopping

Do you ever find yourself uttering these sentences:

- What about me?
- I'm not as good as them.
- I have too much to do.
- There's not enough time in the day.
- I can't be bothered.
- What's next?

These are all symptoms associated with becoming disconnected from what is essential in your life: your purpose. They leave you unable to put any plans of intentions in place that have real value and meaning to you. Over time you stop behaving in a way that produces results. Your character changes. What you end up doing is a whole pile of nothing.

" If you do nothing you get nothing. "
AUNG SAN SUU KYI

You might have the occasional crack at something, but because you're not inspired by it, you have no clear plan. Your sense of self-worth and confidence is no longer there, so you fail to take consistent action, potent action, or any action at all. You have set yourself up for failure and unfulfillment, which perpetuates the feeling of being stuck.

Now here is the weird thing. Everyone gets stuck at times. Everyone experiences the feelings, behaviors and habits from the lists above. *Everyone.*

Successful people, those who live their lives with happiness, joy and fulfillment, and leave a legacy, experience *eudaimonia* (a Greek word that translates as "human flourishing"). Unsuccessful people, those who live in a constant state of blame, excuses, sadness, and lack of fulfillment leave little or no legacy.

There is a stark difference between the two. The characteristics of successful people:

- They get stuck.
- They recognize that they are stuck.
- They seek guidance, support, mentorship, knowledge, and strategies for change.
- They make changes to their behavior.
- They embrace the discomfort of change and take action.
- They get unstuck.

This book is designed to help you if you are stuck and recognize that you are. The fact that you bought this book and have read this far probably indicates that you are, or have been, stuck. Or you realize that if you're pursuing success in life, you will have moments of getting stuck again.

In these pages, I explain the six phases I went through before I got myself out of that terrible situation all those years ago, a process that I have been obsessing about ever since.

For months I was stuck. I lived in zombieland, like a walker from *The Walking Dead* (not dead, but not alive either). Then one morning as I drove to the office, I took a good hard look at a powerpole. I started to calculate how fast I would need to go to move from not alive to dead. It was only a few seconds of thought, but it was enough to jolt me into the realization that, mentally, I was in trouble. This was phase two, the point when I fully recognized that I was stuck.

Phase three was to immediately start to seek help from people who could give me guidance and mentorship. They helped me to realize that my challenges were my choice and of my doing, and that I could make it all go away. I could get unstuck. They helped me see that there was a cause behind my situation, and that cause was me. This was step three.

At about this same time, a good friend tapped me on the shoulder and asked if I would like to create a new business with him. I instantly connected with a deep value that I had lost: the value of creation. This was phase four.

I was starting to change my behavior. With the addition of massive action, I was beginning to move out of being stuck. This was phase five.

Within four weeks of my moment with the pole, I had reached phase six. I was unstuck and back in the land of the living.

My story has a happy ending, but I know that many find themselves stuck, not just for six months like I was, but for years, even decades. One of the most common groups of people to find themselves stuck are the midlifers.

I believe we are at a time in the world when, more than ever, we need our political leaders, our business leaders, and our parents to be great. To be the best examples for the next generation so they can speak their truth and fulfill their dreams.

I wonder if there was a reframe on the words "midlife" and "crisis" to...

Seeing midlife as nothing more than the middle of your life (thirty-seven to fifty-five years of age in Western cultures)

And...

Seeing *crisis* as a "turning point," "a time of decisive change" with a return to the origin of the word. The word comes from the Greek *krisis*, meaning to decide, separate, judge, sieve out.

Do you have to be in midlife to have a crisis? I don't think so. A crisis happens whenever you fail to make decisions and sieve out what matters most from the noise and busywork. To sieve out the unresourceful, the not important, the should and the shouldn't, and pursue with verve a life with fun, freedom, and fulfillment. To have a eudemonic life, to experience what it's like to flourish as a human.

I believe that's what makes this book unique. It's a guide, not just to merely surviving but also to *flourishing* in life. It's a book about getting unstuck and making your life count. It's for you if your "river of why" has taken a shift in direction, and you're struggling to embrace the change. Nervous, excited, scared, overwhelmed or stuck, this book will show you how to get clear on what you really want. It will show you how to develop the framework, character, and momentum to achieve it.

Your Life CEO is about prioritizing your life so you can complete your life's work rather than just do your busywork.

"The unexamined life is not worth living."
SOCRATES

Introduction

> *❝ I find it fascinating that most people plan their vacations with better care than they plan their lives. Perhaps that is because escape is easier than change. ❞*
>
> **JIM ROHN**

In my high-performance coaching practice, I encounter CEOs of small and large businesses, and aspiring CEOs (business owners and entrepreneurs) on a daily basis. In their day-to-day lives, they have confidence, give commands, and seem to have all the answers. But there is something that makes the most confident of CEOs go weak at the knees. Every month, or every quarter, they have to face the board of directors, who want to know:

- Have you made this month count?
- Is the company on track? Is it making a profit, and does the future look good?
- What are the key metrics of the business, including profit and loss, cash flow, and balance sheet?
- What is the current direction of the organization, and what is the future direction?
- What is the share-price value, and how is this likely to be affected in the coming months and years?

Sometimes the CEO will have good news for the board, and sometimes they will have bad news. Either way, what goes on in these board meetings can have serious consequences for all concerned. A huge amount of planning effort in those meetings goes into ensuring the company is working at its full potential, kicking big goals, and delivering value to shareholders.

Let me pose a simple but obvious question. What is more important, a person's share portfolio or a person's life? I hope your answer was the latter.

A CEO who expends a great deal of time and effort into making sure the company is running at full steam may well have a shambolic personal life. Who they are at home is often very different to who they are in the office. Why is that? How can someone be full of confidence, goal oriented, and focused at work and yet experience broken relationships, poor health, and discontent in their personal life?

This book provides the answer to that question and, more importantly, the solution.

Regardless of whether you're a business owner, employee, or stay-at-home parent, you are your own life CEO. And whether you realize it or not, you're accountable to your own internal board of directors. Perhaps your board has been asleep at the wheel and has given you the jolt you need to get back on track. That's okay; know that you're not alone. But you can get back on track, and this book provides the blueprint for doing exactly that.

Maybe your life has felt a little out of control. Maybe you're feeling stuck, in whatever form that means for you personally. The good news is that you've come to the right place. You're about to embark on a journey that's all about empowering you to take back control, and start being the life CEO you were destined to be.

Being the CEO of your life is about realizing that you are the decision maker. You are the boss, and it's all your responsibility. No, don't close the book and stop reading. It's going to be okay. I cover all of this in detail in the following pages.

Just for now, entertain the idea that you are in charge of your life, and that at some level (and you get to decide the level) you are responsible for it.

By moving away from your busywork and doing your life's work instead, you need to decide if you're going to take charge and be the chief of your life. Like a company CEO, there are some key responsibilities to being your life CEO:

1. Decide on your purpose, and the vision for your life.
2. Set some intentions, and create a plan and strategy for how to make those happen.
3. Form a personal ethos or culture that's in alignment with your purpose and values; how you're going to behave.
4. Take action, and allocate time, energy, resources and even money to bring animation to your plans.
5. Give yourself constructive feedback. Celebrate your wins and observe your missteps, and, importantly, learn from all of them. Create profit in your life, and experience fulfillment.

Do these all sound like the roles and responsibilities of a company CEO? That's because they are similar. Creating a successful life is no different from the strategies a CEO uses to build a successful company.

Throughout the book, you'll see these words and this symbol, which lets you know it's time to get out your journal and write.

📓 JOURNAL TIME

I know what you're thinking. I really do. Do I have to do the activity? Can't I just read the book? Yes, you can just read the book, and maybe apply some of the strategies. But as you'll find out in the chapter on productivity, knowing stuff is not enough.

I have taken notes my entire learning life: my bookshelves are full of journals. My favorite notebook is a Spirax red-and-black notebook that costs just a few dollars. During every seminar, workshop, lecture, retreat I attend, I record my impressions in this notebook.

Half of the content of this book is based on the notes, thoughts, and insights I've gained along my knowledge-gathering pathway. My suggestion to you is that you do the activities in this book, take some notes, record some insights, and write some to-do lists.

For the record (pardon the pun) this is how I do it. I use the right-hand pages to record my notes and do any activities. I use the left-hand side for any insights that arise from the activities, any quotations, and also to-do lists. This is where I list books to read, movies to watch, web pages to check out, YouTube clips to view, people to call, and email addresses. By keeping the two groups separate, the action items don't get lost in the notes and activities.

I don't want you to get bogged down doing activities. Be efficient, and don't overthink things. You can always go back later and do the task again. In fact, you probably will, because who you are, your beliefs about what is possible, and your strategies will change (hopefully for the better) as you progress through this book.

So grab your favorite pen, an activity book and get ready to take some notes, do some exercises, record some insights about you and the world. Start an action, to-do list.

Worksheets are available online for you to download and use as you progress through the book. These worksheets are designed for you to use as a template for higher productivity and to save you the time in recreating them yourself. You will see these words and graphic to let you know a worksheet awaits your pen:

☁ ACTIVITY DOWNLOAD

Go to www.LifeCEO.com/Resources. Register with your name and email address for regular access as you progress through the book. You'll be emailed a link that will take you to an exclusive book readers' site for your download as a PDF or Word document.

Finally, this is the Life CEO model I have used as the basis of this book:

> **Knowledge is not power. Knowledge is only potential power. Action is power.**
> **TONY ROBBINS**

AMEWORK FOR
OUR LIFE'S WORK

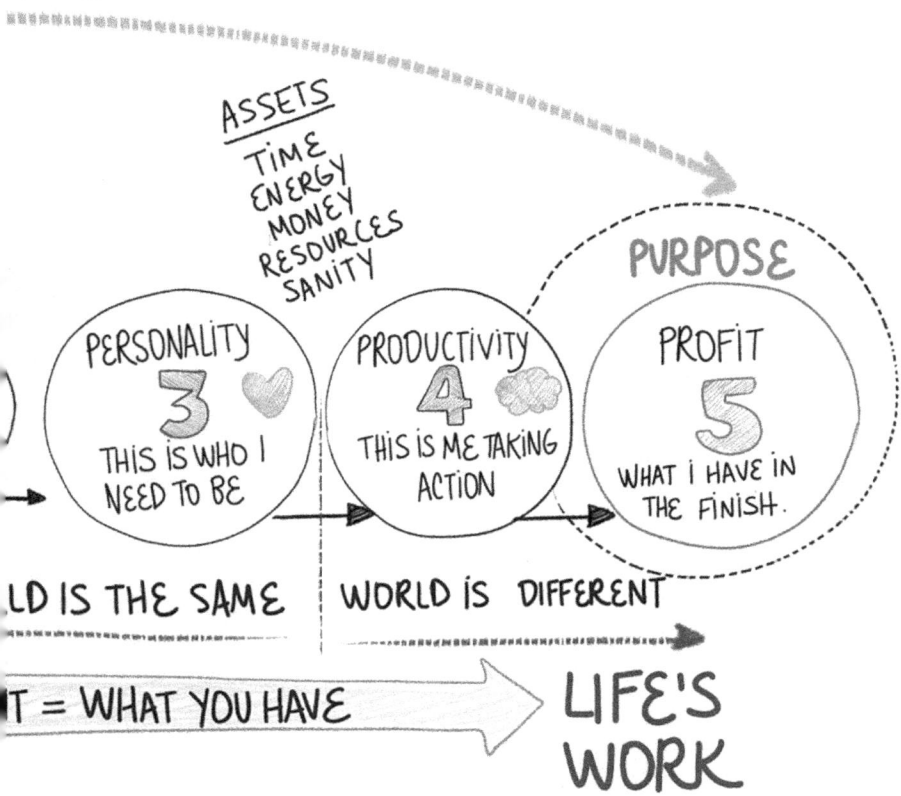

IN WITH
FINISH
MIND

ASSETS
TIME
ENERGY
MONEY
RESOURCES
SANITY

PURPOSE

PERSONALITY
3 ♥
THIS IS WHO I
NEED TO BE

PRODUCTIVITY
4
THIS IS ME TAKING
ACTION

PROFIT
5
WHAT I HAVE IN
THE FINISH.

LD IS THE SAME   WORLD IS DIFFERENT

T = WHAT YOU HAVE   LIFE'S
                            WORK

Part 1
FULL DAY VS. FULFILLED

1 What Does It Mean to Be Your Life CEO?

"At the end of the day, if you're a professional athlete in track and field you are the CEO of your company."
CARL LEWIS

A chief executive officer has one of the most admired jobs in the business world. Everybody thinks CEOs can do whatever they want, are almighty, and know everything there is to know. Not true. The job description of a CEO includes being answerable to the requirements of employees, customers, shareholders, investors, the community, and the law. A CEO's direction, behavior, and actions are directed by the vision and purpose of the company, and the CEO is often answerable to a board of directors.

There are five crucial responsibilities a CEO must perform on a daily basis:

1. **Set the direction of the company based on its core values:** The CEO clarifies and documents the purpose and vision of the company so everyone in the organization knows where the company is headed. The company's values and purpose penetrate all aspects and departments. The mission and responsibilities of each department reflect the vision of the company. Outcome: *clear purpose*.

2. **Create the strategy and business plan**: The CEO sets out the long-term plan for the company, and the short-term goals and KPI's (Key Performance Indicators) so everyone in the organization knows how to achieve the vision of the company. Outcome: *well-designed plans*.

3. **Sculpt the company's tone, culture, and behaviors**: The CEO has a massive influence on the way the company and its employees behave, and creates an environment that dictates the performance, success and potential failure of the company. The CEO creates a setting that helps attract and keep key players in the company; a vibe that lets people know how to speak, dress, move, write email, answer the phone, sell, and design; and an atmosphere of championing or encouragement. The CEO also sets an example of work ethic. Outcome: *the personality of the company*.

4. **Distribute the company's time, energy, resources and money in the execution of the company's vision**: The CEO ensures that action is taken on the plan and things get done, and decides what is achieved at a macro level. And while the CEO may not be the one doing the final act, they provide the guidance for what is to be done, with what and by whom. Outcome: *taking productive action*.

5. **Track the performance of the teams, each department, the company, and, most importantly, their own personal performance**: Being the CEO of a company doesn't necessarily mean someone is good at it. Being CEO is a tough gig, and without the training and developed skills for the job, many fail, and fail spectacularly. Importantly, when the company does succeed, the CEO should acknowledge those responsible for the result, including acknowledging themselves. Being accountable and giving constructive feedback is essential, including when everything goes to plan. Great CEOs celebrate their own personal success. Outcome: *making the company profitable*.

In short, the CEO is responsible for everything, including the success or failure of the company. They are held accountable and are responsible for all departments, including but not limited to operations, marketing, strategy, production, product, finance, the creation of company culture, human resources, health and safety, sales, and public relations. It all falls on the CEO's shoulders.

In the end, it comes down to profit. After the vision, strategy, culture, resources, and CEO's best efforts are taken into account, does the company make a profit? Is there more at the end than there was at the beginning? Is the company, and the world around it, better for the CEO's exertions? Is there a benefit derived from all the work performed and capital invested?

The shareholders will look for answers to all these questions.

You may ask, what has this all got to do with "life CEO"? Everything. Let's break down the words *life chief executive officer*.

Life: from the Old English "līf," meaning life, body, including the condition that distinguishes living organisms from inorganic objects and dead organisms, being manifested by growth through metabolism, reproduction, and the power of adaptation to environment through changes originating internally. It also relates to time, and the living existence or period of living existence of an individual.

Chief: from the Latin "caput," meaning head, leader, the most important individual in a body of people.

Executive: from the Latin "execūt(us)," meaning a person or group of people responsible for the administration of a project, activity, or business that puts plans, orders, and laws into practical effect.

Officer: from the Latin "officium," meaning service or duty; a person appointed or elected to a position of responsibility or authority in a government or society.

So *life CEO* means you are the CEO in charge of your life.

2 Work-Life Balance Myth

> **"**The phrase 'work/life balance'
> encapsulates a depressing outlook.**"**
> **TOM HODGKINSON**

Before digging too deeply into the responsibilities of being your life CEO, I need to sort out what I believe is a massive mistake in thinking. I agree with Tom Hodgkinson (above). I hate the idea of work-life balance. I instantly picture in my mind the illustration below.

On one side of the scale is work, and on the other is life. Crazy! It looks like a never-ending battle of balancing the two. It also insinuates that work is not life. If work is not life, what is it?

In the movie A Family Man, a guy named Dane Jensen (Gerard Butler) is a recruiting headhunter at the Blackridge Recruiting Agency. He works super-hard, and loves the thrill of the hunt. He always arrives home late, and takes calls all day and all night, and at weekends. It's clear that he's juggling his desire to see his family and his commitment to his work. In one scene, he arrives home late yet again to find his wife already in bed, angry that he missed Halloween with his family.

"Do you think I wanted to miss tonight?" he says to his wife. "That I wanted to make those calls at the office?"

"You like making those calls," she replies. "Sometimes I think you don't really live here, you just sleep here."

"The whole Halloween thing is just kids running around filling up with candy," he says. "It's all just sad."

"Sad for you, Dane. Even when you're here, you're not really here. Always thinking about some deal you've got going, or some candidate you're scamming. One day you're going to wish you had this time back. I love you, and it makes me sad for you."

"You know I work damn hard for this family," he spits back at her. "I bust my ass seventy hours a week in that boiler room so you can stay at home. You think it's easy, working commission sales, cold calling, starting each month with a blank slate, waking up at two A.M. with a knot in my gut, hoping to God I can close a deal? And all so my family can have a nice life. And if that means missing a day and being a bad guy, that's a sacrifice I'm happy to make."

When the couple's ten-year-old son, Ryan, is diagnosed with cancer, Dane's professional priorities at work and his personal priorities at home begin to clash. He struggles to maintain balance. He feels trapped. He's stuck repeating the same patterns, and meanwhile his son is losing his battle with cancer. The boss visits Ryan in hospital, and fires Dane after seeing him arguing with his wife.

It took something coming into Dane's life—his son's illness and the loss of his job—before he made the shift from a trapped life to a turned-on life.

Spoiler alert! Once Dane embraces just one of the most important concepts I'm going to cover in part one of this book— finding his real purpose and making each of his missions align with that purpose—everything changes. His son recovers, and he finds his true calling helping other men get jobs so they can take care of their families.

Dane became his life CEO. He stopped doing his busywork and instead did his life's work.

Busywork

Busywork is where you feel pulled in all different directions. Where, every day, you feel like you're juggling seven balls in the air, always dropping one or another. It feels like you're being pulled in all directions on a medieval torture rack with ropes attached to all your limbs. You're exhausted, in pain and unfulfilled, despite being busy all the time.

The image below shows you as a set of scales with seven arms, and you're trying to balance each arm against the other six. It makes me feel uptight and anxious just thinking about it.

DOING YOUR BUSY WORK

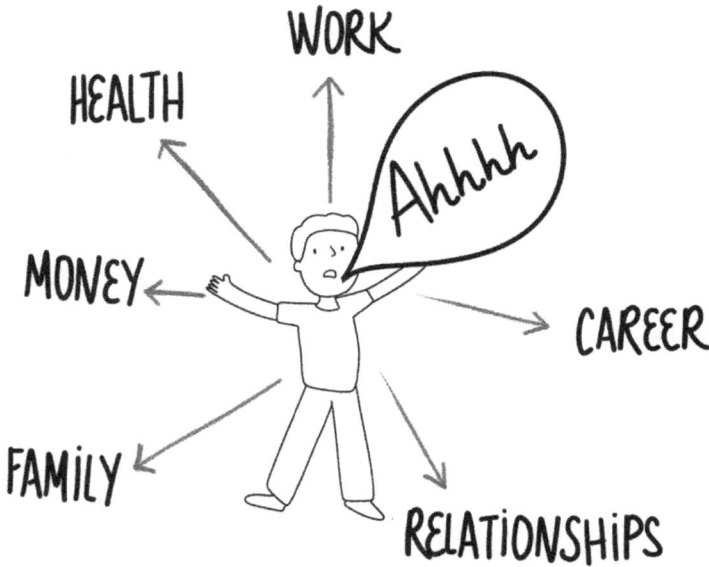

Life's work

By contrast, life's work is where everything is aligned, and driven by a higher purpose. How would that look? Imagine if everything you did helped every other aspect of your life. The better you work, the better your health. The better your health, the better your relationships. The better your relationships, the more money you make.

When you're doing your life's work, there is no work-life balance—juggling different mission balls, feeling pulled in different directions. There is just one big ball to hang onto, one direction to take.

DOING YOUR LIFE'S WORK

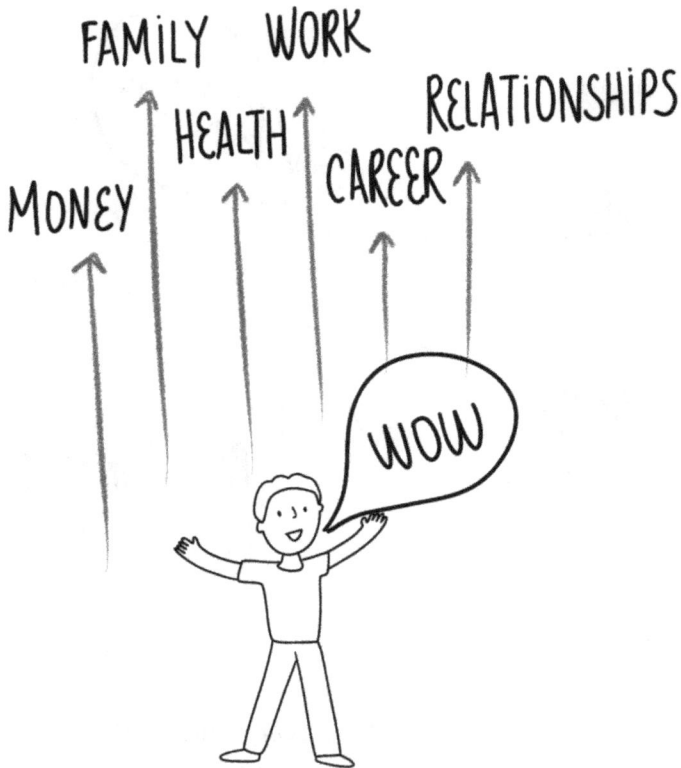

FAMILY   WORK

HEALTH   RELATIONSHIPS

MONEY   CAREER

WOW

Doing your life's work requires that you be a CEO directing different departments within the company. In a well-led company, where each department has a mission that aligns with the company's vision or purpose, the relationships are symbiotic. A better marketing department creates a better sales department, which produces a better product-development department, which creates a better HR department, which creates better leadership for the team, and so on. The company makes more money, and there is higher job satisfaction.

What would your life feel like if you could make that happen? If you could get all your departments (missions) to work together, with mutually beneficial relationships for all. If you woke in the morning knowing that everything you did helped everything else. If there was a force like that pulling you out of bed in the morning.

It is possible, and over the next couple of hundred pages we're going to examine the strategies that will make it happen. But before we do, let's take a closer look at the kind of life you're living at the moment. Like a direction search on a satnav, you have to start with your current location before you can get the directions for your destination.

3 What Life Are You Living?

> " Only I can change my life. No
> one can do it for me. "
> **CAROL BURNETT**

Where you are on the spectrum of life changes the quality of your life. The exciting thing is that you can make a decision about the kind of life you want to live. There are three kinds of lives that people live on a daily basis and I want to take a moment to explore each one, their individual effects, and the choices you have to determine your own life.

1. **The trapped, stuck or caged life**: In my coaching, I have found that many people, at some point in their lives, have moments of feeling trapped or caged. Stuck, in other words. Stuck because of the past, because of their circumstances, because of the expectations of others, or through some other limiting beliefs or fear.

    People in this situation feel like they can't break free. They don't have enough time, money, health, or emotional freedom. And the longer they spend in the trapped life, the more they blame others and make excuses. Their language changes from *could* to *should*, from *want to* to *have to*, and from *won't* to *can't*.

Eventually they believe they have no choice and must be stuck forever in their current circumstances and that things will never change. This leads to feelings of helplessness, overwhelm, boredom, anger, frustration, despair and depression.

We have all seen caged animals. Over time they slowly become resigned to their circumstances and eventually give up. Like animals when they are first caged, people often start by getting angry and frustrated with the world outside their cage, evident in their behaviors and language. They blame the world for their circumstances and feel misunderstood. They are certain the lucky ones outside of the cage are at fault for their situation. This attitude separates them even further from those outside the cage.

The irony is that it's the people *outside* the cage that they most want to be like. They want the freedom. It's the people outside of the cage that can give them the connection. The catch is that, over time, people suffering the stuck life often build up a protection strategy that prevents them from connecting with others (especially people outside the cage who they most want to be like), so their life becomes all about them. They stay in ego, making them less likely to ask for help.

The lucky ones might have their cages rattled by a new event or experience that comes into their life and frees them, allowing them to become unstuck and free from the trapped life. But this external force that rattled their cages may only provide temporary freedom.

The ultimate and best way to stay free from the trapped life is for something to come *out of you*, rather than *into your life*. This means change: a change in thinking, and a change in beliefs and in attitude. It means becoming connected to your true purpose in life, and taking risks, having courage, making decisions. It's understanding that you do have a choice, and you can take responsibility for your life.

The beauty of cages is that they all have doors; it's only you who can shut the door, and only you who believes that it's locked. There is always a way out.

So what is outside the cage, and how do you get out?

2. **The tepid, so-so, comfortable life**: This is life just outside of the cage. It's almost as though you're out of the cage, but you're still in the zoo. In the beginning, this life feels good. It's different; it feels freer. As a result of something rattling the cage, you found the way out. Or maybe you went looking and found the door that way.

Either way, it feels good to be out, even though you're living a so-so life. Good stuff happens in a so-so life.

You might have started to get the stuff that most people have, things that are associated with a good life. A nice relationship, a good job, a nice house, a cool car, time to catch up with a few friends, the kids doing okay at school. The tepid life. And just like tepid water, it's neither hot nor cold. It just is.

Is there anything worse than a cup of tepid tea or coffee?

One day you wake up and ask yourself: *Is this it? Is this all there is? Is this going to be the level of my life experience?* As a coach, these are often the clients I see.

On the outside your life looks good, but inside you're dying. Your relationships are dying, your career is just a job, and your health has started to slide. This stage of life is often a result of your becoming disconnected from what is important and doing what you should do, not what inspires you.

So what is the solution? How do you get out of the cage, and the zoo? And what is outside of that?

3. **The turned-on, supercharged or crushing-it life**: This is a life that is not just out of the cage, or out of the zoo, but one that has moved to your theme park. It's a life filled with passion, focus, and energy. It's

a life that's driven by a clear sense of purpose, that's full of thrills that come from fully engaging in life and all its challenges. It's a life where you feel alive. You wake before the alarm clock, and swing your legs out of bed with a sense of excitement for what the day hold.

It is not a life without fear, but it's a life where you embrace fear. You are not without the ups and downs that often go with the rollercoaster ride of life, but you have a certainty of self, a sense of belonging, and as a result you keep moving forward.

In this life, you are a person of inspiration to others, a leader, someone who is attractive, someone who leaves a legacy. It is not necessarily a life lived at an elite level; it can be extraordinary or ordinary. It is a life with a fulfilling career, a life with a passionate and enriching relationship, with vibrant health and vitality.

It is a life worth living.

Isn't it time you got out of the cage, beyond the walls of the zoo and went off on an adventure in your theme park? As a coach, my goal is to help my clients achieve what they want. If a turned-on life is what you want, I can tell you it is possible.

Before you can get out of the cage and into your life, however, there are a few things to consider.

1. Have wonder. Create a vision of how your life will turn out. Make a picture in your mind of how your theme park looks. If you were out of the cage, and out of the zoo, what would your life be like? Be clear on the details of your ideal life.
2. Create a plan for how you're going to make it happen.
3. Be clear about who you need to be and how you need to behave.
4. Make a decision to change, and become ferociously committed to changing for the better. Do whatever it takes to find the door to the cage, the exit to the zoo, and a lifetime pass to your theme park.

5. Take action. *Move*. Do something to start the process, and don't stop until you achieve your new life.
6. Build a team around you to help get you there.

Being your life CEO is making the decision to play in your own theme park. Can you imagine a company that performed only in the trapped or tepid life? It wouldn't last long. Living the turned-on life, and being your life CEO, is about recognizing that only *you* are responsible for fulfilling your life's purpose.

4 You Don't Need More Time

" Your time is limited, so don't waste it living someone else's life. Don't be trapped by dogma—which is living with the results of other people's thinking. Don't let the noise of others' opinions drown out your own inner voice. And most important, dare to follow your heart and intuition. "

STEVE JOBS

I f only I had more time, you tell yourself. Sadly, this book cannot help you create more hours in the day. But by solving the challenge of finding direction, strategy, character, and action, it will help you make every hour count.

More time is often the place your mind sends you to as an excuse when you feel stuck. So many of us go through our lives today doing what we should do rather than what we really want to do. We believe that greater fulfillment and more happiness will come if only we had more time and more money. More money does bring happiness, but lots more money often doesn't.

Continually hoping that more money is the key to everything is a losing strategy. If it's not money, it must be more time, right? Ba-boom! Nope.

When it comes to time, we all have only twenty-four hours in a day, seven days in a week, and fifty-two weeks in a year. By the time you're in midlife, you have less than ten thousand days left. (By the way, check out this great blog by Tim Urban: *Your Life In Weeks*, https://waitbutwhy.com/2014/05/life-weeks.html.)

The question is: how are you going to make those days count?

There is a better question: How are you going to prioritize your life?

I hope to help you reconnect with the importance of thinking about your purpose. Where are you heading? As you progress through life, your direction changes. You have one direction when you're twelve, another when you're twenty-two, and yet another when you're thirty-two. Now that you're forty-two (or whatever age you are as you read this book), where are you heading?

Your purpose

Midlife is that particular age between thirty-seven and fifty-five. It's often a time of change. You might have had your children in your late twenties, so by the time you're forty-two the children are starting to grow up and you're wondering what's next, what's going to come after they move out. Up to this time, you may have put your career, health, or relationships on standby and now you're asking yourself: *What do I want to do? How do I want to contribute?*

Maybe you haven't had children yet. You could be in your late thirties or even early forties. Maybe you've spent the last twenty years working on your career, and now it's time for a change in direction. Maybe you're starting a family.

Whatever your stage of life, it's time to decide what's essential. What do you want to hang onto? When is it time to let go of those things that are nonessential?

We live in a society that is often driven by acquiring more stuff rather than more meaning. You might already be wondering if your current direction is the one you really want. You might find yourself doing busywork rather than your life's work. This lack of direction, purpose, vision or mission has left you feeling stuck. You think the solution to your problems is more time.

It's not. The solution is not to gain more time, but a more definite sense of your purpose, your direction.

You need to know where it's all heading. You need to learn to connect with what's important. To create a plan that will lead you in the direction that you want our life to move, and, importantly, in the direction of your personal ethos. What do you need in order to fulfill your purpose to walk through your plan, and to take action?

Many midlifers who are stuck, who need to find their purpose, may find it difficult to change. Perhaps you're one of those. With busyness in your life; feelings of obligation to your children, partner, mortgage; the acceleration of change occurring in the world today, you could be thinking it's too late to change, or that change will be too hard.

The belief that you have no choice but to continue with the status quo leaves you feeling trapped, thinking once again that the solution is more time. It's not. The solution is a greater understanding of the plan you need to fulfill your purpose.

Who do you need to be?

Many personal-development books have been written over the years, and they're full of advice on what people need to do. But I think a better question is: Who do I need to *be*? It's not what you *know*, and nor is it who you know. It's who you *be* that makes the difference.

Due to the pervasive influence of social media in the world today, I find that many of my midlife clients compare themselves to others. And they often compare their worst with others' best, which often has a significant impact on their self-confidence and feelings of self-worth.

Without having trust in themselves, and the willpower fed by a higher purpose, many find themselves struggling to be great: great in their health, wealth and relationships. They think the answer is more time. It's not.

The answer to having a great life is getting clear on who you need to *be*; the form or personality you need to adopt. It's understanding and developing the ethos or character you need in order to tackle the terrain on your journey toward fulfilling your purpose.

As a result of poorly executed or flawed strategies (or no strategy at all), many midlifers find themselves paralyzed. Exhausted from doing without direction, and disenchanted from doing without achieving true fulfillment. They are left cogitating on what might be, philosophizing on the principles of change, but unable to make a decision. Unable to cut off from what *is*, to pursue what *is wanted*. They do everything possible except take the next step: the step of *action*. Their world, and the world around them, remains unchanged because they believe they just need more time.

The answer is not more time but more action, follow through or production. Activity is driven by direction, strategy, and character.

In the modern world, there are many life hacks to ensure we keep moving forward, with productively and potency. It might feel good to sit at home on your comfy sofa, sipping a nice pinot in front of the crackling fire, cogitating on life, philosophizing on what might be, but if you want your life to change, you have to take action.

Knowledge is not power; action is.

The word *midlife* is often associated with the word *crisis*. And we are all aware of the negative connotation of a midlife crisis, which usually happens when something unexpected or unplanned for comes into someone's life. Naturally, we think a crisis is something we want to avoid.

In this book, you will discover that a midlife crisis doesn't have to be something to avoid. In fact, it's something to embrace. Huh?

The word *"crisis"* comes from the Greek *kris*, which means to make a judgment or decision, to reach a turning point. It also means to sieve out. If you feel overwhelmed by life, and find yourself doing busywork rather than your life's work, use your crisis as an opportunity to sieve out what's really important, to realize you *do* have a choice and you *can* decide your future.

Are you ready for change? Good. But for things to change, things *must* change. You can't stay the same you and have your world change around you. Some things are going to have to be sieved out.

Being your life CEO is sometimes about making the tough calls. Knowing that sometimes you're going to be unpopular. But you have a job to do; you have a purpose, a mission to complete. A great CEO knows what to sieve out and what to keep.

Warning: This book is not designed to convince you to change. It is not motivational, nor is it inspirational. Inspiration can only come from within you. Please don't read this book if you're not ready for change. It will be a complete waste of your time, money and the paper and ink sacrificed to produce it. I hear *Fifty Shades of Grey* is a good read if you don't want your life to get any better—although it might make some changes to your bedtime routine.

Part 2
OVERVIEW OF THE FIVE STEPS

5 Purpose: Begin with the Finish

> " Begin with the end in mind. "
> **STEVEN COVEY**

I hate to have to roll out that old chestnut of Steven Covey's, but it sums up the meaning of purpose pretty well. Purpose is about deciding what you want your life to look like. It's about connecting with the direction you and your life are heading in. It's not about the finish, because we all know how that turns out. We have the eternal sleep. Death is how it ends up for all of us; we cease to exist in this world as we are now.

Many have a belief in the afterlife, Heaven, Nirvana, Elysium, Zion, or Valhalla. That is not my expertise, and so it's not for discussion here. When I talk about the finish, I'm talking about what will your life look like at that point.

What will it have amounted to? What will be the theme of it? What will people say about you when you've gone? What will be written in your obituary? What will be said in your eulogy? What direction did your life take? What did it mean? Did you matter? Is the world a better place because of you?

As you progress through life, there may be times when your immediate direction changes, but generally the overall theme of it will remain the same.

As an analogy, take a look at the great Murray River that forms the border between Victoria and New South Wales in Australia. Imagine that you put a model boat in at one end and set it off on its voyage (that is you, starting out on your life's journey. Step back and take a look from a distance. The boat has a direction, an overall path that it follows. That is its total bearing or heading. That trajectory is your *why*, your purpose, your life's big mission.

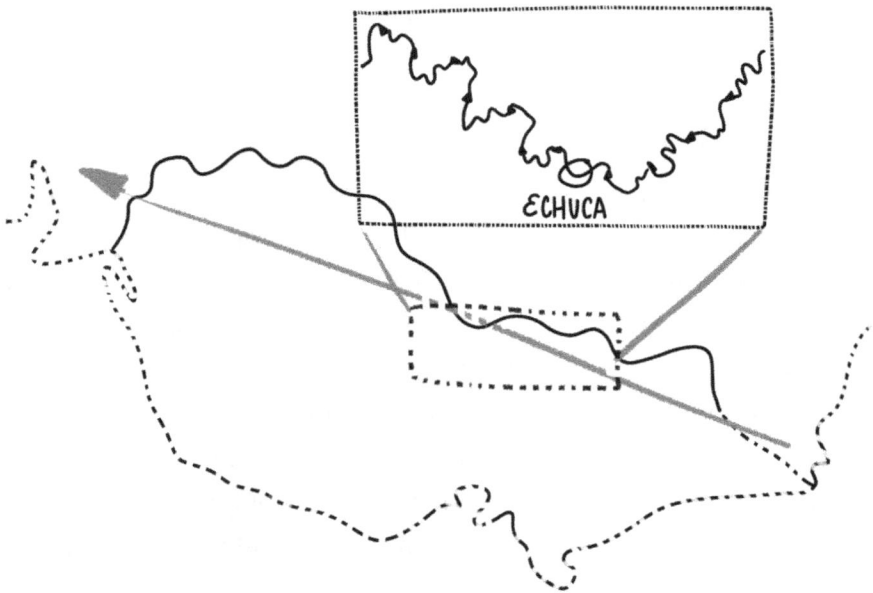

ECHUCA

Imagine your boat on its journey. You see it traveling through many twists and turns. But it maintains its track—its purpose, its *why*. This makes sense if you think of the boat as your life. Your direction at the age of five is different from when you're fifteen, which is different again when you're twenty-five, fifty, seventy-five.

But all those shifts in direction are part of the general course of your life. When you're on your river of purpose, it will be full of twists and turns. It's about recognizing those twists and turns and going with the flow, the flow that feels right. Your *why* journey may not always be comfortable. There will be obstacles in the way, just like a river with logs, rapids and the occasional waterfall. The journey can be rough, it can be tough, but it feels right.

Now imagine you're camping by a river with your family. You blow up the air mattress or inner tube, wander down to the water and get in. You lie back and let the river take you. You feel the pull of the current, the direction it's heading in, and yes, there are occasional rocks. You get stuck sometimes. But with a bit of a wiggle you get unstuck and continue.

That's what it's like when you go through life on *why*, on purpose. You feel like you're being pulled along. You're pulled out of bed in the morning before the alarm goes off. You're drawn in the direction of the right relationships. You attract the right friends. You pursue the right career and make the right choices. It's not always easy, but you feel a degree of contentment. This is what it means to have a turned-on life.

> " There's a difference between, as I always say, the destination, the endpoint, and the journey. The journey has a lot of twists and turns. It isn't always pretty. "
>
> **BOB MENENDEZ**

Now I wonder whether part of the reason you picked up this book, why you feel like you're in the stuck life or the tepid life, is that you've drifted off your river of *why*. Maybe because of a life event, you've ended up on a side river, which becomes a stream and then a creek. There's very little flow in a creek. Even worse, you might be stuck in a swamp. There's even less flow in a swamp. Life has become nothing but hard work with little progress. Very little *eudaimonia* where you are.

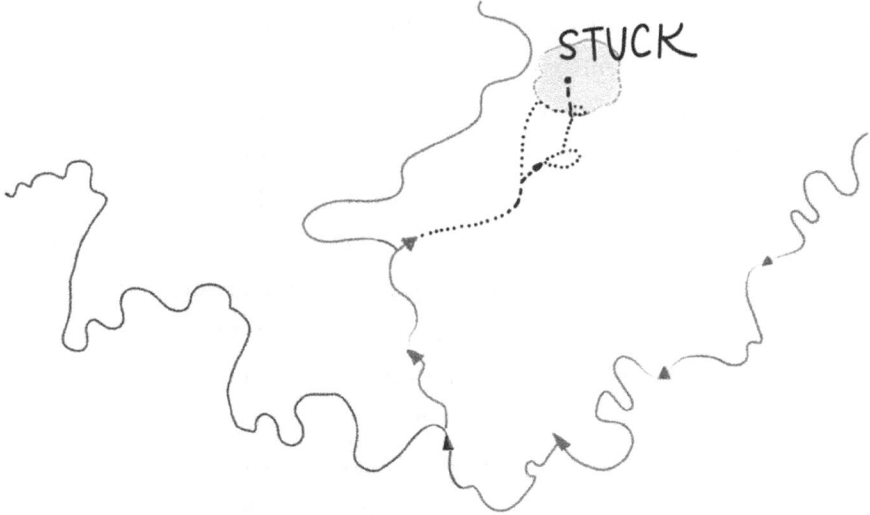

How does this happen? Why do we sometimes end up the creek or the swamp rather than in our river? There's a significant answer to that, which will be covered in the next chapter, but for I offer two common reasons for slipping of the path that I encounter in my coaching practice.

The first reason is that we have a moment (or a few) of shiny-thing syndrome. Something catches our eye and we're distracted by the glint, the shininess. Sometimes we don't realize we're traveling down the wrong path until it's too late.

Be careful of the shiny things that appear in your life. The quick-fix solution, the get-rich-quick scheme, the easy path (not the path with ease), the shortcut. Being on your path, on purpose, is not always easy. When temptation beckons, take a moment to check in to see if what you're about to pursue feels right. Consult your compass, check your map, and make sure you're still on course.

> " It's very tough for me to focus. I'm like: 'Look, something shiny! No, focus. Oh, there goes a butterfly!' "
> **GABBY DOUGLAS**

The second most common reason is that we get *should-on'd*. Someone tells us we should do something. You know how it goes. *You should lose weight. You should change jobs. You should switch careers. You should start a business. You should marry him/her. You should leave him/her. You should make more money. You should buy a house. You should go away. You should settle down. You should, you should, you should...*

When that has happened, have you gone off and done the *should*? No good, no good for you, no good for the world. Stop doing what you should do, and do what you really want to do. Do the thing that feels right, that make you feel you're at ease, even though whatever it is might not be easy.

> " Do what is right, not what is easy nor what is popular. "
> **ROY T. BENNETT**

To sum up, take the opportunity to discover again, or maybe for the first time, what your purpose is. Get connected with it; really understand what turns you on. Take the chance to get clear on your purpose, your missions, and decide what your intention is for your life.

It's this first step—beginning with how you want your life to finish—that creates clarity, and generates the fuel for you to become, and do what it takes, to be your hero again. To live a life with meaning, a life that counts. To feel like you're no longer doing your busy life, and instead doing your life's work.

A great CEO takes the time to decide the direction of the company, to make sure all the company's actions are propelling it in the direction that matters most. As your life CEO, this is a critical step. Don't miss it. It will be your guide for as long as you decide to hold the position of your life CEO.

" What is right is not always popular and what is popular is not always right. "
ALBERT EINSTEIN

6 Plans: Creating a Framework for Success

" Our goals can only be reached through a vehicle of a plan, in which we must fervently believe, and upon which we must vigorously act. There is no other route to success. "
PABLO PICASSO

It's one thing to be clear about the direction you want your life to take, to connect with your purpose, but it's a whole other ballgame turning that vision into something tangible, something that causes a shift in the world around you.

This step is critical in setting a framework, or plan, for how you're going to achieve the life you want. So many people stop at the dream, wishing for things to happen, and end up wishing their lives away. Wishy-washy planning or goal setting is one of the worst things we can do to ourselves. Poor planning or no planning at all most often results in failure.

Imagine what might come of your life if, in the beginning, you were to set out a plan for the day ahead, the week ahead, the month, year, or the next decade ahead. For some, the mere thought of that might generate instant butterflies.

Many may have, at one time, set a goal, but probably not well enough if you haven't reached that goal. As a result, you might have beaten yourself up, had less confidence in your abilities, reduced your self-worth, and, worst of all, decided never to plan again. Instead you have chosen to let "the universe," or God, or someone outside of you make your plans for you.

Here is the thing. If you don't decide what you want your day, week, year of life to be like, someone else will.

> **If you don't design your own life plan, chances are you'll fall into someone else's plan. And guess what they have planned for you? Not much.**
> **JIM ROHN**

A plan, and the goal setting associated with it, will take the big-picture vision of your life and convert it into something tangible. You can have a vision for a fantastic relationship, for changing the world, but for these visions to translate to a change in your world and the world around, you must formulate a plan before you take action.

Imagine a football team with a vision to win the grand finale. In every game of the season, they just run onto the field and start playing. No plan. They just start kicking a ball around. It's probably not going to work out too well for that team, despite their best intentions and wishes.

I built my own home ten years ago. It was the dream home of my wife Michelle and I. In the beginning we dreamed about what it would look and feel like. We bought house, pool, and garden-landscape magazines and books. We search on Google, haunted Pinterest, gathered as much information as we could, all along checking in to see if it was still what we really wanted. *Really.*

Once we had created a portfolio of what our dream home would look like, we took it to a designer and architect to turn our vision, our dream, into something that could be built. Every square millimeter was calculated. His plans showed every possible detail for the construction of our (dream) home. Every aspect, every detail, including a timeline so that I, the owner-builder, could coordinate the tradespeople to minimize time wastage. All the materials necessary were calculated to eliminate waste of money and resources.

Can you imagine what it would have looked like if a carpenter had arrived on site to build our house, just grabbing bits of wood and nailing them together? Again, it probably would not have ended well for the carpenter, or the family (mine), who had to live in the house.

Creating a framework for your life is essential to ensuring that you get stuff done. Later in the book, I will introduce you to the T.R.A.C.K. Method of goal setting, which is one of the most influential ways that I know of turning dreams, wishes, and good intentions into reality. Using the method correctly, and to its fullest, will ensure that any goals you set are as good as done.

Gone will be the days of disappointment. Instead, your life will be full of milestones of success. Your days will feel more fulfilling as you get clear on what you want, when you want it, and how you're going to go about achieving it.

If you recall the river example from the previous chapter, remember that although you may be in your river of *why*, it will still have the occasional buried log or rock, and hidden rapids. Be kind to yourself. Not everything will go to plan (as I discovered when I got home one day and found that the old house we were removing partway through the build had fallen off the tray of the truck and was leaning up against our new home).

As your life CEO, the plans you create will help keep you on track with your decisions and actions. Importantly, they will help you allocate your time and money in the direction of what matters most, to produce a profit in your life in alignment with your purpose.

Note: When I say I was the owner-builder of my home, I didn't actually do a great deal of nailing, sawing, painting, screwing, and sanding. In fact, I didn't do any. But I did have a cool leather tool belt, and the tradesman pants and shirt to go with it. Not that I wore the shirt that often, because I had to work on my tradesman tan.

7 Personality: Decide Who You Be

> " Between stimulus and response, there is a space. In that space is our power to choose our response. In our response lies our growth and our freedom. "
>
> **VIKTOR E. FRANKL**

Since my first child, Bella, was born, my wife has driven the kids around in a Land Rover Discovery. It's been a great car, able to handle the rough treatment that a family of five can throw at it. What I love most about it is its flexibility, its ability to adapt to a range of conditions. From extreme ice and snow, to long stretches of freeway bitumen, to downright scary steep hills.

The Discovery, like many other four-wheel drive vehicles, has a knob in the center console called the "terrain response selector." When you start the car, it goes to its default setting, which is set up for driving on regular roads. If the driving conditions change, the vehicle doesn't perform as well if it remains in road mode, so, with a twist of your wrist, you can change the whole behavior of the vehicle.

We got to experience this feature on a family trip to the snow at Mt Hotham in Victoria. We drove there on a beautiful bright day, with not a single snowflake on the road. We parked on the top of the mountain and headed off to do snow things. Two days later, and after a big dump of snow, we trekked back to the car, only to find it covered with and surrounded by snow. After we cleared away some of the snow so we could get in, I turned on the ignition and selected the snow setting on the dial.

At first nothing appeared to change. But underneath, the behavior of the car definitely changed. The ABS brakes, the traction-and stability-control systems, the locking action of the differentials, the shift timing of the transmission, and even the throttle response of the engine all behaved differently now because I told the car it was in the snow.

You are no different. You have the ability to choose your behavior at any moment. Yep, at any moment, and within seconds. You've done it many times in the past. Have you ever driven in your car, singing to yourself, and had someone cut you off, making you break hard? Maybe you jumped up and down in your seat, and start ranting and raving about the other driver's carelessness and stupidity. One minute you were happy, the next you were a raving lunatic.

Now, this is not a don't-get-angry, be-at-peace-and-full-of-love book, although that would be cool. In fact, I believe it's useful at times to get angry. After all, we are all human. It's normal to be sad, or angry. (The only person I know who doesn't choose emotions, because he can't is, Dr. Spock in *Star Trek*. But you are not a Vulcan.)

> ❝Generally speaking, if a human being never shows anger, then I think something's wrong. He's not right in the brain.❞
> **DALAI LAMA**

These next few words may be a lot for you to absorb, but they are very important. No one makes you angry; you *choose* to be angry. No one makes you sad; you *choose* to be sad. No one makes you happy; you *choose* to be happy.

That's right, you choose your own behavior. It's good news, but sort of bad as well. The bad news is that you're responsible for all those crazy emotional moments you've had in your life. The good news is that you're responsible for all those crazy emotional moments you have had in your life. They have all been of your own choosing.

You are response-able for the way you feel. (You will see this word often throughout the book. It comes from the Latin *respons-*, past-participle stem of *respondere,* "to respond".) This word is key to understanding. Who you are (your behavior) at any given moment, for any given circumstance, can be different, and you get to choose. You are response-able.

I often clients tell me that they just want to be themselves. I always ask them: "What is yourself?" I believe we are *always* ourselves, because who we are is our choice and we cannot be someone we are not.

The person I am as I write these words is different to the person I was when I went for my morning run, which is different to the person I am when I'm with my kids, which is different to the person I am when I'm coaching, and so on. But all of them are me.

Making a start

I love the word *ethos* (probably because it makes me feel like a philosopher). It comes from the Greek (no surprise there) and means "custom, habit, or character." It used to describe the distinctive character, spirit, and attitudes of a people, culture, and era.

In this third step in the process of getting unstuck and creating change in your life, we look at who you need to *be* to fulfill your purpose, and achieve your goals, through action. I believe that it's not what you know, nor is it who you know, it's who you *be* that makes the difference.

Everybody seems to be looking for the quick fix. They're asking Google, their teacher or their coach: *How do I do it? What do I need to do?* They're also saying: *I need a to-do list. I need to do more. If only I could get it done.*

You do not need more to-*do* lists if you want to change your life; you need more *to-be* lists. It's the quality of your *be*ing and not your *do*ing that needs attention. (I will get to the doing a little later in the book.) So many fail at carrying out their best intentions because they attempt to do whatever it is without first becoming.

I'm often asked by clients what they need to do to lose weight. I tell them to ask Google. They tell me about the diets they've tried, which of course haven't worked. Now, I have to say that I think almost all of the diets out there do work, but they won't work if the client is not a weight-loss person. What do I mean by that? What would a weight-loss person's ethos be? Their character, spirit, attitude?

Here's a quick list of attributes, and I'm sure you can think of at least three others:

1. Determined
2. Disciplined
3. Organized
4. Strong-minded (has willpower)
5. Focused

> **It was character that got us out of bed, a commitment that moved us into action, and discipline that enabled us to follow through.**
> **ZIG ZIGLAR**

To succeed in getting what you really want, you must first decide what it actually is that you really want. Then make a plan (create a framework). Then decide whom you need to *be* in order to do the things that create change.

Who you are right now is responsible for the results that you're currently getting. You probably got something from of that behavior in the past, and who you are right now is still serving you in some way. If you want to change your circumstances, you need to change your behavior, your ethos, your character.

This step is one of the most important in the process of getting you unstuck—out of trapped and tepid and into the turned-on life. You will take a look at the stories that you run in your unconscious that keep you trapped. You will look at your state (terrain-response control), and develop new and powerful strategies to decide whom you are going to be in order to create the life you really want.

This will not be easy. There will be some well-worn paths in your brain, routes that need some rewiring. They're the natural paths that you take right now, but with time and practice you will establish new ones, or reactivate old versions. This is an exciting step in the process of you unleashing your greatness again.

As your life CEO, you'll be able to set the culture, tone and ethos for your personal company brand. When people think of you, how are they going to describe you? We often describe companies in terms of behavior, not just in terms of product. You are responsible for setting the behavior for your company, and creating one of the world's most powerful and respected brands. *You.*

Until then, be great.

8 Productivity: Where the Rubber Meets the Road

> " Isn't it amazing how much stuff we get done the day before vacation? "
>
> **ZIG ZIGLAR**

Knowledge is not power; action is. In my coaching practice, I often see clients who have spent time creating a purpose statement, designed a plan to achieve it, and even set some well-formed goals, but nothing has come of it. Why not? Because they never got up from the chair in front of the computer and took action.

Nothing in the world will change if you don't take action. It's the follow-through that creates change. You take action, and in some way the world starts to change. It can be a call, a conversation, an email, a walk or a run—any kind of movement. The crucial thing is that you have taken action.

Taking action is easier if you're clear on the reason *why* you're taking action, and have a well-formed plan. Also, if you have the character; that is, you know who you need to be. In other words, you started with the *finish* in mind, have created an excellent *framework*, and have decided on the setting you need to *be*.

I won't give you a long list of productivity hacks because there are trillions of books, YouTube clips, podcasts, courses, etc., on different ways of *doing*. In fact, one of the most searched Google terms starts with "How to..." I will give you my own personal hacks that I've found the most useful in helping me allocate my assets of time, energy, resources, money, and sanity. These are all the assets that any CEO has to allocate, based on the plans that have been created.

As your life CEO, you will need to make decisions around the allocation of what are limited assets. You do not have unlimited assets. All companies (even trillion-dollar ones) understand that there are limits to the allocation of assets. A good CEO knows where to allocate them and where not to, and when it is appropriate to say no. A good CEO will also be aware of where cuts need to be made in the best interests of advancing the company's mission, and making a profit.

You will learn my strategies for making decisions around the allocation of my assets. As your life CEO, making decisions will be one of the most important actions you will make, and like all CEOs, sometimes you'll get it wrong. That's where the final step in creating a life that matters comes in.

9 Profit: Report Back on Your Results

> **Life is divided into three terms - that which was, which is, and which will be. Let us learn from the past to profit by the present, and from the present, to live better in the future.**
> **WILLIAM WORDSWORTH**

Ever pursued something with vigor, put all your heart and soul into it, and when you got there realized it wasn't what you wanted? Where you found that the result was empty? This is the result of pursuing a *should*, not your purpose. You finally get to the finish line and don't feel fulfilled.

If you follow the strategies I put forward in *Life CEO,* this will stop happening. It won't stop people *shoulding* on you, but it will help you distinguish between on-purpose and off-purpose pursuits. There's nothing worse than giving up the assets of time, energy, resources, money, and sanity to find out that what you got wasn't what you really wanted. It can be soul-destroying, particularly if you've compromised your values in the process.

> **For what shall it profit a man, if he gain the whole world, and suffer the loss of his soul?**
> **JESUS CHRIST**

When we compromise our values and standards, often we don't achieve what we set out to achieve. In this part of the book you will learn to look at the outcome and determine if it was the result of poor planning, poor state management, not enough or wrong action, or because it was not in alignment with your purpose.

Like any CEO, being your life CEO means you need to create a reporting season, where you report back to the stakeholders in your life. You take the time to assess your progress toward fulfilling your purpose. Are you on track with the goal you set yourself? If so, celebrate, give yourself a bonus. If not, it's time to seek advice, internally or externally, and find out why things are not going to plan.

As with any CEO, after the profit announcement come the questions: What's next? Where is the company going now? Based on what's been achieved so far, where is the next opportunity for growth?

But unlike a company CEO, if the results aren't great you don't get to step down and hand in your resignation.

Or perhaps you did. Maybe the reason you picked up this book is because, at sometime in your life, you did step down as your life CEO, and very quickly someone else stepped in to take your place, running your life according to their agenda and purpose. Or perhaps no one stepped in, and your company was left to float through life a shelf company. (A shelf corporation, shelf company, or aged corporation is a company or corporation that has had no activity. It has been created and left with no activity; metaphorically put on the shelf to age. Ouch!)

Don't step down as your life CEO. Stay in charge, get clear on your purpose, set some new plans, check your culture, and take action again.

Part 3

STEP 1

PURPOSE: BEGIN WITH THE FINISH

10 Deciding: Influencing the Outcome

> "Winners are people with definite purpose in life."
>
> **DENIS WAITLEY**

So often in life we do what we should do rather than what we really want to do. Getting clear on your life's purpose and creating a life-purpose statement may sound heavy, and in some ways it is, but it's not so much heavy as powerful. Then, by using this life-purpose statement, you will formulate your life's missions. They are the vehicles you will use to fulfill your life's purpose.

Each of these missions will have a mission statement. It will also have a list of intentions, which itemizes the behaviors and actions you intend to follow to keep those missions in alignment with their and your life's purpose.

Once you're clear on your life purpose and your missions, you'll be able to formulate plans that feel good, and that will be fulfilling. You can set goals that are inspired and achievable. Behave in a way that is in alignment with who you need to be to achieve your goals, and take the actions that bring your life's purpose to fruition.

So why is *why* so important? Let's see what the research says.

Famous psychiatrist, Viktor Frankl, an inmate of the Auschwitz concentration camp, found what he deemed the key to surviving the

Holocaust: living a purposeful life. This link between life purpose—
having a *why* for life—and longevity is not new in the scientific
literature. The evidence shows that a higher purpose is associated with
decreased mortality in both older and younger adults.

More than that, though, studies have linked life purpose with a
lower incidence of certain diseases, improved brain aging, and better
overall mental health. These results are all linked to the physiological
mechanisms of the body and its ability to deal with physical,
psychological and chemical stressors, while maintaining homeostasis
(body balance).

For instance, individuals reporting more life purpose have lower
levels of chronic inflammation, including lower circulating levels of
interleukin-6, a chemical responsible for inflammation in the body.
Purpose in life has been associated with a healthier endocrine system,
cardiovascular health, and waist-to-hip ratio, as well increased high-
density lipoprotein cholesterol. Importantly, sleep improves as well.

One excellent study looked at the association between life purpose
and regulation of physiological systems involved in the stress response.
This study aimed to investigate the prospective relationships between
life purpose and allostatic load over a ten-year period. The term
"allostatic load" refers to the collective and varied physiological
liability experienced by the body as a result of its attempt to repeatedly
adjust to environmental challenges via allostasis. Allostasis, therefore,
refers to the physiological change that the cardiovascular, autonomic,
neuroendocrine, immune, and metabolic systems simultaneously
undergo in situations of stress.

The studies found that higher life purpose predicted lower levels of
allostatic load. Further, life purpose was also a strong predictor of the
differences in beliefs about how much influence individuals can exert
over their own health.

> " There is nothing in the world, I venture to say, that so effectively helps one to survive even the worse conditions as the knowledge that there is a meaning in one's life. "
>
> **VIKTOR FRANKL, Man's Search for Meaning**

Dealing with stress

Another study looked into whether having a purpose in life could stimulate the reframing of stressful situations to deal with them more productively, thereby facilitating recovery from stress and trauma.

They examined adults (aged 36 to 84 years) from the MIDUS study, and tested whether purpose in life was associated with better emotional recovery after being shown a negative picture. They looked at eyeblink startle reflex (EBR), a measure that shows sensitivity to emotional state. Greater purpose in life predicted better recovery from the negative picture or experience, which suggests that feeling that you have purpose and meaning in your life could contribute to a more healthful and adaptive regulation of negative emotional responses.

Having a higher purpose in life may provide motivation to learn from and adaptively review negative events and avoid brooding, to quickly refocus on one's goals and purpose.

This current study looked at the time structure questionnaire (TSQ), an instrument designed to measure the degree to which individuals perceive their use of time as structured and purposeful. They showed that TSQ total scores correlated positively with a sense of purpose in life.

Interestingly, it also showed that self-esteem, reported health, present standing, and optimism about the future, type-A behavior, and more efficient study habits all have a positive effect on the TSQ.

It was also no surprise to learn that depression, psychological distress, anxiety, neuroticism, physical symptoms, hopelessness, and anomie had an adverse effect of TSQ; that is, their use of time in a structured and purposeful manner was poor.

The link to income

Show me the money. Does having a life purpose result in having more money? Research has demonstrated that individual dispositions can predict individual-level economic outcomes such as personal net worth and income. For instance, conscientiousness, and a proclivity toward being organized and industrious, tends to predict greater financial success concurrently and in the future. What about purpose?

One study examined a sense of purpose as a predictor of current and future income, and net worth levels. The results showed that participants who reported a stronger sense of purpose had higher levels of household income and net worth initially, and were more likely to increase on these financial outcomes over the nine years between assessments.

What's the moral of the story? Perhaps that finding your purpose is well worth it.

So, you've got some money, you're using your time wisely, you're healthy... but what good is it if you don't live long enough to enjoy it?

We know that having a purpose in life increases your health span, but does it also increase your lifespan? One study sought to extend these findings by examining whether purpose promotes longevity across the adult years. They demonstrated that purposeful individuals lived longer than their counterparts.

In fact, for every standard deviation increase in purpose, the risk of dying diminished by 15 percent. In other words, having a purpose appears to buffer against mortality risk across the adult years.

So you will probably live long enough to make it to the old people's home, still with some coin in the bank. The good news is that you will get your money's worth out of the retirement home if you live with a purpose. The study assessed the association between purpose in life and its effect on health and mortality in community-dwelling elderly persons (about eighty years of age). The results showed that a high level of purpose in life was associated with a substantially reduced risk of mortality by up to 57 percent, compared to those with low or no purpose.

Heading in the right direction

Get ready for a cool, but sometimes challenging section of the book. This might be tricky, or even hard work, for some, but the end, you will have a clear sense of the direction you need to be heading in.

There will be plenty of thinking and writing for you to do. Whether you do it or not will be up to you. It's *all* up to you; it's all a choice. But for things to change, for your life to be better, for you to have more fun, freedom, and fulfillment you will need to do something that might not feel good at the time but will be good for you in the long run. Whether you do the exercises or not, you are the reason for all your current results, and will be the reason for all your future results.

The framework we're going to follow in this section is shown in the graphic below.

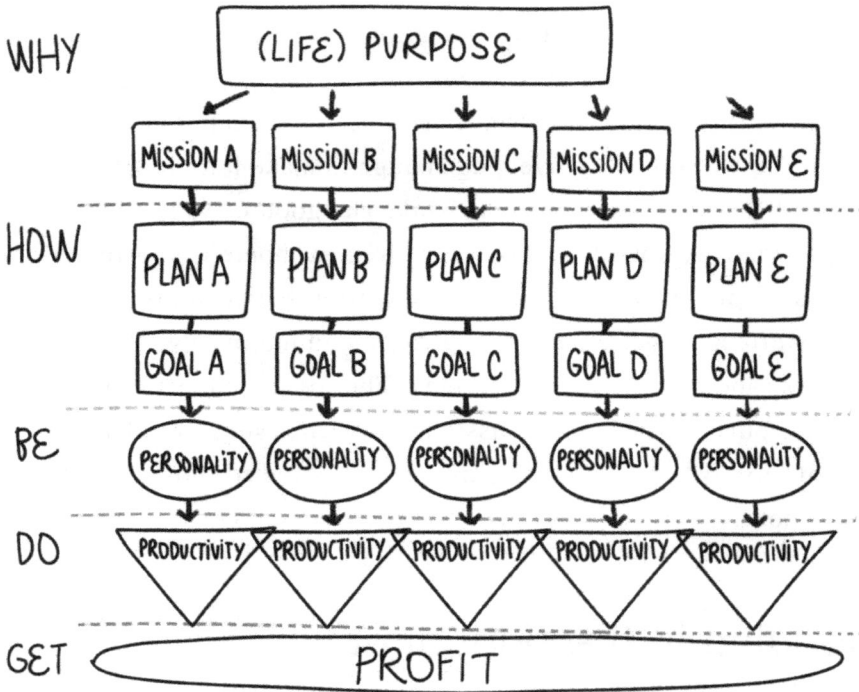

WHY	(LIFE) PURPOSE

WHY	(LIFE) PURPOSE
	MISSION A · MISSION B · MISSION C · MISSION D · MISSION E
HOW	PLAN A · PLAN B · PLAN C · PLAN D · PLAN E
	GOAL A · GOAL B · GOAL C · GOAL D · GOAL E
BE	PERSONALITY · PERSONALITY · PERSONALITY · PERSONALITY · PERSONALITY
DO	PRODUCTIVITY · PRODUCTIVITY · PRODUCTIVITY · PRODUCTIVITY · PRODUCTIVITY
GET	PROFIT

Motivation

One of the things I'd like you to have an awareness of is the difference between motivation and inspiration. You've probably heard the story about the donkey, the carrot and the stick. It goes a bit like this. If I want a donkey to move forward in a specific direction, how would I do it?

Option one would be to dangle a carrot in front of the donkey. We call that "towards motivation," and it works. It would, in the beginning, get the donkey to move forward.

Option two could be to walk behind the donkey with a big stick, whacking it on the rump. We call that "away motivation," and that works as well.

The catch with option one is that, over time, the carrot will shrivel up. Or the donkey would realize it's never going to get the carrot and give up. The catch with option two is that you would get sick of whacking the donkey on the rump, and the animal would stop. Sometimes your motivation is high enough to get you kick started, but it's unsustainable. Motivation is the application of an external force, and that's what causes the donkey to move.

Inspiration, on the other hand, comes from within. People often use words like *want* or *need* when talking about motivation. There's a big difference between motivation and inspiration. Inspiration comes from within, and it lasts forever as long as it's connected with life purpose.

I could use a sports team as an analogy. The coach might say, "If we don't win tonight, you're all going to cop a beating." Or, "You've all got to go and have cold showers." Or, "You've all got to run a one-hundred-kilometer race."

Or the coach could say, "If you win tonight, I'm going to buy you all dinner." That's motivation.

By the way, "away" motivation is much more potent than "towards" motivation. We will do a lot to avoid pain.

Inspiration

To be at ease in your life, you need to be *inspired*. Let's take a look at that word for a minute. Its origin is from the mid-fourteenth-century *enspiren*, meaning "to fill (the mind/ heart with grace); also "to prompt or induce (someone to do something)." From the Latin *inspirare* comes the meaning, "inflame; blow into." The general sense of "influence or animate with an idea or purpose" is from the late fourteenth century. I love this definition from Dictionary.com: "To be aroused, animated, or imbued with the spirit to do something, by or as if by supernatural or divine influence."

Most great sporting coaches begin with inspiration. Most coaches get the person connected with their purpose, to know why they're on the field. When you're on *why*, when you're on purpose, when you're inspired, you get out of bed before the alarm clock goes off. You're excited to get into the day because you're inspired.

You're on purpose. That's where you want to play.

11 Dream Again

> **"The biggest adventure you can take
> is to live the life of your dreams."**
> **OPRAH WINFREY**

Sadly, many of us have stopped daydreaming. We reach midlife battle-scarred and hardened, having lost our ability to imagine and dream big. I often look at a little boy, or little girl, and I can see in their eyes that they are dreaming. They might be walking along holding their parent's hand, swaying their body, taking everything in, and at the same time I know they're creating their version of how they would like it all to turn out.

Children have no limits on what is possible. They're going to become heroes. A fire fighter and save someone from a burning house. A doctor and save the injured patient. A police officer and protect society. A parent and raise children. A fighter pilot and protect the country. An astronaut (that was me) and discover distant worlds. A dancer and entertain the world. A vet and save animals.

You probably used to daydream, too. You were going to become a hero. You were going to leave a legacy. You were going to live a life a mattered, maybe even an extraordinary ordinary life.

Just this morning before I sat down to write this chapter, my wife Michelle and I were sitting up in bed with our Saturday-morning cup of tea, with all the kids crowding the bed (our kids are aged eighteen, sixteen and fourteen). We were talking about the movie we all went to see the night before called *Dunkirk*. It was about the evacuation of Allied soldiers from the beaches and harbor of Dunkirk, in the north of France, during World War II. Lots of Spitfire planes doing dogfights in the sky, very cool.

As we discussed the movie, I made the sounds of fighter planes, machine guns, helicopters, and jets. Michelle told the kids that I'd probably dreamed of being a fighter pilot as a kid and ran around the house making those sounds all day. She was right. I did dream of being a fighter pilot (before I switched to being an astronaut).

Does this sound familiar to you? I wonder if you could start to dream again. Many midlifers make the mistake of believing that they're too old, too rigid for change, or that change is too hard. It's true that over time our bodies become less flexible, our minds can become less able to adapt, and yes, change can be hard.

But if you really believe that that's all there is, stop reading now and go back to your stuck and tepid life. But if you believe that your life could change, that you do still have the resources to make a change, then let's get you dreaming again, starting right now.

Start by writing a list of all the things you dreamed of being when you were a kid. *All* of them, as crazy as they may seem to you now. The purpose of this exercise is not for you to start pursuing those dreams now (although you could), but for you to start daydreaming again. Let's bring the dream muscle back to life again.

It's okay you can't remember everything. See if you can get just a few, then just a few more. I wonder if you can remember seven to fourteen of them. Take as long as you need to remember and write.

📖 JOURNAL TIME

Stop reading, grab your journal, open to a blank page and write at the top "My Old Dreams." Now start writing.

How did you go? Did you get it done? Did you take a few trips down memory lane?

Now spend just a couple of minutes looking at the list you created and look for a central theme of those daydreams. What were you doing? Who were you a hero for? What was the moral of those daydreams?

📖 JOURNAL TIME

"The moral of my daydreams is..."

Now that you've taken a look at your old daydreams and started the process, how about trying for some new daydreams? If you were to pretend that anything was possible, that you got unstuck and out of tepid, what would be possible? If you were to overcome your fear, sort out your beliefs, and develop a strategy for action, what would you daydream?

Take yourself back to when you were that little girl or little boy, when you believed anything was possible. When you dreamed of becoming a hero, of making a difference.

This get-it-all-out session is an opportunity to dream big. Be silly, be outrageous, be selfish, be crazy, be courageous, be naughty, but also be authentic, and believe it's all possible. In fact, write down the things that you *don't* think are possible but are nice to dream about anyway.

> ❝ I like nonsense; it wakes up the brain cells. ❞
> **DR. SEUSS**

At forty-nine, I still dream of being an astronaut. I can't remember trigonometry and I get dizzy if the action is too fast on a movie screen, so my chances of becoming one are probably zero to none. But I still dream about it.

📖 JOURNAL TIME

Take as long as you need to dump as many unspoken and unwritten thoughts on what you daydream about:

- What might you love to do and be if you could?
- Where might you live?
- Who might you meet?
- What might you experience?
- What job would you have?
- Where might you travel?
- What legacy might you leave?

Well done. That can be a tricky exercise. What I encourage you to do over the next few weeks, and for the rest of your life, is to make a note of those daydreams in your journal, and maybe even add to them.

> ❝ You have 86 billion brain cells waiting
> to be activated by a big dream. ❞
> **DR. BEN CARVOSSO**

12 Designer Diary

> **Efforts and courage are not enough without purpose and direction.**
> **JOHN F. KENNEDY**

Where do you want your life to go? What's the path that you're on? What is your purpose for the next period of time, whether it's three, five, or even ten years? If *you* don't decide these things, if *you* don't make a decision about where you want your life to head in the next ten years, someone else will.

This is worth repeating. If *you* don't decide, someone else will. It might be your parents. It might be your partner. It might be your boss. It might be the government. Someone else will decide for you.

I'd like to set you some homework. To set the scene. To take a moment to look at what could be the underlying purpose of your life. Call the assignment "My Designer Diary." It's straightforward. I want you to think about where you are right now, and project yourself into the future ten years from now.

I've said previously that your *why*, your purpose, is a general direction. So think about how would life be years from now if you were to get right in your river. Right in your flow. If you were to experience more ease in your life and your river, and started to become the person you need to become. You begin to develop the character traits, ethos, culture and habits that someone with that kind of *why* would develop.

Then you start to do some of these things. You start to make some of the decisions, take some of the actions, and employ some of the strategies that will help you achieve the things that you want to accomplish in your life. Things that are on mission, on purpose, in the river of why that make you feel like there's ease in your life.

Pretend, just for a moment, that for now you're not quite in your river. You've read this book, and over the next few days, weeks, and perhaps even months for some of you, you get on *why*, on purpose. Become who you need to be, do what you need to do.

Where will you be in ten years?

It's ten years later. You're getting into your bed, or your hammock, or wherever else you sleep, and you're writing in your diary. You're going to write about this day (ten years in the future). How did it feel to live this ideal day? This perfect day, which, if you could live it forever, would make you die happy. This day is a product of you having been on purpose for ten years. Being who you need to be. Doing what you need to do. How does it turn out?

> ❝ I never travel without my diary.
> One should always have something
> sensational to read on the train. ❞
> **OSCAR WILDE**

Your diary entry might go something like this:

"Wow, what a day. This was one of the best days ever. This morning I got up at six o'clock and it was dark outside. I put on my running gear and went for a run. The run was so special. It's part of my morning ritual. As I was coming home, the sun was coming up, just starting to twinkle through the trees. Not only was the sun twinkling through the trees, but there was also an incredible smell that started to develop as the sunlight hit the trees. It rained last night, and there was a beautiful kind of eucalyptus-y, pine needle-y fresh, fragrant smell coming out of the earth. As I ran up my driveway, I looked at my house. I'm so proud of the home that I've created. It's more than just a house. This place is a home, and it's the home where I've raised my three children. As I walked in the front door, my wife was getting out of bed. She smiled and gave me a kiss. She asked if I wanted a cup of tea. We sat at the kitchen table and we chatted.

This is one of my diary entries, and yours is obviously going to be different. Think about all the various aspects of your life ten years from now. Where are you living? What job do you do? Where do you work? What time do you get out of bed? What do you eat? How old are you? Who is in your life? Where do you wake up? What do you eat for breakfast? What's the view like from your house? What kind of conversations do you have throughout the day? (Not just with other people, but with yourself as well.) What thoughts do you have during the day? Who do you hang out with? What do some of the more mundane aspects of your life look like? How do you spend your day? Who are your friends? What do you do each day that gives you personal fulfillment? What kind of legacy might you leave?

This diary entry that you write should encompass just one typical day, not a special holiday or other kind of unique day. This is just a normal day. It's an extraordinary ordinary day, but keep in mind: if you could live this day every day, you would die happy.

Don't just answer the questions from the above list. Write more, and write in as much detail as you can. Describe your day in images, sounds, feelings, and thoughts. You could even put some data in there, a few numbers.

JOURNAL TIME

"The moral of my daydreams is..."

Open your journal to a blank page and start writing.

Remember, your diary entry is made up. It's not a goal. It's not something you'll be held accountable for. Don't carve it in stone or write it in blood. It's just an idea of how, maybe, just maybe, life might turn out for you ten years from now. As we all know, life can happen. There's no way of accurately predicting how our lives are going to be in the future. But there is a very real underlying purpose for doing this exercise.

Later on in this book, I will ask you to read this diary entry and look for the theme. When you read a book, whether it's fiction or nonfiction, you might be asked by a friend to tell them what the book is about. What is the moral of the story?

When you look back on this diary entry a little later, that's what you will do. You will look for the moral of the story. The underlying theme of this person's life. Your diary entry will be a summary of you being on purpose, who you need to be, doing what you need to do. What is the underlying theme of your life? What is important to you?

This is a great exercise, but I've got to tell you, it's not easy. I often set this activity for my coaching clients, and fully fifty percent of them don't do it. The most common reason for not doing it is that they're wallowing in the mangroves, trying to get back to the river, but it seems so far away. The whole idea of contemplating how their life could be seems so foreign, so far away, and so complicated that can't bring themselves to do the exercise.

Another reason people don't do this diary exercise is that that have too much fear about who they might need to become to achieve that kind of lifestyle. They may have low self-worth, low self-confidence and little self-belief, and live in fear of who they may actually need to become to achieve that sort of life.

That's okay. And you don't have to do the exercise either. But I strongly encourage you to do so.

> " Even if you're unhappy, just pretend that you're happy. Eventually your smile will be contagious to yourself. I had to learn that. I used to think, 'I'm being fake,' but you know what? Better to be fake and happy than real and miserable. "
> **EVANGELINE LILLY**

Now I'm going to ask you to pretend. Just pretend, for a moment, that you could get on *why*, that you could get on purpose, in your river, and start experiencing the ease again. Just pretend. I'm not asking you to actually do it. Just pretend you could.

I'm asking you not to become it now. Don't even start to do some of the things you may need to do to create that ideal day, that future diary. I'm asking you to just pretend. Pretend that by the time you've read this book, you will be on *why*; you will be who you need to be. You're starting to do the things you need to do, and your life has begun to move in the right direction. Just pretend.

Good luck with the diary entry. Enjoy the exercise. I hope that you write pages and pages, in detail, about your ideal day ten years from now.

13 It's Time to Make a Statement

> **❝You just decide what your values are in life and what you are going to do, and then you feel like you count, and that makes life worth living. It makes my life meaningful.❞**
> **ANNIE LENNOX**

Hopefully, you've been doing some thinking over the last couple of chapters, thinking about what your life might look like if you were to make some changes. If you were to get on purpose, set a plan, become who you need to become and take action.

In this chapter, we're going to help you get clear on what is your current purpose, or your *why*. In what direction is your deep purpose or river of *why* flowing at the moment?

A purpose statement captures in a sentence or paragraph the reason for your life. What are you here to do? What is going to be your life's work? Who are you going to impact on your life's journey? What legacy will you leave? Think of a statement that might be found on your headstone.

This will become the guide for all your future large and small decisions. It will guide the missions in your life: family mission, health mission, career mission, business, mission, etc. It will become your place of inspiration.

It's not a corporate, gold-plated mission statement that is meaningless to the people it's supposed to represent and inspire. For example, here is the ANZ bank's mission (purpose) statement: "Creating a better, more balanced world. Our purpose is to help shape a world where people and communities thrive. That's why we strive to create a balanced, sustainable economy in which everyone can take part and build a better life."

If I were to ask one of the ANZ's customers, or any of their staff, probably none would identify with that mission statement in relation to the bank. And I'm sure that if the bank died, those words wouldn't be on its tombstone.

A corporate mission statement is not what you are writing. Your purpose statement will inspire you to be your best. It will guide your plans, goals, behaviors, and actions every day.

If we take a look at this statement from Tim Cook, Apple's CEO, to prospective Apple employees, we might get a better feel for what drives Apple's behavior and makes it the United States' biggest company: "Apple has always been different. A different kind of company with a different view of the world. It's a special place where we have the opportunity to create the best products on earth— products that change lives and help shape the future. It's a privilege we hold dear."

And another statement that Tim Cook offered in an interview shortly after Steve Jobs passed away: "We believe that we are on the face of the Earth to make great products and that's not changing. We are constantly focusing on innovating. We believe in the simple, not the complex. We believe that we need to own and control the primary technologies behind the products we make, and participate only in markets where we can make a significant contribution. We believe in saying no to thousands of projects so that we can really focus on the few that are truly important and meaningful to us. We believe in deep collaboration and cross-pollination of our groups, which allow us to innovate in a way that others cannot. And frankly, we don't settle for anything less than excellence in every group in the company, and we have the self-honesty to admit when we're wrong and the courage to change. And I think, regardless of who is in what job, those values are so embedded in this company that Apple will do extremely well."

Wow, that makes sense. Have you ever used Apple products, or dealt with the support you can see reflected in this statement? Disclaimer: Over the last seven years our family has invested in Apple, with two iMacs, one MacBook Pro, two MacBook Airs, four iPads, three Apple TVs and eight iPhones.

Your purpose, or *why*, is in a constant state of flexibility, and around every ten to twenty years or so it will go through a slight shift. Now, a minor shift is not a ninety-degree turn, more a 2–5 degree flex. So understand that the life-purpose statement is right for now, and it's okay if you come back to revisit it every year and eventually find it needs a tweak. I probably tweak mine every two to three years, mostly in words but occasionally at a level of core purpose. You will evolve, and so can your life-purpose statement.

Guidelines for success

Let me give you a couple of guiding thoughts to set you up for success:

- You cannot force your life-purpose statement. It's something that will ooze out of you with careful and thoughtful questioning. It will be tricky, often frustrating. Sometimes the core value, emotion or belief you're trying to capture will be on the tip of your tongue or pen, and yet you're unable to get it out. As Yoda said, "Patience you must have, my young padawan."

- It will help to put you in an inspirational environment. Remember that your state is governed by your focus, language, and physiology. All this can be influenced by your environment. Find an environment that brings out your best. Personally, I love finding a fabulous five-star restaurant or hotel to sit in to build the vision for my life. I use this environment when I do my ten-year designer diary (chapter 12). For you, it could be the beach, a holiday home in the mountains, sitting by a river in front of a campfire (I've done that, too), or just in your favorite room in your home. Wherever it is, find the place that brings out your best.

- Don't judge every word, wondering what will others think. This isn't for others; this is for you. Keep it simple but powerful.

- The thought of fulfilling that purpose should create a sense of excitement, and at the same time frighten you just a little (or a lot). The grander your life's purpose, the more growth for you and the planet, but at the risk of more fear of who you might need to become and what you might need to do. This statement will set the standards for your life. In the wise words of Franklin D. Roosevelt: "Happiness lies in the joy of achievement and the thrill of creative effort."

- As you go through the process of creating your life-purpose statement, remain flexible. I'll give you a template to follow, but you're free to make up our own or change mine until it feels right for you. There are no rules when creating a statement that will become the guide for your life.

- Importantly, have *fun*. This might feel weird, and there might be some difficult moment, but I encourage you to keep a smile on your dial. It will help in creating a statement that lights you up.

Creating your life-purpose statement

Before you do the following exercise and create your statement, it's crucial that you have done your designer diary (chapter 12), and skipped a couple of chapters forward to complete your values exercise (chapter 23). Both of these activities will help you create the vision and find the words that will build your life-purpose statement.

Take a moment to read over your designer diary again and ask yourself whom you're serving in that diary. What person or thing that is bigger than you is your life impacting? Who will your legacy impact?

Now grab your top five values (or ten) and a thesaurus. I love http://www.thesaurus.com, which you can access on your phone via an app. Sometimes you need to use a different but same word to help the wordsmithing of your final statement.

A note on wordsmithing. When you do this exercise, just follow the formula spelled out below. Don't worry if you don't create beautifully a poetic, flowing sentence. You will have the chance to fix that up later. Just get started on it.

JOURNAL TIME

LifeCEO.com/RESOURCES

Open your journal to a blank page and follow the five steps:

1. Create one list of words listing the people you want to serve, and another listing the values that are important to you.
2. Now create the structure: "My life purpose is to serve _____ by being _____, and _____, and through becoming _____ and _____ for myself and others who wish to learn and grow with me."

3. Now fill in the blanks with the names of people from your first list, and your top five to ten values words from your second list. You might need a few goes at it, and it might feel a little frustrating. It's worth rewriting the sentence each time you make a change until you start to feel the flow, but don't change the overall sentence yet.

4. Now you can start molding the whole sentence to suit the words you have used.

5. Review and finish the statement. Write a final version on a blank sheet of paper and pin it up for a day or two. Keep reworking it until it feels right. You will know it's right when it puts a smile on your face and makes your heart race.

My own personal example from 2005:

1. People I want to serve: family / mankind

   Values that are important to me: drive / powerful / loving / focused / energized / wisdom / leader / creator / balanced / courage / mentor (inspiration)

2. "My life purpose is to serve _____ by being _____, and _____, and through becoming _____ and _____ for myself and others who wish to learn and grow with me."

3. Two attempts to write my statement:

   a) "My life purpose is to serve *my family* by being *focused*, and *energized*, and through becoming *a leader* and *balanced* for myself and others who wish to learn and grow with me."

   b) "My life purpose is to serve *my family and mankind* by being *focused*, and *energized*, *with leadership* and through becoming *powerful* and *balanced* for myself and others who wish to learn and grow with me."

4. Tidying up the statement:

"My life purpose is to serve *my family and mankind through focus energy, and leadership* and *with balance and power of love* for myself and others who wish to learn and grow with me."

5. After reviewing and finishing my statement:

"My life purpose is to serve my family and mankind, through focused energy, and leadership and with the balance and power of love for myself and other, I will inspire all those who wish to learn and grow with me."

Another review three days later (2005): "My life purpose is to serve my family and mankind, through leading with energy, inspiration and a sense of adventure, I will encourage all those I contact to build their dream and live an outstanding life."

Another review eight years later (2013): "My life purpose is to serve and create with energy, adventure, and abundance. To love, learn, lead and through playful inspiration, encourage others to build their dream, and leave a legacy."

Another review three years later (2016): "My life purpose is to serve and create with energy, adventure and abundance, a creative mindset and playful inspiration, I will leave a legacy in all those I connect with, so by choice, they build their dream machine and live an amazing life."

As you can see, the process of writing your mission statement is ongoing. The initial writing period may take a couple of hours, but it will continue to evolve during the rest of your life.

It is essential that you finish the statement. Don't leave it hanging just because it's not perfect. Trust me, your life won't be perfect, either. Just complete the statement for now, and start using it as a guide in your decision-making. Use it to formulate the statements for your life's missions in the next chapter.

As your life CEO, you *must* have something to guide you. This is a statement that you will learn by heart; it will help you do what's important and make your life count.

Don't file it away, but don't do the opposite and consider it carved in stone either. This statement is for you. It's *your* guide, and no one else's. Feel free to print out a nice copy, frame it and hang in your study. Or make it a screensaver on your computer. Or write it on a small card that you can carry in your wallet. Put it somewhere that allows it to stay top of your mind.

This is a great thing you have done. It underpins everything you will do from this point forward, and I don't just mean in this book but for the rest of your life. It will be your guide, as CEO. It will give you clarity around what is important and will help you know when not to compromise.

It is a *life-purpose* statement.

14 Your Mission, Should You Choose to Accept It

> ❝When you discover your mission, you will feel its demand. It will fill you with enthusiasm and a burning desire to get to work on it.❞
>
> **W. CLEMENT STONE**

We have spent some time looking at your life's purpose and creating a statement for it. The next important step is to look at the methods you will use to fulfill that purpose.

A company has departments: marketing, sales, HR, finance, product development, and so on. Each department has a job to do, a mission to fulfill to contribute to the companies.

It is the same with you. As your life CEO, you need to consider the different aspects of your life that you'll use to play out your life's purpose. They could include:

- Family
- Relationships
- Health
- Money
- Business
- Career

- Fun Stuff
- Partner / spouse
- Parent
- Brother / sister
- Spiritual
- Hobby

I encourage you to keep the number of missions to more than five but less than seven. More than seven will result in severe overwhelm. This means that some of your missions might need to be chunked together; for example, *parent*, *brother*, *partner* might all get chunked under *family*.

Remember, these missions will be in constant flux as aspects of your life evolve. When you're ten, your missions are different to when you're twenty, and again when you're forty, and again when you're sixty, and so on.

What are your current missions? What are the different aspects, roles or vehicles in your life right now? What might be coming up in the next twelve months?

📖 **JOURNAL TIME** ☁ LifeCEO.com/RESOURCES

Make a list of all the different areas of your life, the various roles you have, and the places where you spend significant chunks of time. Then take that list and divide it into five to seven different categories.

Great work. Here is the thing about missions: while they are different, they are all working toward the same end purpose—your life's purpose. It's a bit like a sporting team, which is made of various players who all have different roles, behaviors, and actions. They all come together to fulfill the goal of winning the match. Take soccer, for example:

- **Forward**: Usually placed behind the striker, this player uses speed to make crisp, accurate passes.
- **Goalkeeper**: Prevents the ball from entering the goal; the only player allowed to touch the ball with their hands.
- **Striker**: Offensive position whose primary role is to score goals; this player plays a forward position in the opposing team's zone.
- **Stopper**: Stays back, marks an opposing forward, and prevents that player from being in a scoring position.
- **Sweeper**: Stays back, anticipates defensive mistakes by teammates and makes up for them; this player is not required to carefully mark an opposing player.

Each player has their own plan as part of the whole. They play by different rules, have different behaviors and characteristics, and take different actions, but everything comes together (hopefully) in the end, with the winner having the most goals scored.

Creating a mission statement

Now we'll take a look at each of your missions and create a simple mission statement that will help keep you on track. Plus, we'll add to that statement a list of guiding intentions that will further help you act in alignment with your mission and larger life purpose.

" A mission statement is not something you write overnight... But fundamentally, your mission statement becomes your constitution, the solid expression of your vision and values. It becomes the criterion by which you measure everything else in your life. "

STEPHEN COVEY

JOURNAL TIME

This exercise can be a lot of fun. It allows you to be more specific than you might have been when you created your life purpose.

1. Write down one of your missions, but this time write it in a way that is fun, and feels inspiring, even a little poetic.
   Example 1: Money mission = financial-freedom mission
   Example 2: Career mission = paid-inspiration mission

2. Write a sentence or short paragraph that represents that mission, something that reflects your life-purpose statement. It will likely contain a selection of your highest values (top twenty). Make it inspirational, fun, and something that will set the tone for your behavior and actions. Start with: "My _____ mission is to..."

3. Now follow up that statement with a list of intentions for the way you will behave, and the actions you will take to fulfill your mission. This should an outside how your mission would play out in the world.

   I intend to be...
   I intend to do...
   I intend to act...
   I intend to think...

4. Review and finish the statement. As with your life-purpose statement, I encourage you to write a final version on a blank sheet of paper, pin it up for a day or two, and keep reworking it until it feels right. Again, you will know it's right when it puts a smile on your face and makes your heart race.

Now repeat that four-step process for each of the roles in your life. You could do it all at once or spread the process over a few days or weeks. However you do it, at least start on one so you get a feel for the framework for creating a mission statement. Remember the guiding thoughts that we discussed around writing your life-purpose statement:

- Don't force it.
- Put yourself in an inspirational environment.
- Don't judge your words.
- The mission should create a sense of nervous excitement.
- There are no rules telling you how to do it.
- Have fun.

Following are some examples of mission-statements.

Financial-freedom mission: "My financial-freedom mission is to create a level of wealth that allows my family and me to live our dreams in a state of abundance and freedom." Therefore, this is what I intend to do:

- Be patient with the growth of my wealth.
- Seek out opportunities that will provide the income to build this wealth.
- Invest that wealth wisely for ever-increasing financial growth.

- Be quiet and humble as my wealth grows.
- Always work in an environment of fair exchange.
- Surround myself with a trusted team of advisors that can nurture and grow my wealth.
- Teach my children about money and its use.
- Use my financial freedom to help.
- Always keep the value of money in perspective.

Paid-inspiration mission: "My paid-inspiration mission is to inspire the leaders of our planet. By serving them, I serve many, and due to the life-changing value I provide, I'm rewarded personally and financially for that service. I am paid to save lives." Therefore, this is what I intend to do:

- Seek out opportunities that will allow me to connect with our leaders.
- Surround myself with a team of inspirational advisors who can nurture me and contribute to my success.
- Stretch myself through embracing uncertainty for more certainty.
- Lead a life of example.
- Keep the bigger picture in mind; be grateful, and ensure that my actions are good for me, good for others and good for the greater good.
- Educate myself on how to become the best coach I can be.
- Look for ways to compress for quality and leverage for maximum impact.

Sharpen-the-saw mission: "My sharpen-the-saw mission is to build a body and mind that supports me in achieving my dreams." Therefore, this is what I intend to do:

- Exercise on a daily basis in a way that charges and fills my body with life-giving oxygen.

- Fuel my body with food that supplies the nutrients to build strength.
- Stretch my mind on a daily basis by filling it with positive, stimulating thoughts.
- Read a book that stretches my mind.
- Journal my life experiences.
- Practice placing my mind and body in a zero state.
- Put my sleep time in rhythm.

Playtime mission: "My playtime mission is to put joy, laughter, fun, excitement, challenge, friendship, simplicity, and love into my life continually." Therefore, this is what I intend to do:

- Be spontaneous.
- Be organized with my time to create the flexibility and space to play.
- Create and keep friendships.
- Remain alert to the beauty of simplicity.
- Seek out opportunities.
- Put more laughter on my face.

Happiness lies in the joy of achievement and the thrill of creative effort.
FRANKLIN D. ROOSEVELT

The wheel of life

We have worked on designing your life's purpose and missions so you can go into each day with a guiding vision for how you want it to turn out. Before we leave this chapter, I want to leave you with an insight about where we often spend our time. Why is it that we sometimes find ourselves pursuing some missions more than others? And why does life sometimes feel like it's hard work, that it's rough and not complete?

You may have seen the wheel of life before. You know, the diagram that is often displayed at personal-development seminars. There is a circle (the rim of the wheel), which is where your plans and goals sit. It has lines (the spokes), which are your missions. Everything meets in the center (the hub): your purpose.

WHEEL OF LIFE - YOUR MISSIONS

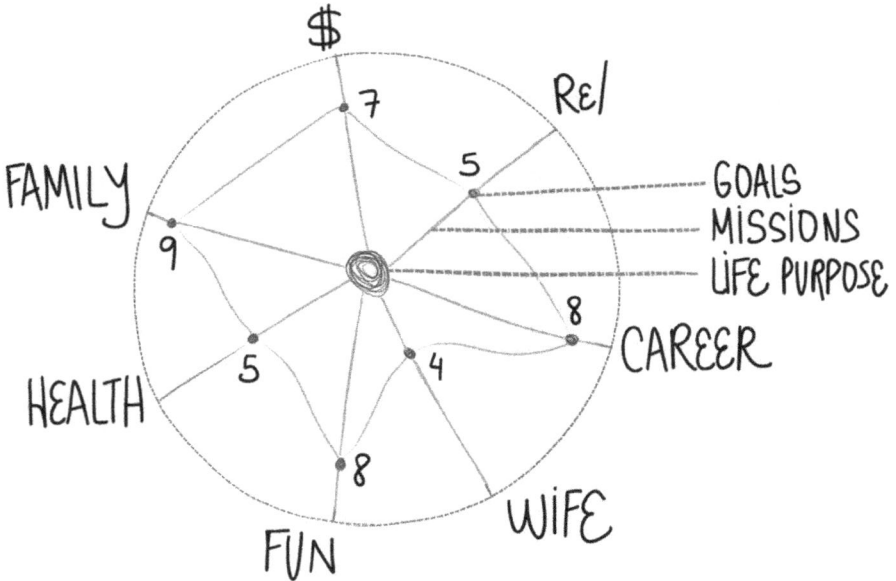

$
7
Rel
5
FAMILY
GOALS
MISSIONS
LIFE PURPOSE
9
8
CAREER
5
4
HEALTH
8
WIFE
FUN

When you do that wheel-of-life exercise, you're usually asked to fill out each of the spokes with a different aspect of your life; a different role or mission that you have, such as parent, husband/wife/partner, or businessperson. Your career could mean another role, or perhaps there's a favorite hobby you spend a lot of time on.

When you fill out the spokes, you rate each role or mission on a scale of zero to ten. Ten means it's a fantastic role. You are indeed fulfilling that role. You feel great about it; you have joy in that aspect of your life.

Zero means the role sucks big time. You're not putting any energy and effort into it, and it doesn't feel right. In fact, you feel entirely unfulfilled.

You then start putting a mark on each spoke from zero to ten. After you've done that, you join the dots. The theory is that if your life is balanced, you will have a smooth, round-looking wheel (unlike the illustration above).

JOURNAL TIME

LifeCEO.com/RESOURCES

Have a go at this exercise yourself. Draw a circle, add your spokes (missions), then put a mark on a scale of 0–10 on each of the spokes. Join up the dots with a connecting line. How does your wheel of life look?

What do you like to work on? Where do you find yourself setting goals? Looking at your wheel is an opportunity to notice the areas of your life that leave you feeling unfulfilled, that need some attention, energy, time, money, and focus.

When I have coaching clients complete that wheel of life, I've often noticed something interesting. I ask them: "Where would you like to work today in your coaching? Where would you like to set a goal today?"

Guess which roles they pick? The ones that they're already doing well. The roles that might be a seven, eight, nine or ten out of ten. They don't pick the roles that are a three or five out of ten.

Sound familiar? Have you ever found yourself focusing on the areas of your life that are already working?

The reason you do this is simple. You have successful strategies and methods for those roles that you're doing well at. But your strategies suck when it comes to other roles in your life, the roles that you're not doing so well at. To work on those areas would be tough, so you don't. You continue to work on the areas that are great, and don't work on the areas that aren't great.

Over time, the divide between the two becomes even greater. And the greater the divide, the more uneven your spokes and the rougher the ride.

" Life is like riding a bicycle. To keep your balance, you must keep moving. "
ALBERT EINSTEIN

Is your life rolling well? If you looked at your wheel and connected the dots, would it be going *clunkety-clunk, clunkety-clunk, clunkety-clunk*, or would it be rolling smoothly? Does your wheel feel balanced? Does your life feel balanced?

When your life feels balanced, you stop feeling like you're busy. You stop feeling like it's all hard work. It feels easy. Instead of feeling like busywork, it feels like you're doing your life's work.

To use the company analogy again, there are different departments, but each department does not get the same allocation of time, energy, resources, or money. But by allocating the assets to a department that is on mission and pursuing the company's purpose, all departments benefit.

Balance in all areas of your life comes from making sure there are symbiotic relationships between all areas of your life, and, as your life CEO, you take responsibility for their fulfillment. Keep this in mind when we get to the planning and goal-setting chapters. Where are you going to put your focus first?

15 Taking a Closer Look at Purpose

> **" Our greatest human adventure is the evolution of consciousness. We are in this life to enlarge the soul, liberate the spirit, and light up the brain. "**
> **TOM ROBBINS**

If you are up to this chapter of the book, you're well on your way to creating the life you really want. That feels more like you're doing your life's work rather than just your busywork. One thing I love about my coaching work is seeing the growth and transformation that takes place in people's lives when they get their mindset sorted. More than that, though, is how fast it happens and how much they evolve.

Don't get me wrong. I know that habits can be tough to change, and many times I have found myself cycling over the same stuff with clients. It can get a little uncomfortable as they battle with embracing the change that's required while still trying to hang onto the new.

So if you found yourself doing this in the last chapter, or find yourself doing it in future chapters, know that that's perfectly normal. Things can get messy and confusing for a while. Then there will be change and personal growth, resulting in a better you and a better world.

Life is great, but then it starts to feel a little boring, tepid. Then you make a change, things get messy and confusing... and so it repeats.

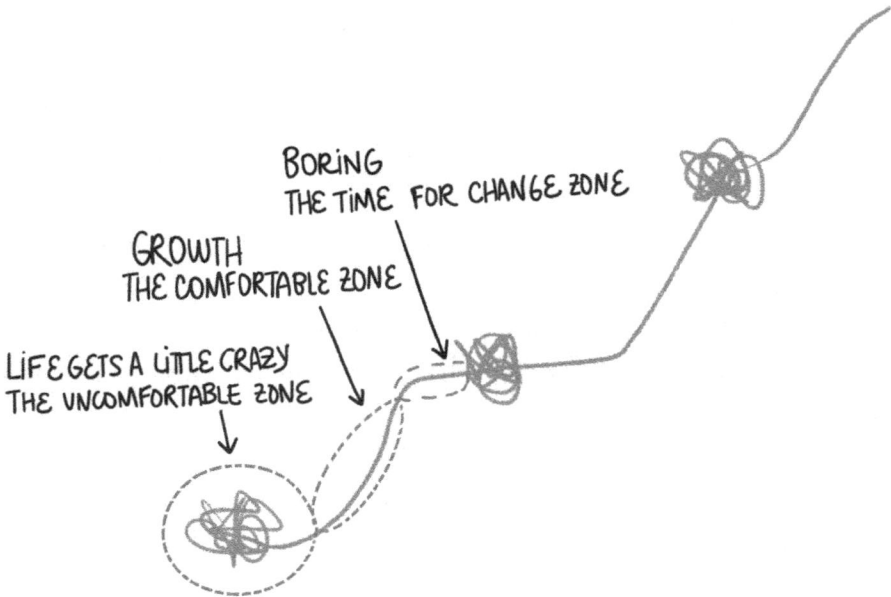

That cycle can vary weekly, monthly, or yearly, so be okay with change, be kind to yourself. If change doesn't happen straightaway, know that change is always a component of life if you want to be a better you and leave a better world. *Eudemonia* (human flourishing), the pursuit of the highest of human good, and its associated Aristotelian word, *arete*, the attainment of excellence in life, are both words depicting movement towards improvement.

Remember that as you evolve and become a better version of you, so might your life's purpose evolve (every ten to twenty years), and undoubtedly your missions will evolve and change. The life-purpose and missions work you do is something to revisit once a year or so. Periodically, allocate half a day to sit and reflect on your purpose and missions, and fine-tune them as the new and different versions of you and your life evolve.

But that's enough about the Greeks.

The Japanese have a word for purpose: *ikigai* (生き甲斐). It means "reason for being." Everybody, according to Japanese culture, has an *ikigai*. Discovering your *ikigai* (what you have just done), the Japanese believe, is often not easy, but when achieved it gives you the highest satisfaction and joy in life.

Wikipedia explains the words come from the term *ikigai* compounds two Japanese words: *iki* (生き), meaning life or alive, and *kai* (甲斐), meaning an effect, a result, worth, use or benefit. It is a reason for living (being alive): it gives meaning to life and makes it worth living.

The word *ikigai* is usually used to indicate the source of value in a person's life, or the things that make someone's life worthwhile. These can be grandiose things, or simple things, like being a leader, business owner, teacher, parent, or artist.

I believe that the missions in your life are what bring life to your purpose. Continue to find yours.

Make your missions count

Don't settle for small. Some time ago I had a defining moment. I had just started the transition from owning a successful radiology company to my coaching career. It was a Friday night in early December, and I was attending a Christmas function with my wife. It had been a busy finish to the year with our kids, so she decided to head home early, and I would catch a lift with one of the attendees a little later.

At about eleven-thirty P.M. I got a call from her, and there was dread in her voice as she asked me to come straight home. I got a lift home straightaway. I found her sitting on the edge of our bed with a look of horror on her face. "John just called," she said. "The money is gone."

My friend John had introduced me to an investor (of other people's money), and it appeared he had been committing fraud on more levels than you can imagine. A big chunk (like, really big) of our investment money was gone, and gone for good. Money that we had been counting on to clear some debts. Money we had been asking him to return for some weeks in the lead-up to Christmas.

I felt sick; a deep-heartache, dizzy, faint kind of sick. I knew this put us in a precarious situation with our finances. That we had days, or perhaps weeks, to get our finances in order.

The following Monday, I arrived at the practice and informed my team that we had to reduce costs immediately, and, sadly, many of them would have to finish up in the coming weeks. There was no room for stories, for making it seem better than it was. It was a raw and painful conversation, but it was action I had to take if we were to get through the next six months.

I decided that we would "simplify for more," words that became my theme during the following year. To save money, I looked for more ways of simplifying how we did things. But there was a catch. I was associating the word *simple* with *small*. I realized that, slowly but surely, I had started to think small. The big dreams were gone, and but that was okay, I told myself, because I was simplifying. *No!* It wasn't until a couple of years later that I realized how small I had been playing. The big dreams weren't there anymore. Big dreams meant big complication, not simplification. Ouch.

When has this happened in your life? Have you been playing small, thinking small, having small dreams? Stop. Start thinking big again.

What would you need to pursue to fulfill your mission and life purpose? It could be a small thing, but what if it's a big thing?

Thinking small will stop you from completing your mission. Don't let failures make you think small.

Friends that lift you

Here is how I came to this realization and got out of thinking small. I started hanging around people who were thinking big (see chapter 34 on commitment to excellence and see how important it is that you engage with people who are moving in the direction you want to).

When you associate with people who think big, it can be a challenge. Your ego will tell you all sorts of stories about yourself, or about them. But hang in there. If they're the right people, they will encourage and champion you to be better, to raise your standards for yourself. They will share their dreams and help you dream again. They will open your mind to what is possible, and help you create more and better visions. Who do you know who could help you think big again?

Okay, enough talk and cogitating about the big-picture stuff. It's time to make some plans.

Part 4

STEP 2

PLANS: CREATING A FRAMEWORK FOR SUCCESS

16 Plot Your Course

> " Set your course by the stars, not by the lights of every passing ship. "
> **OMAR N. BRADLEY**

U se a timeline to create some intentions. Goal setting, goal setting, goal setting. *No, I'm not doing it again. I've done it before, and I'm doing it again. It just doesn't work. The last time I set a goal, I didn't get it. It was really disappointing and zapped some of my confidence.*

Sound familiar?

Have you ever set a goal and not achieved it? Or even worse, set a goal, achieved it, and realized you didn't really want it. That it was someone else's goal, not yours. One of those "you should" situations rather than "I really want." If you have completed the first part of our five-part formula—that is, get clear on your purpose and how you want your life to turn out—this next step will help you get what you *really* want.

How can you set a goal you really want and actually get it this time? In this chapter we explore in detail the steps that will lead you to succeed in achieving your goals. Not once, not by some fluke chance, but time and time again, for years to come. Would that be cool?

So let's get started. Before we create some official goals, however, start thinking about what plans you need to make. Get all the stuff that you think you want out of your head and in front of you so you can start to put it into perspective, and decide what to tackle first on your journey to more fun, freedom and fulfillment. It all begins with...

Mind maps

In 2001 my mother bought me a book called *Head First,* by Tony Buzan, a serious advocate of the mind map. The book was full of weird drawings that looked like tree roots spreading out everywhere. I didn't get it at the time, but I now know the massive benefits of mind mapping.

In the previous chapter, you defined what your central purpose is. The overall direction you want your life to take. You also looked at the different missions and roles in your life. You took a closer look at those missions, and set some intentions around how you wanted each one to look.

" You are never too old to set another goal or to dream a new dream. "
LES BROWN

Now, with those intentions, you need to actually start doing some things. We're now going to look at what it is you want to do, given that central purpose. Given that aspect, that mission, that you currently have in your life and your intentions around that mission.

What do you want to do? What do you want to achieve? Do you want the world to be different, and if so how? How do you want to make an impact?

This is where you start making a plan. There are lots of different ways you can do this, but I love mind maps. A mind map lets you take all the stuff that's in your head and lay it out in front of you. That allows you to see it clearly, to see it in context, so you can create timelines around the things inside your head.

There are three ways you can do this.

First option: Get yourself a beautiful big piece of paper. Really big. In the very center of that paper, write your purpose. You might create a nice big circle and write your purpose statement in it. Once you've done that, draw some branches coming off it in all different directions, a bit like that wheel of life in the previous chapter.

All those branches will lead to another circle, which would be your mission, or role. One branch might go out to being a parent. One might go out to health. One might go out to your career. These branches represent all the roles or missions in your life.

Coming off one branch—let's say it's the career branch—you might have other branches representing different aspects of your career. One could be career development. It could be rituals that you want to create in your career. It might be communication within your career. It might be interaction with teams within your career. It might be the next step you want to take in your career.

The career-development branch then has its own branches leading off it. You might have seminars, YouTube clips, courses, books and research. Different aspects of your career that would lead to career development. Coming off books might be the intention to read six books a year on career development. You might have the intention to do one course per year. Each of these spokes leads to the next. You're breaking it down into more and more detail as you go.

Now do that for every other aspect of your life. In the end, you will have this massive image of all the missions in your life, and all the things that relate to each of those missions, and everything you want to achieve relating to each of those missions.

It will lead back to your central life purpose.

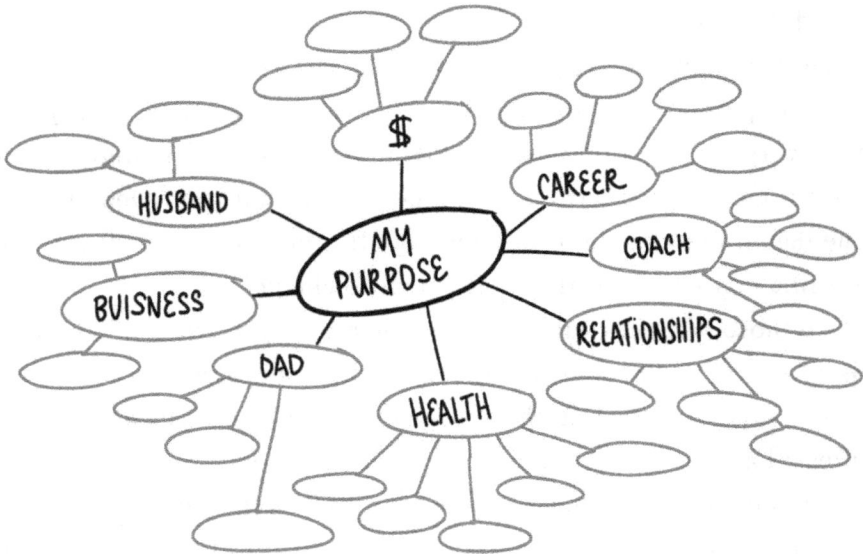

Second option: The second way to mind map is by using computer software. There is some great software out there that allows you to use your computer, mobile phone, or iPad. I use a program called SimpleMind (https://simplemind.eu), which is easy to use and affordable. I think there's even a free version. It's a great piece of software that I use to create my mind maps.

Third option: This method of mind mapping involves a strategy I've used in the last couple of years. You will use a giant piece of cardboard or other rigid material to create what I call an "intention board." I use something called Corflute, which is like plastic cardboard and is obtainable from your local hardware store. Whichever material you use, go really big (2m x 1.5m) because you want plenty of space.

Tack it onto the wall and get a stack of Post-it notes. Divide your intention board into sections. Put the different roles or missions that are in your life on the left-hand side. Create a timeline of years along the bottom. Now take your Post-it notes and start dumping, straight from your brain, the different things you want to achieve in each role and write each one on a Post-it note. Stick them on your intention board on the right-hand side.

When that's all done, stand back and look at your board. Examine each mission. You might have put one for health. Do you want to run a marathon? If so, do you want to run it this year or next year? Or is it something you want to do in three or four years' time? Once you've made your decision, put the note in the column relating to that particular year.

My missions include cool stuff. Stuff that is interesting, that challenges me and causes some growth. For example, I would like to get my pilot's license. That would be a cool goal. There would be so much growth, challenge, and learning involved in that. Maybe not this year or next, but possibly the year after. Add that to my board. I would love to go on a safari. Maybe that would fit four years from now. Add that to my board.

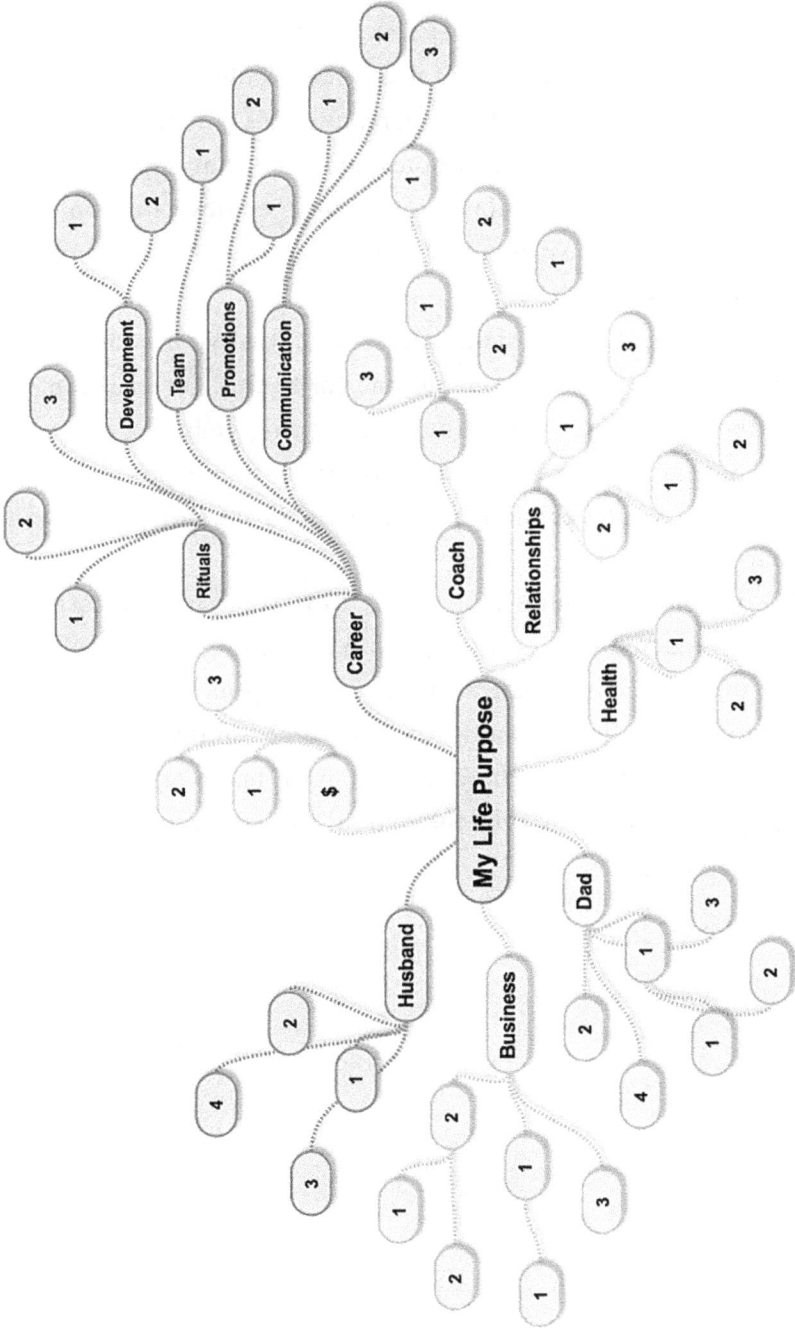

GOALS

DAD

HUSBAND

$

FUN

HEALTH

Re/

18 19 20 21 22 23 24

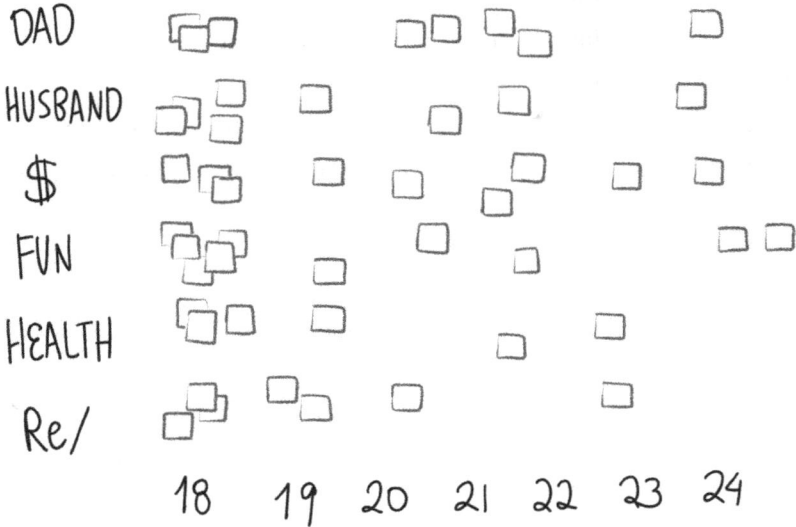

Over a period of about an hour or so, I think of all the different things I want to achieve, and all the various aspects of those things, and add them to my board. I let it all sit there for a few days, glancing at them occasionally throughout the day. I might decide it's a bit unrealistic to do the safari in four years. It might be better if I did it in five. So I shift it to the five-year column. I do this with all my intentions, deciding which are feasible and which are not. When I do think something is right, I remove the Post-it note and, with a permanent marker, write the intention.

This intention board lives in my study and I check it every day. It has everything I intend to achieve in the next five to ten years. At the start of every year I look at my intentions from the previous year and ask myself a few questions. What did I achieve? What do I still want to achieve? What do I no longer want to achieve?

I recommend you do the same thing at the start of every year. It's a great opportunity look at your mind map, whether it's on a computer or a piece of cardboard, and review it. You might decide to take off some of the things that are there and move them to another part of your timeline. Or you may decide to delete something altogether.

Mind maps. They make an incredibly powerful tool for you to take the stuff that's in your mind and put it out there in front of you. It's no good keeping it all in your head.

JOURNAL TIME

Either buy some computer software (SimpleMind is good), or get yourself a large sheet of paper, and start mind mapping each of your different missions or roles, and the things you want to achieve in those roles. Not necessarily this week, next month, or even this year, but that you want to achieve in your lifetime. Based on your current mission and purpose, where you're headed, what do you want to achieve? How can you take those missions, those intentions, and make a difference in the world?

At some point, the world has got to change. When my wife and I decided to build a home, we started with a vision, an intention. The architect drew up a design of the house, and put a strategy in place involving a timeline, tradesmen, etc. That's exactly what you're doing with your mind map. You're taking your intentions, and creating a strategy. (In the chapter on goal setting, you will learn how to take those intentions and turn them into goals.)

BHAG vs. NHAG

I hope you wrote down some big intentions in the mind-mapping exercise. Years ago, one of my coaches introduced me to BHAG and NHAG. He explained that the G stands for *goal*. I think it would be better to think of the G as standing for *game plan* (intention). (As you will find out in chapter 17, goals are different from intentions.)

BHAG stands for "big hairy audacious goal." That's the big goal. It could be to build your own home, go back to school to study, get married, lose twenty kilos, or run a marathon. These are big game plans. You should have lots of these. If you haven't, go back and add some. What are some of the big, audacious, scary, audacious things you want to achieve that are in line with your purpose and mission?

Sometimes those big goals can look scary, and that brings us to the benefits of NHAG, which stands for the "next happy audacious goal." These are the things that will take you on the path to achieving your BHAG. All BHAGs have lots of NHAGs in them.

There is an old joke: "How do you eat an elephant?" Answer: "One bite at a time." Your NHAGs are bite-sized chunks that result in your BHAG. Make sure you have lots of NHAGs in your intentions map.

If, for example, one of your BHAGs was to build a home, some of your NHAGs might be to research five areas to live in; contact ten real estate agents; meet with two builders; buy land; and decide on a home. These are all "next happy audacious goals" that will lead to the BHAG of building your own home.

Now it's time to take some of those cool intentions—your dreams, and especially some of those NHAGs—and turn them into goals.

17 Create Plans with a Deadline

> ❝A goal is a dream with a deadline.❞
> **NAPOLEON HILL**

Have you ever set a goal? Have you ever set a goal and not achieved it? Have you ever set a goal, not achieved it, and decided never to set a goal again? Have you ever become overly general with your goals to help set yourself up for success? Your goals become a bit fluffier, don't they? You try not to be too specific. You make it broad, so when you shoot, hopefully you'll hit something.

Or maybe you've just lowered the bar. You've set a goal, not achieved it, beaten yourself up a little bit, set it again, not achieved it, beaten yourself up a little bit more, until eventually you think: *I don't like that feeling anymore. I'm not going to do goals anymore.*

What about those times you actually got the goal but didn't get the other thing? *Oh, I got it, but I didn't get that other thing, so not really a win.*

Dealing with the "should"s

The other thing that sometimes causes us to fail at our goal setting is to have goals that are *shoulds*. You know: *I should lose weight. I should exercise more. I should make more money.*

A good friend called me one day and asked me to do a session with him. I told him I was free that afternoon and to come on down. When he arrived, he told me he wanted to do a goal-setting session. He had been in Sydney Harbour on a massive luxury yacht with some wealthy people who had told me he should make more money. "Cool," I said, "so you want to make a money goal. What's your goal?" He told me he wanted to make half a million dollars that year. "Great," I said. "Let's do that."

> " Make sure you visualize what you really want, not what someone else wants for you. "
> **JERRY GILLIES**

So we started to work through the goal-setting exercise. When we reached the end of it, I suggested we check to see if that's what he really wanted, to see if the goal was kind to him and in alignment with his values and life purpose, and his mission around money.

Well, that didn't go well. He had no clear sense of his life purpose, and no idea about what his money mission might look like. So next we did a quick values check-in. I asked him what his values were around money, and he told me that he hated it.

"Hang on," I said, "didn't we just set a goal to make half a million dollars?"

"Yeah. No. I hate it," he said.

"When you think of money, what do you think about?"

"I can't stand it. It gets between my family and me."

"What else do you think about money?"

"You've got to sacrifice to get it."

This went on for another ten minutes, when he told he didn't really want to make half a million dollars. You see? He'd been should-on'd.

" Learning what you don't want is how you know what you do want. "
ROBIN WRIGHT

Have you ever had that happen? When you feel like you should do something, and maybe you even start pursuing it. You might set a well-formed goal and decide to head down that path. You might get halfway down the path and realize it isn't for you. Or you get to the end, having achieved the goal, but you still feel unfulfilled.

Most likely, though, you will fail at the goal because it isn't in alignment with your purpose or mission. There's no ease in pursuing it, and many of your values are in conflict, so you sabotage the goal on some level. The setting of *should* goals is a disaster, and that's why getting clear on your life purpose, and creating mission statements and intentions for the different roles in your life, are all essential to avoiding them.

Focus

Some time ago I was reviewing one of my old goal folders and came across one I had set a long time ago, just after we had our first child, Bella. At the time we already had one child, but we wanted to have two more. So we set a goal to have two more children. We did our normal goal-setting process, and although it was not as detailed as now, we actually planned the date and place of conception of our third child: *Fiji in April 2001.*

So we had our second child, and forgot about the goal of conceiving our third child in Fiji. We were just happily chuffing along. In April of 2001, we were in Fiji. We hadn't planned to be in Fiji when we set that original goal, but there we were. About two weeks into our holiday, Michelle found out that she was pregnant.

We had set that goal three years earlier. That's the power of focus. You get what you focus on consistently, and you get it faster if you have a deadline attached to that focus, better known as a goal.

> ❝ Deadlines refine the mind. They remove variables like exotic materials and processes that take too long. The closer the deadline, the more likely you'll start thinking waaay outside the box. ❞
> **ADAM SAVAGE**

The T.R.A.C.K. Method©

Each of the letters in my strategy, the T.R.A.C.K. Method, stands for a key component of powerful goal setting. As I work through the letters, I hope you will follow along in your journal. At times you might need to go back a step or two because you've discovered that the goal you set is not one you really want, or because it's a poorly worded or defined goal. That's okay. This is your first run-through, just getting to grips with the method.

After you've set a couple of goals, you'll be better at it. In fact, the process can take as little as thirty minutes to set a well-defined goal that you can and will achieve.

Imagine creating a plan for each of your missions. Every three months, set one goal for each area (mission or role) of your life. You will end up with several beautifully constructed, well-defined, set-for-success goals completed in less than four hours.

Before we start, pick one of your missions and, following on from the plan you set for that mission, write down a goal you want to achieve.

JOURNAL TIME

LifeCEO.com/RESOURCES

Write down in a sentence a goal you would like to achieve in one of your missions. Don't worry about if it's right or not, just write it down. It will form the basis for you to refine it in the T.R.A.C.K. Method.

And now I'll break down each letter in the T.R.A.C.K. Method.

T = time/tangible

Time: It's important to be clear about the timeframe when you make goals. All the research shows that you will perform better if you have a deadline. I believe it's also important that the timeframe for your goals is no longer than ninety days. I like the number ninety because it's close to a quarter of a year, and I love rounding into chunks, but's also a timeframe that's manageable. It's not too soon, and it's not too far away. You can see the end in sight.

What if you have a goal that will take a year to achieve? For a start, I wouldn't call that a goal, I'd call it a plan. You could start with the intention of achieving something and create a plan that maps out a year of activities. Then, within that plan, you could have goals that take ninety days to achieve. So you would have four goal periods in which to accomplish that plan by the end of the year. Breaking it into chunks like this will help keep the end in sight.

Let's take another example. If you had a plan to lose, say, fifteen kilograms, you might you set a goal to lose eight kilos in ninety days. Then, set the next goal to lose another seven kilos.

You might have a plan to save $1,000. You might decide that it's going to take you six months to save $1,000, so in the first ninety days you aim to save $500. Make the goal $500. Get very specific on that.

Get very specific with your strategy to get the $500. When you reach the ninety days, give yourself a high-five. You got the $500. Now tell yourself that you're going to get the next $500.

Set yourself up to win along the way. This will give you mini (or massive) celebration points along the way to fulfilling your plan.

Tangible: This is also very important. A goal must be something you can measure. To illustrate this point, I'll give you a couple of examples of something you might want, but can't set a goal for. If you had a goal to feel more motivated, how would you measure it? You couldn't. You couldn't put it on a set of scales, or measure it with a tape measure.

A goal must have a unit of measure, e.g. kilograms, meters, dollars, points, etc. There must be a number in the desired goal. Motivation cannot be an outcome because it's not tangible. You can't put it into a wheelbarrow; it doesn't have physicality to it. Motivation is a state or tone, not an outcome.

People often tell me that their goal is to be happy. Could you put yourself in a happy state right now? Go on, do it just for ten seconds. Go hard at it. Get happy. Okay, you did it. You can determine your state immediately. If I told you to go into a sad state, you'd start to think about some sad stuff. Maybe you'd start to slouch in your chair. Before you know it, you're doing sad.

What you focus on—your language and your physiology— determines your state, or tone. You can do that in an instant. So when you set goals, make sure that they're really goals. That they're real outcomes and not just statements of what you want to achieve.

When I coach clients, I'm often in a highly energized state. I move faster. I speak faster. I have more energy and a *lot* of passion. This is the perfect state for my clients to be in if they want to move ahead in their lives, so in effect I'm creating the environment that will support them also getting fired up and taking action.

When I go to a new client who doesn't know me, I know they don't want a crazy guy walking in. So before I get to the door I take a breath and put myself in discovery state. It's a state of curiosity, a state of calm. I do that within one breath. I change in an instant. Then I walk in the door in a different state.

You, too, can do that any time you want. Switch it on and switch it off. People often tell say to me, "I just want to be myself." What does that mean?

Every Tuesday night, my family watches an episode of *The Walking Dead*, a zombie-apocalypse TV series. We sit on the couch, slouching, in our jammies, with cups of tea, just hanging out, allowing ourselves to get taken on a roller coaster of emotions. In that instance, I'm in the *Walking Dead* state, chilling out with the family.

Then there's the state I have when I'm exercising.

You can choose that at any time. It's not a goal. It's not an outcome. It's a state. Just remember that. Outcomes require steps. They're not something you can achieve in an instant.

Now, I'm not saying that you can't want to feel, lighter, happier, healthier, faster, or stronger. You can, you just can't have it as a goal. You can, however, set a goal that, as a result of pursuing and achieving, means you will get to experience those emotions, feelings, and moods. In fact, to achieve the goal you will *need* to experience those moods.

Here are a few examples that show great goals versus goals that are not so great:

- Lose weight versus lose five kilos lost by September 30 (ninety days)
- Have more energy versus walk every day, burning at least 300 calories until March 30 (ninety days)
- Think positive versus read one Mindset book every two weeks until December 30 (ninety days)
- Save money versus save $1000 in investment account by December 30 (ninety days)

Your goal needs to be tangible. If I was your accountability buddy (more about this later), you should be able to prove to me, by showing me the evidence, that you have achieved your goal.

JOURNAL TIME

Take your original goal that you wrote down in the beginning and tidy it up. Make sure it has a time frame that is within ninety days and is tangible. That it's something you can measure. Be clear on the measurement; which will be the documentation to show you have got it.

R = real/one hundred percent responsible

Real: This is also very important. It's not something you have to write. Instead, you'll have two checkboxes to mark off. When you set a goal, the question to ask yourself is: *Is this goal realistic?*

I'm saying, stretch yourself. I'm saying, do some stuff that is a stretch. Something that's going to make your heart race, but do ask yourself: *Is this real? Can I really have this?*

For example, if I set a goal to be an astronaut, would you think that was real? Is it realistic? Or if I set a goal to be the world's best basketball player. That's not real. It is for somebody, but not for me. Check with yourself: is it real? Yeah. Check.

☑ REAL
☑ RESPONSIBLE 100%

One hundred percent responsible: Are you willing to be, and can you be, one hundred percent responsible for your goal? Maybe I set a tangible goal, with a timeframe that within two weeks Michelle is going to dye her hair bright purple. That is my goal—for my wife to have bright purple hair. Can I be a hundred percent responsible for that outcome? No, because I'm relying on somebody else.

Make sure your goal is one that you can be a hundred percent responsible for. That does not require someone else. That you're willing to take responsibility for. Are you willing to be responsible and achieve the goal? Many of us don't check that box. We have an idea, and we do some goal setting, but we never decide that we're going to be truly responsible for it.

Missing this one-hundred-percent-responsible component of goal setting is something I see often in my coaching practice, and in society, particularly in institutions.

For example, a bank might set a teller a KPI (Key Performance Indicator) or a goal of selling one insurance policy per day. However, this goal is not fair to either the bank or the teller. It is setting up both for failure, uncomfortable conversations, and feelings of pain. Why? Because the teller cannot be one hundred percent responsible for a customer purchasing an insurance policy. Therefore it cannot be a goal. The goal could be, however, to ask ten customers per day if they have insurance. This is within the teller's control. It could form part of the bank's plan and lead to the fulfillment of the intention to increase insurance sales.

You might set a goal to get a certain score on a test. While it might be a great intention to get an A on a test, you don't know the questions that are going to be asked. Therefore the test is outside your control or responsibility. You can't set an A as a goal. You can, however, set a goal of doing two hours' study every night, or doing five practice tests, or doing revision questions every day. These goals are within your control. You can be responsible for them, and they are tangible. And as a result of pursuing these goals, you may end up getting an A, or not. Either way, you are setting yourself up for success, not failure.

The more success you have, the more self-confidence you will have. This is a key area where people and organizations set themselves up for failure. Make sure you set goals you can be responsible for.

JOURNAL TIME

Draw a couple of checkboxes under your goal and ask yourself: *Is it real? Can I be one hundred percent responsible?* If you check both boxes, great, move on. If not, it's time to go back and take another look at your goal. If your plan is truly what you want, create a goal that is real and that you can be responsible for.

A = adventure account

It's one thing to create a goal with a clear, tangible outcome that appeals to the logic part of your brain. But for you to have the energy and persistence to pursue the goal, it must be inspiring. That is, it must connect with your *why*, your life's purpose. It must trigger your core values and stimulate the feeling you want as a result of getting the goal.

Here is where you'll take the *logic* of the goal and add in the *heart* of the goal. You'll write an adventure account of your goal in such a way that it sounds like it's already happened. As you write your account, it's important that it brings out the feeling you want.

For example, you might set a goal to lose five kilograms. Your goal might look something like this: *Boom. It's a couple of days before my goal deadline, and I've just looked down. The scales show I've lost five kilos. I feel fantastic.* As you glance up from the scales, you see yourself in the mirror. *Wow, my body has started to transform. I'm feeling so much better about myself. My energy is increasing. People are starting to comment on how I'm looking at work. My clothes fit better. Everything has changed.* As you stand there, your partner walks in, slaps you on the behind and says, "You look amazing."

That's a pretty cool scenario, right? That's an adventure account of you achieving your goal. Rather than just a goal to lose five kilos. There's a difference in your brain. Your brain thinks differently about it if you stand here and think: *I'd like to lose five kilos.* Your brain responds: *Okay, good, let's have a crack at that.*

Compare this to you already telling your brain that you've got it and it feels amazing to have it. You're basically saying to your brain: *I've already got the goal. It's a done deal.* Your brain responds: *Wow, how did we do that?* Your brain starts looking for the answers to get you there. If you've already got it, your brain starts to work out how to get there way more powerfully than if you just think about something you'd like in the future.

If I asked you how you could have more energy in the future, you would find yourself looking for an answer. That's what writing an adventure account will do for your brain—create questions that it will go looking for answers to. Be sure to write the goal with clarity and emotion, with language that shows it already done. It will start you moving immediately, no need to get out the whip.

Maxwell Maltz wrote a book years ago called *Psycho-Cybernetics.* According to Maltz, the mind doesn't know the difference between an actual experience and something you think about vividly. That's pretty cool. Your mind doesn't know the difference. This means that when you create a vivid picture of something in the future, your mind doesn't know the difference between that and something that's real. It will start looking for a way to get that to happen.

C = constructive/cool name

Make sure your goal is constructive and has a cool name. That it's going to be a positive outcome for you and everyone around you, and that it's stated that way, with a fun, catchy name. Remember, emotion drives motion, and motion drives emotion.

It's important not to set a goal like not wanting to put any more weight. That's not a constructive goal. It doesn't sound cool. It's got to be constructive, stated in the positive. It's where you want to go, not where you *don't* want to go. It's what you want, not what you *don't* want.

Let your creative juices flow as you write what is almost a diary note; that is, a constructive adventure account of your goal.

📖 JOURNAL TIME

Have fun. Take the logic of your goal and insert it into a paragraph that reflects you achieving the goal. What does it feel like to be there? What are you seeing, hearing, thinking, experiencing, and noticing around and inside you? Who did you have to become? How are you different now that you've achieved it? Who has been impacted as a result of you achieving your goal?

Some examples of goals I have set in the past:

- Cool-stuff goal: Red Ducati Monster 696. Wow, it's my birthday, and I took my new Ducati Monster 696 for a ride. Whenever I start that engine, there's an amazing burble and vibration as I give it a rev. It looks fantastic, as do I in my full (black with

Ducati logo) leathers. Riding it is a thrill. I feel connected to the road and my surroundings. I have an incredible sense of freedom. I'm so grateful.

- Bring-back-the-mystery goal: Mystery night every two weeks, with a total of six in three months. This goal has been awesome. I've spent three-plus cool hours with my wife in a place of mystery and adventure every two weeks. It's created a space that allows us both to grow closer together. It's enhanced our love and bond, and has reminded us of what is important. It makes us smile, our hearts to race, and our blood to flow.

- Stay-lean-get-strong goal: Stay at 74–76 kilograms, and create a twenty-percent increase in leg press (130 kilos), seated row (70 kilos). Incredible! It's the end of June, and I've stayed lean, with a twenty-percent increase in strength. I look amazing, and feel strong, useful and capable. I haven't let in the old, and I feel like I'm a great example for others—inspirational and attractive. People want to know my secret. I'm maximizing my health, my performance, my energy, and have built up my mojo.

One of the reasons I share these goals with you is because so often people think goals need to be a money or business thing, maybe because they're easily measurable. But it can be something for your relationship. It can be stuff for your health. It can be cool stuff.

Life any great CEO, you need to set goals for all aspects of the company. Each department has its own mission, complete with plans and goals. Goals with deadlines.

K = kind to you and others

Remember my earlier story of the man who came to me wanting to make half a million dollars? We did a check-in, and it wasn't kind to him. It was going to create conflict for him down the track, and potentially others as well. There are two methods you can use to decide if your goal is something you really want, and is something that it is kind to you. One is a mission check-in, the other is what I call "the agenda questions."

Mission check-in: Go back and take a look at your mission statements. Each one should contain your core values. Read over your mission statement and check that there's no conflict between your goal and the statement. Will your goal not only support the mission it relates to but all the other missions in your life as well?

For example, let's say you set a business mission to generate more income by traveling to the city (two hours away) to make sales appointments with potential clients three days per week. Sales goal: three city sales appointments three days per week. Now, there's nothing wrong with that as a goal. However, if you did a check-in with your other missions, you might find a conflict. Let's take a look.

Family mission has as part of its statement the intention to spend quality, high-energy and present time with the family, as a priority. Can you see that the sales goal might be in conflict with this mission?

Health mission talks about finding ways to sharpen your saw (create high-performance physical, chemical, and mental health) while in other missions. This mission will be central to, and never compromised by, all other missions. It's possible that the sales goal might be in conflict with the health mission. Or maybe not.

What if, as a result of doing this missions check-in, you decided to pursue this goal, and you added to it. You add health goals of spending three days a week listening to a podcast that stretches your mind, and drinking an additional two liters of water per day. As a result, on the way into the city during your trip, you use that time to listen to a podcast and drink your two liters of water. Instead of a conflict, you have now created two goals that will work synergistically for a better outcome.

This process doesn't need to take long—about three to five minutes tops—but it could save you a massive amount of pain later, when you find yourself failing at the goal because of some life purpose, mission or values conflict. Ninety-five percent of the time your goals will support your missions, and it's all happy days.

📖 JOURNAL TIME

Now take your new goal, and the relevant mission statement for that aspect of your life, and look at the goal against the mission statement. Is the goal in alignment with the mission statement? If you sense a conflict, ask yourself how you could shift the goal to eliminate that conflict. An even better question would be to ask how you could shift this goal so it supported your other missions and goals. This might mean you have to rewrite the goal, but better to do it now rather than find out later that the goal was set up for failure.

Agenda questions: The four questions you are going to ask yourself are designed to bring out the hidden agendas to achieving or not achieving your goals. The best way to do this is to create four boxes and simply write as much as you can in each box about these four questions:

1. What *would* happen if you *did* pursue and achieve this goal?
2. What *would* happen if you *didn't* pursue and achieve this goal?
3. What *wouldn't* happen if you *did* pursue and achieve this goal?
4. What *wouldn't* happen if you *didn't* pursue and achieve this goal?

I have to tell you that the last question almost always sends me into a trance, but it's a great question. I've often found that it reveals a hidden agenda that might be the clincher in not achieving the goal.

DID

WOULDN'T ———————————————— WOULD

DIDN'T

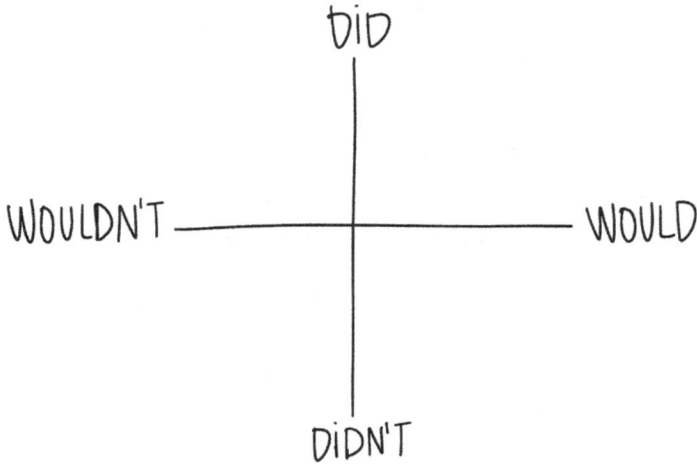

The best way to explain this process is to use an example. Let's take a woman who has the intention of saving $8,000 for a family holiday. She's broken it up into four quarterly goals of saving $2,000 in ninety days. Here are her agenda questions and answers:

- What *would* happen if I *did* pursue and achieve this goal?
  a) I would be able to get away with my family.
  b) I would learn the habit of saving.
  c) I would feel more confident.
  d) I would experience new and different things.
  e) I would be focused and disciplined.
- What *would* happen if I *didn't* pursue and achieve this goal?
  a) I would be at home and work instead of holidaying.
  b) I would stay a spender not a saver.
  c) My kids would see my lack of discipline.
  d) My life experience would remain local rather than global.
  e) I would have money to spend on other things like clothes and food.

- What *wouldn't* happen if I *did* pursue and achieve this goal?
  a) I wouldn't have to stay home this Christmas.
  b) I wouldn't be able to buy as many clothes or go out as much.
  c) I wouldn't waste my money.
  d) I wouldn't miss out on alone time with my family.
- What *wouldn't* happen if I *didn't* pursue and achieve this goal?
  a) I wouldn't go away with my family.
  b) I wouldn't get to experience other countries, or expand my mind and the minds of my family.
  c) I wouldn't have to budget and watch my money.
  d) I wouldn't need to change; I could stay the same.
  e) I wouldn't have to take time off work to go away.

There are a lot of statements in there that reinforce the pursuit and setting of that goal. There are, however, a few that could sabotage the goal. Here are three I would be wary of:

- I would have money to spend on other things like clothes and food.
- I wouldn't need to change, I could just stay the same.
- I wouldn't have to take time off work to go away.

You can see how these might just cause her to sabotage the goal. But as long as she's aware of them, and as long as they're not unkind to her or others, there's no reason why she shouldn't pursue the goal. In fact, now that she is aware of them, she can formulate a plan in case they start to rear their ugly heads.

A personal example for me was the Ducati goal in the example above. I didn't actually pursue that goal in the end, because when I did the agenda questions one of my answers was: *I would possibly die from a bike accident if I did get the bike.*

114

Initially I ignored that agenda answer, but over a week it kept playing on my mind until I realized I couldn't resolve it, and it would always be a conflict. So I stopped pursuing the goal.

The other thing that comes out of the agenda questions is fuel to support your goal. And I have often found that some super-cool stuff has come out of the questions, which I then add back to my adventure account.

The more you can create inspiration around your goals, the more likely you are to achieve them.

📖 JOURNAL TIME

Open your journal to a blank page and draw your two lines with the words *did*, *didn't*, *would*, and *wouldn't* at the ends. Start answering the questions. You might find that the diagonally opposite answers sometimes match, and that's okay, but ask yourself, what else? Dig deep. Your answers will feed or fail your goal.

Race time 1hr 55min

Run the Half Marathon @ "Run Melb"

Sunday July 24th 2016

I will cross the Finish Line and get an SMS with a time of 1hr 55min

Wow. What an adventure and challenge that was. So excited to have completed my first half marathon in under 2 hours. I feel fantastic. So excited to have proved the power of mind over matter. To have fulfilled my decision that despite a broken foot "I would always run".
The camaraderie leading up to the event and at the event itself, reinforced the importance of hanging out with people that champion you.
I am on such a high.
Well done Benny

Determined, Courageous, Strong, Focused, Disciplined, and Consistent

Follow my training program.
- Train smart and hard. Do the miles. 3x / week
- Eat like a high performer, eat to win.
- Surround myself with the doers, the mentors that inspire, challenge and raise my standards.
- Keep the body in repair.

Keys to successful Goal setting

T	☑	Time
	☑	Tangible
R	☑	Real
	☑	Response-able
A	☑	Adventurous Account
C	☑	Constructive
K	☑	Kind to you and others

While some additional points to consider will be covered in other chapters on personality and productivity, it's worth highlighting some key insights while we're talking about goals.

Who are you becoming?

This is, again, something that I coach when I'm with a client. Goal setting is the question: Who do you need to *be* to achieve this goal? What kind of person? In my Ducati example, it would have cost money so I would have needed to work hard, think big, and do what others were not doing.

For my stay-lean-and-get-strong goal, I need to remain energized, inspired, and work hard. To bring the mystery back, again I'd need to be energized, attractive, and have creativity. Why do I use the word *attractive*, by the way? It means being passionate. Being playful. Being present. When someone is playful, present and passionate, you will be attracted to them. You want to hang around them. I had creativity, because if I'm going to bring back the mystery, I'm going to have to be creative. It can't just be dinner down at McDonald's or the local restaurant every fortnight.

📖 JOURNAL TIME

Take one minute to write down the qualities you need to bring to this goal. What would you need to believe? How would you need to behave? What would your mood, tone, or state need to be? What energy would you need to bring for the goal to be achieved? What kind of attitude?

Time to make a change in the world around you

Lastly, what do you need to do? What action do you need to take? Whenever you set a goal, it's important to do something towards that goal immediately. Straightaway. Within seconds of you putting down the pen and finishing writing the goal, take some action towards that goal. For example, with my Ducati goal, some of the action I could have taken would have been to start conditioning Michelle to the idea; check out bike sales and get the notifications; start a savings account; book a test drive; investigate finance deals.

I could have started the first two immediately.

JOURNAL TIME

Write down three or four things that you could do, immediately, this week. In fact, write down one thing that you could do tonight. They don't have to be massive things. They could just be little things that start the process.

18 Accountability and Motivation

> ❝ One person's embarrassment is
> another person's accountability. ❞
> **TOM PRICE**

A few years ago, I decided that I was going to sell my allied healthcare practices, sell our house, move the family back to Melbourne, and shortly after that go to Italy to live for a couple years. My coach at the time, CJ Mertz, contributed to me developing this goal-setting strategy. At the time, I was seriously inspired to pursue the next shift in my missions on the way to fulfilling my life purpose. He, however, added some motivation to the inspiration to ensure I succeeded.

For those of you who want to know, I'm going to show you how to do this. By the way, I got the goal, and I'll tell you what the motivation was in a moment.

Do CEOs have accountability? Absolutely. They are accountable to all stakeholders, their teams, shareholders and the board. Creating accountability while being your life CEO is an opportunity to create someone outside of yourself to report to. It's almost like creating your own one-person board that you agree to report to and make a commitment to with regard to your performance.

Remember the donkey with the carrot and the stick from the earlier chapter? Well, this next strategy combines all three. It's like taking goal setting and putting it on steroids. Your goals will come faster and with more certainty than ever before. I must warn you, however, that this is not for everyone. But if you're willing to be a little uncomfortable in the pursuit of what you really want, then read on.

I will work you through this strategy by doing the strategy as we go. So take your journal out and get ready to write, laugh, cry, sweat, and feel your heart race.

1. **Pick your accountability buddy**: An accountability buddy is someone who keeps you accountable to the goal you have set. This is the person you choose to hold you in a state of being accountable, liable, or answerable. Your buddy has a great deal of response-ability; they must ensure that you do what you say you are going to do. They will celebrate with you when you do, support you along the way and, importantly, enforce the penalty if you don't achieve it. Your buddy is there to ensure you get the carrot if you reach your destination, administer the whip along the way, and release your penalty on you if you don't. Your buddy is your one-person board.

   Only do this if you're sure you want to. You don't have to do it. You can still achieve the goal without the accountability. If you choose to do it, it's important that you are completely transparent to your accountability buddy. They must know, specifically, how you're going to measure your goal. There can be no fluffy, vague, or grey areas around what is goal achievement and what isn't.

   Your buddy must be someone who cares about you so much that they will enforce the penalty. Despite your pleas for mercy, they will have none. A resolution and contract of your commitment to the goal are all they care about and holding you to account is their duty. They must understand the responsibilities involved with being an accountability buddy. Which, by the end of this chapter you will be able to explain.

Choose wisely. Don't pick someone who you know will fold when the going gets tough. Pick someone who will champion you, support you, challenge you, and enforce the penalty if required.

This probably sounds overly dramatic, but accountability only works if you're going to be held accountable. So, who's it going to be?

JOURNAL TIME

Pick one of your goals, and having decided on your accountability buddy, start writing: "My name is," _____ and I've resolved to my accountability buddy _____ that I will achieve the following goals." Now write down the goals you have decided to achieve. This is what you will give your accountability buddy.

2. **Decide on your reward**: You're going to give yourself a reward. We have a special part of the brain that loves rewards. Loves gifts. Loves special treats. This is the fun bit. The reward is not getting the goal. The reward is something else.

For example, if your goal is to run the interstate marathon, what reward might you give yourself for achieving it? How about a couple of days at a nice hotel on the Gold Coast? You might say: *Man, not only am I going to get fit, I'm going to achieve this goal and tick the marathon box off, and I'm going to have a couple of cool days on the Gold Coast.* The brain starts getting excited about that.

If it's a fitness goal, you might say: *I'm going to buy myself some new runners when I get this goal.*

If it's a money goal, you might say: *I'm going to buy myself a new suit if I get this. Or some new shoes.*

If it's a career goal, you might say: *I'm going to buy myself a new office chair.*

You can tie in the reward with the theme of the goal, or not. I suggest you keep the value of the reward at the same level as the difficulty or value of the goal.

Once you've decided what your reward is, you need to go out and buy or organize the reward straightaway. You don't get to use it, but you do get to look at it (although not if it's a painting or a TV). Every day you will look at your goal sheet and rewards and be motivated by inspiration, carrot (getting the reward), and stick (giving the reward away).

JOURNAL TIME

LifeCEO.com/RESOURCES

Write down something that would be a cool reward for achieving your goal.

3. **Decide on your penalty**: The next thing you're going to decide is your penalty for not getting the goal. When I do this in a workshop, usually everyone starts to look worried, and you should, too. What you decide needs to really hurt.

For example, your goal might be to run the marathon but you don't do it. You don't train, and you decide to forgo the registration for the event. No, no, no. It's got to be painful, *really* painful. Or not, right? Don't do this unless you're willing to create some stick. (Remember, you don't have to do this.)

A mate I trained with at the gym told me one day that he had a goal: to lose ten kilograms. I asked him if he was sure about this, absolutely positive. He assured me he was.

"I want you to give me some accountability for it," I told him. When he assured me once again that he was sure, I said, "Great. First of all, what's the reward for getting it?"

He thought about it and said, "I'm going to get myself a new gym outfit."

"Great. What's the penalty?" I asked him.

"Oh, I'll come and mow your lawns for two weeks."

By now you will know that mowing the lawns for a week just doesn't cut it. It's too easy. I knew which school my friend's children went to so I suggested he donated $500 to the school as a penalty.

You know you've got it right when you get that uncomfortable, heart-racing, nauseous, faint feeling. And that's when the voices start. *Do I really want this goal? Am I really willing to be responsible for that goal? What if I don't get it? How could I get out of it?*

The penalty part of the accountability process calls you to check in with yourself as to your desire for this goal, its realness, and your ability to be responsible.

I began this chapter by saying that my coach helped me achieve my goal of selling my practices and so on by adding accountability. Well, my goal was to sell my practices by September 31, which gave me six months to do it, and also to sell my house. My penalty was that I would have to move my family into a caravan park until the house was sold.

With such a massive goal and a serious penalty, I had three buddies to make sure that I was accountable. I had to sell the practices. If I didn't sell the practices, I had to go to my friend's house and mow his lawns every week for six weeks. He lived three hours away. That would have hurt.

This penalty might seem extreme, but I was determined not to fail. Do you think I pulled out every stop to ensure I achieved my goal? You bet I did.

With that level of penalty, you need a strong accountability buddy, possibly even multiple buddies. Create some leverage for yourself, if you want. If you don't want, don't do it.

📖 **JOURNAL TIME**

Write down your penalty. Remember, it must truly hurt. Whatever you're thinking of right now, it needs to be ten times more potent in its level of pain and suffering.

4. **The bonus penalty**: The third step in the process was a penalty if you didn't achieve your goal; the fourth step doubles down. If you didn't achieve your goal, not only did you cop the penalty, but you also have to give the thing you were going to reward yourself with to someone else. Yes, that's right, you give your reward to a person or organization you don't particularly like.

It mustn't feel good giving away your reward. For instance, if it were a new suit, you wouldn't choose to give it to the op shop to benefit someone else—unless you don't like op shops. Instead, you might give the suit back to the store you bought it from and not ask for a refund.

📖 **JOURNAL TIME**

Write down the name of the person you're going to give your reward to. Ideally it will be a person or organization you don't particularly like.

Once you have completed your accountability sheet, you need to take action on the goal and the accountability (this accountability sheet is also available for download at theonbutton.com.au). For the accountability, you need to:

- have a conversation with your accountability buddy about the rules of engagement, and make sure you're clear about the goal and the penalties
- go get your reward
- pin up your goal and your accountability sheet.

Good luck, and remember, this is optional. The T.R.A.C.K. Method of goal setting works by itself; accountability just adds motivation to your inspiration.

Review with templates

Now let's do a quick review. This is one of the most important chapters in the book. It's the chapter that connects your life purpose with action. It's the go-between, the thing that will take a great idea and turn it into reality.

I encourage you to go to theonbutton.com.au, click on the resources tab, and download the T.R.A.C.K. Method templates. You can fill out the sheet on the computer. Search for some cool pictures to add, or print them out, or cut out a picture from a magazine.

The idea is that in the end you'll have five to seven copies of this poster to display for the next ninety days. For ninety days, every day when you wake up, there will be only five to seven things you need to focus on. That's much more achievable than a massive goal that might be three years down the track, with multiple parts to it, and is possibly out of your control. Set yourself up for success.

So, have a crack at filling this out. The first box at the top is the cool name of your goal. Goals have to have cool names. This is you putting the tangible thing in there. How will you know that you've got the goal that you're going to set?

Next, write an adventurous account, focusing on all the cool stuff that's going to come. It's constructive, so it positively. It's an adventure account of having achieved the goal. Then do a values-and-agenda check-in. Is it what you really want? Is there anything that will stop you from achieving it? Finally, find an inspirational picture that means something to you.

Done. Now repeat the process for each of your missions as part of the plan associated with that mission.

19 Some Distinctions Between Goals

" Challenge is the pathway to engagement and progress in our lives. But not all challenges are created equal. Some challenges make us feel alive, engaged, connected, and fulfilled. Others simply overwhelm us. Knowing the difference as you set bigger and bolder challenges for yourself is critical to your sanity, success, and satisfaction. "

BRENDON BURCHARD

One of my favorite high-performance coaches is a guy called Brendon Burchard (see quote above). What I love about his coaching work is his concept of making sure that the effort that's put into something produces a reward. When setting a goal, make sure it moves you in the direction that you want to go in. After getting clear on your purpose, setting a plan, creating a goal, managing your behaviors, and taking productive action, ensure that there is a profit at the end. Remember, profit means gaining an advantage or benefit, making progress.

The equation

This equation I learned from Brendon can be applied to any aspect of your life, but especially to business. It is Brendon Burchard's Ultimate Business Formula (for Entrepreneurs).

T.E.R.M.S. < $ROI + FB + PD + L

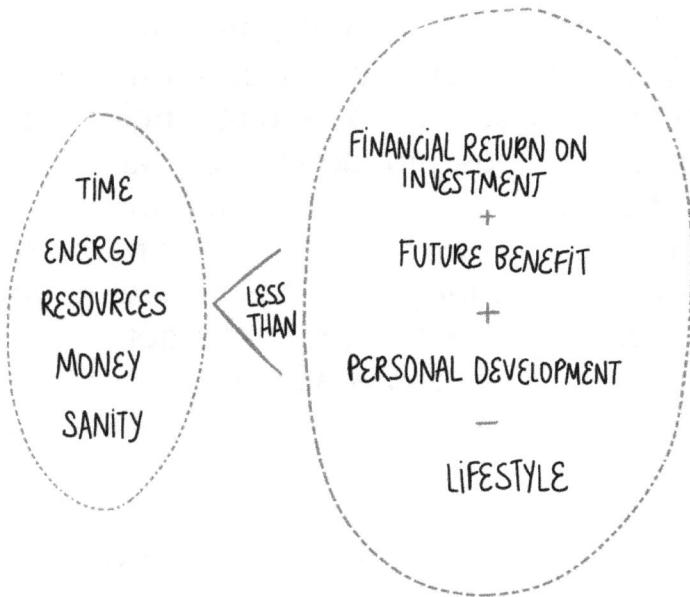

TIME
ENERGY
RESOURCES
MONEY
SANITY

LESS THAN

FINANCIAL RETURN ON INVESTMENT
+
FUTURE BENEFIT
+
PERSONAL DEVELOPMENT
–
LIFESTYLE

This formula comes from the notion that entrepreneurs must evaluate opportunities in a slightly different way to traditional large businesses because they often have fewer cash and resources available. Entrepreneurs will sometimes use intuition to guide their decisions because a result is often not just about the money but also the lifestyle, or personal benefit, they gain.

This is key to being your life CEO. You have limited assets. There are only twenty-four hours in a day. Only so much money in the bank.

Only so much energy you have each day—not to mention the amount of sanity you can hold onto before going mad.

Let's take a closer look at that equation again. It means that the amount of time, energy, resources, money, and sanity you put into something must be less than the financial return on investment, future benefit, personal development, and lifestyle.

There are two parts to this equation to consider. Firstly, what you put into something is not always what you get out. For example, if you spend money on your business you might gain more lifestyle. For example, you might employ a virtual assistant, which costs money, but you gain by having a better lifestyle. As a parent, you might give up some sanity (what am I talking about, "might"?) for the future benefit of you and your children by setting house rules and sticking to them.

Secondly, for this equation to work, recognize that what you put in must always be less than what you get out. Now, before you start thinking you can put in zero, it doesn't work like that. You must always put in *something* (we will talk more about this in the Productivity step a little later).

Cogitating produces nothing. It's through action and application of T.E.R.M.S. that you will see a result or benefit. It's important that this result is a profitable one. That is, after the expenses of T.E.R.M.S. you have a greater income of $ROI + FB + PD + L. This produces a net profit. Net profit in your business, relationships, health, family, and career.

Decide

I've used the word *decide* a lot in this book. What does it mean exactly? As I mentioned in the preface, to decide or to sieve out is one of the origins of the word *crisis*. But the word "decide" comes from the late fourteenth century ("to settle a dispute") from the Old French *decider*. It also comes from the Latin *decidere*, meaning "to decide, determine," literally "to cut off" from, to resolve and make a determination.

When setting a goal, it's important to be decisive. Your decision might not actually be the right one, but as one of my mentors, Dr. Doug Heron, used to say, "I might be right, or I might be wrong, but I am in no doubt."

> " Decide what you want, decide what you are willing to exchange for it. Establish your priorities and go to work. "
>
> **H. L. HUNT**

Take the first step. It's important when setting goals that you take the first step in getting your goal moving. No matter how small it is, take the first step. The moment you set a goal and put down your pen, you must take action. Setting the goal doesn't mean taking action because the world hasn't changed. Taking action means setting something in motion that cannot be taken back. Make the call, send the email, search online for the next step, get up from your desk and start building it.

Create some kind of ripple in the world that tells you that you have started, that you have moved a little closer to achieving your NHAG (see chapter 16). Taking the first step consummates the decision.

The journey

It's not always about the destination but who you become on the journey to the destination. The needs of purpose are the needs of a better you and a better world. The goal sets the path for you to experience life and become who you need to be. Keep in mind the person you need to be. Be clear on that from the beginning, as it will make the journey easier. And recognize that you will also become who you need to be in the pursuit of the goal.

> " You cannot change your destination overnight, but you can change your direction overnight. "
> **JIM ROHN**

To-do lists

Let me start by giving you some to-do list facts compiled by Sasha Cagen, the author of *To-Do List: From Buying Milk to Finding a Soul Mate: What Our Lists Reveal About Us*, compiled a list of to-do facts. Cagen, considered the world's leading to-do-list-*ologist*, is collecting thousands of to-do lists for original research on the way people use their lists:

- She found that 83 percent of to-do-list makers preferred the tactile experience of writing their lists with pen and paper. The satisfaction of crossing things off was key. Interestingly, people often felt more accountable when a list was in their own handwriting.
- Up to 50 percent admitted to writing down tasks they had already done, then crossing them off. That gave them the sense of having achieved more, and they had another opportunity to run their pen through another completed item.
- Cagen discovered that more people cross off tasks (66 percent) than check off tasks (21 percent). Four percent write an "X" and five percent do nothing at all.

131

- Most importantly, 96 percent said their lives were better with to-do lists, 89 percent said they enjoyed making lists, and 28 percent identified as obsessive list makers.
- Lastly, 26 percent of list makers also had a "don't-do" list (most of the items on this list involved people not to date or sleep with).

A to-do list can be a very powerful tool. There are lots of strategies for to-do lists, and the key is to find one that works for you. I'll run through the process for the way I do it.

Something for everyone: I start by looking at each area (mission) of my life at the start of the week (Sunday night), and write a list of all the things I want to achieve for the week. I make sure there's at least one thing to be done in each area of my life. Some of these to-dos are repetitive. For example, I have exercise scheduled in my calendar, but I still add it to my sharpen-the-saw mission to-do list.

You don't have to have equal numbers (equal allocation of assets) of to-dos for every aspect of your life, but ideally there will be something. Connecting your to-do list with your missions helps get them done. When an item gets raised from just a task to be completed to a mission to be fulfilled, the chances of you doing it go up.

Intentions list: I am kind to myself and write these down as "intentions to do." Life happens, and sometimes I don't get everything done, so I'll add it to the next week. I don't let it disappear. If I don't get a task done, I simply add it to next week's list. Put everything on your list that you want to get done. It doesn't have to be done now, but it does need to be done.

If it's a big list, leave some things off this week and put them into another list down the track. The exception to this rule is if the to-do item is part of a goal, such as walking for thirty minutes a day. This is not optional; this is a commitment written in the form of a goal. This is a KPI that you, as your life CEO, must complete. It becomes a "big rock," as Steven Covey would say. It goes in the life jar first, and everything else works around it.

Easy stuff, in easy time: I make time during the week for the quick tasks. Anything that I think will take less than ten minutes I handle in a scheduled time slot during the day. I call this "easy stuff," and usually I take care of it just before lunch. This includes emails and calls that I can check off quickly. This makes my list look good. Plus, it's often the small things that make a big difference.

Big stuff, in block time: I schedule in the big things on my list. I make time for them in the week ahead so I can create the mindset and space to get them done. I always ask myself at the start of the week: Who's waiting on whom? Who is waiting on me, and whom am I waiting on?

Often projects get stalled because we're waiting for someone to get back to us. We assume we're on their to-do list, but we're not. Put them on your to-do list and check in with them so they will do what you need them to do. For those waiting on you, that email you were sent in reply to your request is another request. Make sure you get back to the sender. Put it on the list.

Write them down: One of the keys to to-do lists is to write them down. I use a small day-to-a-page diary that allows me to keep adding and crossing off things as they get done. Please do not use scraps of paper. Keep all of your to-dos in one place. They make for a great read at your yearly review. Yes, there are a million apps out there that you can use on your smartphone, but nothing can replace paper and pen for to-dos.

Part 5

STEP 3

PERSONALITY: DECIDE WHO YOU BE

20 Storytime

> " Wherever my story takes me, however dark and difficult the theme, there is always some hope and redemption, not because readers like happy endings, but because I am an optimist at heart. I know the sun will rise in the morning, that there is a light at the end of every tunnel. "
>
> **MICHAEL MORPURGO**

Why are you the way you are? Your personality—which is expressed through your behaviors, actions, language, and communication—comes from a collection of stories that you have stored in your mind. Stores that you have accumulated throughout your life. Stories that might or might not be true.

If you have ever read a good book, or seen a great movie, you might have wondered whether the story was true. It seems so convincing. Are the stories in your head about how the world works true? Where did you get them?

A super-interesting guy by the name of Morris Massey came up with a model of where we get our stories, and how we manage to convert them from mere stories into truths. In our heads, anyway.

Stage 1: The imprint period (1–7 years)

In this period, a child's brain is like a sponge; it wants to find out about everything. Nothing is off limits. You've seen little kids (and been one). They just have to touch everything, taste everything and smell everything. They are into everything. They want to take in everything. With a child of this age, all emotionally significant events tend to go straight into their subconscious mind.

During this imprint period, children have not yet developed their mental filters. Their parents are the most critical people in their lives. Parents play a key role in helping lay down the foundational neuronal networks that will form the framework for all future learning. Children might ask questions and engage in conversation with you, but their learning will not come from what you say, but what you do.

The old saying, "Do as I say not as I do," definitely does not work at this age (if it works at any age). The good news is that it's not just one event that affects the child's life (although, if emotionally significant, it can have an impact). It is multiple exposures to similar events that paint the final picture in their minds about how life works.

Wow, let's dump a bit of pressure on any parents reading this book, Dr. Ben. Well, yes, your behavior potentially has a big impact on your children, and other people's children. And I say potentially because no matter what happens to you, or around you, you can choose the meaning you put into it. I believe that the role of parents is to give their children a range of experiences that then create for them a range of future choices and options.

But, hey, it's not just parents. It's TV, the Internet, school, friends, teachers, brothers and sisters, food, music, books, toys—everything your child sees, hears, feels, and tastes. It's every experience. Everything.

Those first seven years are full of significant experiences that lay the framework for children to develop empowering values, beliefs, and standards. Equally, many children will also be exposed to some experiences that may lay the framework for some disempowering values, beliefs, and standards.

This is the time where you decide what is right and what is wrong. You start to create your truth about how the game of life is played. Remember, this is not *the* truth but your interpretation of the truth. It's during this time that you lay the foundations (start drawing our map) for everything. You decide on the principals for what you value, and your beliefs about yourself and the world. You learn how the physical world works, including what you think about time, and energy. Your language and the importance of words develops, and your attitudes to life. And much, much more.

It's also during this first seven years that you develop your ego, the part of the brain that protects you from danger, and from the things that challenge your sense of truth. At about the age of three, you start to see ego appearing, in the form of a filter, and it's this filter that sometimes gets you in trouble (more about this in chapter 21). It's also the thing that keeps you safe.

I remember all my kids, and my friend's kids, having no fear of water when they were small, especially around the swimming pool. One day my wife and I were sitting with another couple right by the pool. My daughter, Bella, was seven, and the other couple's daughter was two. Now, at the age of two there is no filter. The two-year-old child's ego hadn't yet appeared to keep her safe, and the world was for exploring. So she explored and fell in the pool.

The problem was that it wasn't a fall with a splash, but rather a silent slide into the water, unnoticed by the adults all engaged in conversation only meters away. Bella came over and interrupted our conversation by saying, "Anja's on the bottom of the pool." I looked in, and there was Anja looking up with a happy, relaxed look on her face. Luckily, the story ended happily. Bella's dad instantly jumped in and pulled her out completely unharmed.

This is a great illustration of a two-year-old child's lack of filter, and a seven-year-old child's filter that told her a toddler on the bottom of the pool is not a good thing.

By the age of seven, your filter is well and truly in place, and ready for the next stage: the modeling period.

Stage 2: The modeling period (8–13 years)

In the modeling period, children begin to model the behaviors of the people around them. Until this age, they don't see a difference between themselves and their parents, but now they begin to notice that there's a difference. They become aware of self, and of parents and other people.

Between the ages of eight and thirteen, they start to try things out and get a feel for how their beliefs of the world work. They are still impressionable in this period (and will be for the rest of their lives), especially when it comes to significant experiences, those defining moments where a lot of emotion may be involved.

All the time, however, they are checking in with their original map of the world. Their filters were established by the time they turned seven, and they're now looking at the world around them for evidence that what they know about that world is true.

They are not looking for unbiased, peer-reviewed, double-blind-study evidence. They want to know if what they think about the world, and how the game of life is played, is true. There is a bias in the evidence-gathering process.

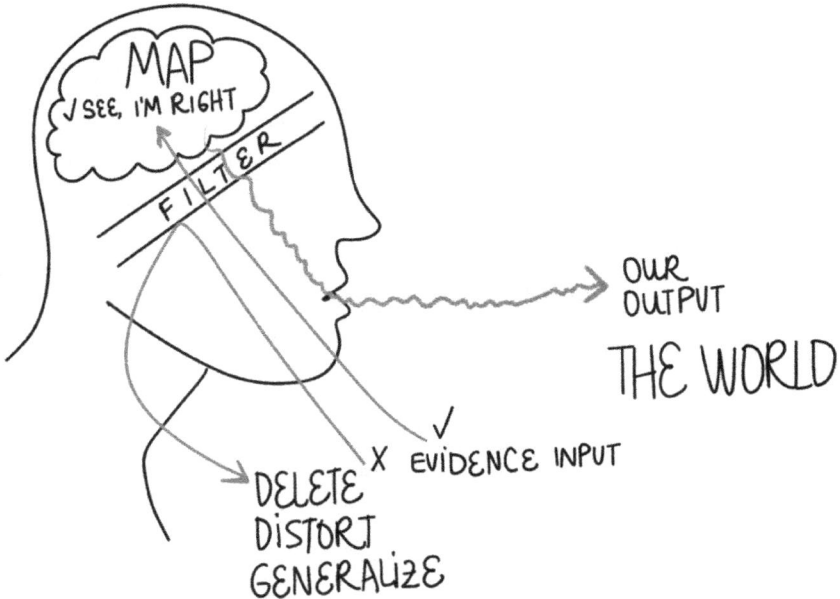

I will explain how this bias, or filter, works.

Deletion: "That didn't happen…": When something happens in your world (something you see, hear, feel, or taste) that is important to you, or that you agree with, something that is a match for your view of the world, something that is a reflection of your map, it comes into your body and is checked by your filter (ego). If it's a match, it goes through the filter and enters the unconscious and conscious. Your mind says yes, that's exactly what I thought. I knew I was right. Your map of the world just got reinforced. Now you're even more certain that what you think is true.

Now comes the scary thing. When you experience (see, hear, feel, or taste) something that is not important to you, or that you disagree with, something that is not a reflection of your map, it comes into your body and again is checked by your filter to see if it's a fit. If the answer is no, your filter discards (deletes) it from existence.

141

We have all had these experiences. You know the ones. You say something to someone, and a week later, when you're discussing the event, your recollection is completely different from theirs.

I say this is scary because you're doing this all the time, including right now, as you're reading this book. You might read things that are not a match for your map, that are not important to you, or that go against your current view of the world. Your unconscious simply deletes them from existence. Your eyes see the words, but your unconscious filter rejects them.

Distortion: "What it really means is…" This is where you take something that you experience, and you distort it. The word "distort" comes from the Latin *dis-torque*, meaning apart, to twist to one side. And this is exactly what you do when you come across something that's not a match for your map or view of the world: you twist it to one side, *your* side. You manipulate and distort the experience at the filter stage so it can fit your view of the world.

We all do this, with all sorts of things, including language. When someone speaks to us, we take the words they say and twist them to suit our view of the world, which is really our view of us. Because of this filtering process that deletes and distorts everything you see, you cannot (warning: this is a *Matrix* moment) see anything that is not you. You can only see what is you.

There are many great examples of this, and a coaching client named Sue shared one with me years ago. Sue was a manager of a café, and when she was at work late one afternoon the power went out. None of the tills or lights was working, so she decided to close down the café. She rang her boss to let her know. Sue's female boss was appreciative of her actions and rational thinking, and ended the conversation by telling her she was "cute" for doing what she had done. Sue told me that when she got off the phone, she was angry with her boss for telling her she was cute. She felt belittled by the comment. She said she didn't feel respected and that she'd been made to feel like a child.

It turned out that the letters C.U.T.E., when identified as the word *cute* and run through Sue's filter and her model of the world, had become distorted from their original meaning; she took it to mean that she wasn't worthy of respect.

Children might also begin to model or emulate the behavior of people they look up to, such as pop stars, actors and the characters they play; their parents, teachers, siblings, or even other friends. Certain mental filters such as individual values also begin to form at this age.

They're now beginning to form a sense of self, an identity of their own. From eleven to thirteen, they start playing around with different roles and different ways of being based on their role models. This is the beginning stage of adolescence, the transition from child to adult.

Generalization: "Most people or things are…" This process develops as an important way for children to learn and handle the vast amount of information that reaches their senses every day. This is the process of learning and creating assumptions so that the data they gather can be applied to the accomplishment of any task. For example, a toddler who acquires the ability to open a door for the first time rapidly generalizes their new talent so they can open all sorts of doors.

This generalization can come from just a few experiences, or just one if it's powerful enough. You could generalize a negative experience through the rest of your life, and as a consequence create problems later on. For example, seeing a large spider crawl across your brother's face and your mother freaking out at the same time might make you scared of all spiders for life (I can still picture the spider).

This is when you form your conclusions about what is the same as what, or what causes what, what is good compared to what is bad. How you feel about the color blue. You might experience life from generalizations such as: *Love hurts. Nickelback songs carry meaningful life insights. Ferraris are awesome. Successful people get up early. Money doesn't grow on trees.*

Generalizations also help you manage information by grouping stuff together in chunks. Normally, the conscious mind can only handle seven, plus or minus two, items of information at any given time, so generalizing helps you manage large bits of data. Think of phone numbers, which are easier to remember when you put them in chunks: 0412376893 becomes 0412 376 893. Cars: brand, BMW; model: 1 Series; type: 135 Coupe (with the added generalization that BMWs are also awesome).

Stage 3: The socialization period (13–21 years)

The delete, distort, and generalize filters go to work as you start to move into the socialization period. This is when you go out into the world and start finding your tribe; people that are like you and your model of the world. This is when you start trying out your model of the world in the world. During this period, you are also largely influenced by your peers. You are further influenced by the media, especially when what you read and hear resonates with your values and those of your peer groups.

Joanne was a client in my coaching practice a couple of years ago. She was a successful CEO (of a company, but not her life), fit, attractive, intelligent, and interested in being her best. Sounds perfect, right? The catch for Joanne was that she was on her third marriage, and once again she was fed up with being treated poorly by her husband. He was never home, and when he was he would yell at her and argue, and at times verged on physical violence. She said he had cheated on her a couple of times, and even though she had forgiven him she believed he was doing it again. She wanted me to help her change so she could be a better wife and keep her husband.

When I asked about her previous marriages, she said they had all ended up the same way, with her husband leaving for another woman.

If you recall the model I presented above, what I said to her at the end of her session might make sense. "Sounds like your husband is perfect for you," I said.

Now, I know that sounds harsh, but here is the history behind it. Joanne had grown up in a home with parents who were verbally and physically abusive to each other. From the time she was born to the age of seven, she developed a map for how the game of marriage was played. During those first seven years, she gathered as much information as she could about relationships and marriage. By seven, her "truth" about marriage had been formed.

The next seven years (8–14) was when she started to gather more evidence that her model of the world, and the game of marriage, was true.

Imagine that Joanne is walking down the street with her girlfriends and they pass a couple kissing and cuddling on a park bench. One of Joanne's friends says, "Oh, look at that couple kissing." Joanne says, "What couple?" Because of Joanne's model of relationships, her filter deletes the couple. Her eyes see them, but her filter deletes it before it reaches her mind, protecting and maintaining her truth.

Or she might say, "They're behaving that way because they're in public. If they were at home, they wouldn't be kissing." This time her filter distorts what she see to it still fits her truth: married people are physically and verbally abusive to each other.

Or she might say, "Before they get married, all couples kiss each other. But when they get married, they yell and punch each other."

Now imagine that Joanne is watching a TV show where the man comes home drunk, gets into an argument with his wife, and she slaps him across the face. The husband yells abusive comments at the wife and storms out. Joanne's filter let's this go straight through to her unconscious mind, as it's a perfect match for her truth, and further evidence of her model of a married couple.

Guess what happens to Joanne in the next seven years (ages 15–21)? What friends does she hang out with? What boys does she attract into her life? Are there any boys who mistreat her? They make a perfect match for her. Her filter prevents her from seeing those boys who would treat her with respect and kindness, and instead only lets her see the boys that reinforce her truth. Is it any wonder that, twenty years later, Joanne is on her third marriage to a man who is a perfect match for her?

Now, I'm not saying that an abusive relationship is anyone's fault, but I am saying that both parties are one hundred percent response-able. Being in this relationship is a choice, and that's a great thing because it's also a choice to be out of the relationship.

If you are in an abusive relationship, connect with your purpose, set some plans in place, connect with your power, surround yourself with people who will support and champion you, and take action. Make a shift.

As your life CEO, know that nothing is true, and that you can chose. You are responsible for your life.

Now, what can you do if you think your model of the world is not serving you? Let's take a *Matrix* journey and look at why the menu is not the food.

21 The Roadmap Is Not the Road

❝We see things not as they are but as we are.❞
H.M. TOMLINSON

A few months ago my wife and I went for a date week in Port Douglas, Queensland. It was just the two of us, so I wanted it to be special. I spent hours researching the best resort to stay in. They all sounded great, so I started looking through their galleries of pictures. The resorts looked amazing. I booked a resort that had a massive pool with a giant swim-up bar, and spacious rooms with balconies that stretched forever.

When we arrived, we found that the images were same and yet different to the actual resort. The pool was not massive but moderate, the swim-up bar was not giant but adequate, the room was not spacious but small, and the balcony was a squeeze rather than a stretch. The pictures were not the resort.

I'm sure this idea seems simple enough. After all, who would confuse a roadmap with a road, or a menu with a meal? But people often become confused over what they think of as reality.

Let's look at another example. Asian restaurants and McDonald's love to put a picture next to the description of the meal and price. Big, beautifully stacked burgers with the perfect distribution of lettuce, tomato, bacon, and beef patty, all lightly placed between two perfectly shaped burger buns. Then you open the box and find a squished burger with a flaccid beef patty, one slice of tomato, and a pickle hanging out the side. It looks like something put together by a hormonal teenager wishing they were at home playing Xbox, and that's because it probably was put together by a hormonal teenager wishing they were at home playing Xbox (that's a quick insight to my map of McDonald's).

You get the idea. The images, movies, and text we read don't give us the truth, but rather a representation of the truth. It's the result of our filters (beliefs, values, standards) being applied to the thing. This filter, just like the filter you can apply to photos you take on your smartphone, creates an internal representation of the truth. The catch is, you don't know the difference. You think the world is what your internal representation of the world shows.

This filtering process comes from all the deletions, distortions, and generalizations we apply to the information we see, hear, feel, taste, and smell. The filter only allows us to see a reflection of who we are. We experience the world not as it is but as we are.

One more example. It's not the truth, but an example. Years ago there was a street directory in Australia called *Melway*. The team that put together this directory went across Australia creating maps of the country. Mr. Melway (not his real name) told them what to record, what was important, and to be sure to add hospitals and railway stations. And so they did. The map of Melbourne in *Melway* is obviously not Melbourne but a *representation* of Melbourne, with some features that were considered important when the map was created.

Mr. Navman sent his team out to map Australia, with instructions to include petrol stations and schools. And so they did. Again, the map of Melbourne is just a *representation* of Melbourne, based on what Mr. Navman thought was important.

Then Mr. TomTom did the same, and his map was also good, but it wasn't the full truth. Then Google did it, with Google Maps, and Apple with Apple Maps. Even with all the incredible technology and imagery, these maps are still not the truth. They are snapshots-in-time representations of the truth.

We create our own maps of the world through our experiences and the meaning we give them. We are especially affected by important events.

> **"The world is a looking glass and gives back to every man the reflection of his own face."**
> **WILLIAM MAKEPEACE THACKERAY**

Defining moments

A defining moment is a particular, important event that happened in your past, usually in your childhood. Most adults have five to nine defining moments in their past. The only thing that makes an event important that it feels important *to you*. What other people think about its significance is not relevant.

These events, either positive or negative (again, you get to choose), cause significant shifts in our maps and how they represent the world. An event can involve health, money, relationships, career, education, parents, siblings, grandparents, or anything else that you make important. Just like Mr. Melway made hospitals and railway stations important.

These are events that you give weight to, and as a result they cause your map to change. Your representation of the world changes. What you delete, distort and generalize changes. You will see the world differently because *you* are different, and you can only see what is you.

Here is where it gets a little scary. If your map of the world changes, any previous beliefs about the world must also change. Defining moments often cause your old representations of the world to change. That is, your memories often change as a result of defining moments. When you say that you remember something, what you mean is that you're remembering the current representation of that memory. Yes, that's right. Even your memories, no matter how clearly shaped, are deleted, distorted and generalized based on your current map of how the world works—your current representation.

So do you have to wait for a defining moment to shift your map? What happens if you come to the realization that it's not working? There's good news. You can shift your map at any time by using the power of the "?".

Questions

Have you noticed that this book is full of questions? That's because every time I make a statement, you take that statement (like you're doing right now) and run it past your filter, check it against your representation of the truth, and either delete, distort or generalize what you just read. Your representation of this book is a reflection of you. You can only experience this book as you are. That's where questions come in.

When you're asked a question, it will usually slip past the filter. Let me give you an example.

I might say to you, "I love rainy days. They're the best, and they're good for you."

You might respond by saying, "Are you kidding? I hate rain, it ruins everything." This is a direct reflection of your representation of rain.

But what if I asked you these questions: "Tell me three things you love about rain." Or, "Does rain serve any benefit?" Or, "Did you know that rain has special nutrients in it that feeds plants better than a garden hose?" Or, "What's the best experience you've ever had in the rain?"

These questions will get past your filter and cause you to go looking for the answer. This is of course what I do in my coaching practice.

" We cannot solve our problems with the same thinking we used when we created them. "
ALBERT EINSTEIN

The above quote illustrates the only catch when you give yourself questions. Given that you can only see what is you, it gets tricky to use questions on yourself because you can only ask questions that are a representation of your current truth.

For example, if you believed you were ugly, you would probably not ask yourself the question: "Why am I so beautiful?" Or, "What is it about me that makes me so hot?" Instead, you might ask: "Why am I so ugly? Or, "Why do people think I'm dreadful?"

When you consult with a quality coach, they ask questions from future thinking. Questions that cause you to find the answers to the future that you really want. A future that feels fulfilling and in alignment with your true purpose. That's why I keep encouraging you to do the questions and exercises in this book.

At times you will look at the question and answer: "I don't know." Stick with it. It makes sense that you don't know, because the question is not one you're used to asking yourself. As a coach working with clients, either I will stay in the boat with them until they find an answer, or I will ask a better question to help them find it.

Stay in the boat with yourself. If you don't want to wait for a defining moment to shift your map of the world and how you represent it, then quality questions are the answer.

Great CEOs are curious CEOs. They regularly consult with their board, advisors, and team. They have mentors. They mix in clubs and organizations that are forward thinking, and they ask questions that cause their map to be challenged. Being your life CEO has within it the responsibility to ask future-thinking questions.

In the next chapter, we'll tackle some quality questions to help you shift some beliefs about yourself and the world around you.

22 Beliefs

> "I would never die for my beliefs
> because I might be wrong."
> **BERTRAND RUSSELL**

Beliefs are things that you are sure are right. They are your interpretation of something. I love those words by Gandhi: "We live in a meaningless world that we put meaning to."

A quick example to kick off your understanding. In my coaching practice, I have navy blue carpet with a white fleck in a symmetrical pattern. Someone might look at that carpet and believe that it's too dark, that the white fleck looks like a bit of dust, that a light-colored carpet would have been better. Someone else might look at it and say they love the navy blue because it gives the practice a warm, professional feel, and that the subtle, barely noticeable, white fleck helps hide any stains. In fact, they might say, it's the most sensible choice I could have made.

Who is right? Neither and both. Both are right based on their beliefs. As we now know, they formed those beliefs according to their maps.

You see or experience something, you take what you think is important from that experience and add meaning to it. You then build a story based on that meaning and create a belief. All your future actions are a result of that belief. The entire world that you see, and your experience of it, becomes a reflection of you.

That might seem a slightly bitter pill to swallow, but the good news is that you can be the change you want to see in the world. You just have to shift your beliefs, and the world will change, too. Cool!

Money equals rip-off merchants, or freedom, or too hard, or success. You decide.

Relationships equal cheaters, or love, or too much effort, or great sex. You decide.

Job equals annoying bosses, or contribution, or paying the bills, or teamwork. You decide.

What you do is important, but more important is who you *be*. The action you take is always driven by your beliefs about yourself and the world. If you're finding that your actions are not working, that you're not getting what you really want, maybe you have some beliefs that are holding you back, that are not supporting the new version of your life that's in alignment with your life purpose and missions.

You might believe that you have some great beliefs that support you and are totally in alignment with your purpose and missions. If so, don't change them, leave them be. (I wonder, though, if there are just few that could do with a tweak, or maybe even trashing so you can insert a new one.)

It could be time for a belief upgrade

When we have a belief that holds us back, we call it a limiting belief. Because beliefs are created from experiences, and then played out through our actions, they are then reinforced. They grow stronger and stronger, until for some they become unshakable beliefs. Some will be unshakably good beliefs, and some unshakably not good (limiting) beliefs.

I don't know what is good or bad for you. Only you do. A good belief supports your vision for your life, and a not good one limits that vision becoming a reality.

We often find that our beliefs are hidden in our thoughts (what we say to ourselves) or language (what we say to others). Here are a few examples:

- I always... stuff things up, make a mess, fall over, find a way, arrive on time.
- I never... get it right, find the time, save, make mistakes, get angry.
- I can't... win, decide, lose weight, get a job, lose, smoke, let myself go.
- I can... make mistakes, be known to break things, get stuff done, love.
- I am... a loser, weak, not organized, tired, strong, fast, efficient, happy.

JOURNAL TIME

LifeCEO.com/RESOURCES

Finish the following sentences with at least five examples:
- I always...
- I never...
- I can't...
- I can...
- I am...
- People are...
- Life is...
- Money...
- Love and relationships...

Now keep going. Start looking at all the different missions you have in your life and the different roles, and ask yourself what your beliefs are around those aspects of your life.

It's great to know what your beliefs are because they will help you understand your model of the world, what it all means. That doesn't make it true, however; it's just your interpretation or representation of what is true.

Now let's take a look at your beliefs and see if there are any you might like to change.

📖 JOURNAL TIME

Grab your pen and circle all the beliefs that serve you. That means all the beliefs that you think support your vision for your life, your purpose. They're also the beliefs that feel good, that excite you, that encourage you to keep an open mind. Are they going to create more abundance and growth?

Got a few circled? Awesome. Now it's time to tackle the others, the ones that don't support your vision of your future life; that don't support your purpose, your missions, and the legacy you want to leave.

📖 JOURNAL TIME

Take all those beliefs and write them down the left-hand side of a fresh sheet of paper. Next to each belief, create a new version. It should be one that addresses that particular belief and puts a new meaning to it, and supports your future vision for your life. For example:

- Old: I am hopeless at managing money.
- New: Organizing money is easy.
- Old: I give up easily.
- New: I never give up on what matters most.

Now that you've done that exercise, it's time to reprogram those beliefs through the power of language, repetition, example, and action.

23 Values

> A mission statement is not something you write overnight... But fundamentally, your mission statement becomes your constitution, the solid expression of your vision and values. It becomes the criterion by which you measure everything else in your life.
>
> **STEPHEN COVEY**

I love the quote by Roy Disney: "When your values are clear to you, making decisions becomes easier." When you know your values, you can look at any situation and decide whether that thing you are about to do will match your values.

Values are not something you create; they are something you find out or discover. They have been formed over all the years you have been alive.

As we have discovered, understanding your map of the world means your values have been formed and reinforced since birth. They have been created, like your beliefs, by your exposure to family, friends, religion, school, country, economic upbringing, the media, TV, the Internet, and the books you have read. They determine how you react and interact with the world around you.

Values are the emotional states or tones that you want to experience on a regular basis.

Your current life is a result of your beliefs, values, standards, and rules. Your level of wealth, the quality of your relationships, the strength of your health, and the worth of your job are all reflections of your values.

Values determine much of your day-to-day behavior, what you're attracted to and what you're repelled by. Values have an order of importance and are ranked in your mind. Also, they are not specific in nature, but represent a bigger picture.

There are the two main forms of values:

1. Away-from values (what you want to move towards)
2. Towards values (what you want to move away from)

Here are two values that might work together and likely drive the creation of financial success:
   a) Towards value: wealth
   b) Away value: poverty

Here are two values that might work against each other, blocking the attainment of health, since to become physically fit could require hard work:
   a) Towards value: fitness
   b) Away value: hard work

The ranking of values also helps reinforce the values and the level to which they drive you and your behavior. There are two main types of values:

•   Ends values
•   Means values

As the old saying goes, "One is a means to an end." A means value potentially creates an ends value. For example, money might be a means value to the ends value of success.

Your roles may have different values. Values can also be allocated to different roles or missions within your life. So you might have values for health, career, relationships, money, etc.

The meaning of your values is person specific. Everyone has their own interpretation of what value means. For example, the following values mean different things to different people: love, success, abundance, health, compassion, humor, tolerance.

Do your values serve you? Sometimes you might find that your values do not serve you. In your conscious mind, you want to pursue something, and while it might feel right, and be connected with a deeper purpose, you just don't seem to be able to get there. There's something holding you back. Sometimes that something will be an internal-values skirmish, a skirmish between your towards and away values, your hierarchy, your meaning of that value, particularly when engaging in a conversation that involves values, or just the value itself.

For example, you might sincerely want to become healthy, but you don't place enough value on energy, vitality, fitness or health. So no matter how hard you work at it, your other higher priority values will always win. If money, relationships, fun, creation, and focus are your top values, health and fitness don't get a look in.

Let's take a look at your values and see how they stack up.

📖✎ JOURNAL TIME

Get out your journal and divide a blank page into two columns. As a heading for the first column write *Towards Values* and in the second write *Away Values*. (For a list of towards values, see the resources section at the end of this book for a downloadable list.) Now do a massive brain dump onto the page of everything you can think of that you value or dislike. Remember, this is not an opportunity to create values, but instead to discover them. Here are some questions to get you thinking:

- What have you loved doing over the last couple of weeks? What is the underlying value? For example, if you love gardening, gardening might be a means value for what end value? Creation, nature, organization, etc.

- Have you been angry or upset this week? What has annoyed you? For example, clients running late for appointments could be a means value for which end value? Time, respect, organization, etc.

- When are you happy?

- What do you love doing? If you have spare time, what do you do?

- What do you hate doing? What do think is boring and a waste of time?

- Who do you admire? Why?

Also, remember that as much as possible you want to focus on end values not means values. To help take the value as far as you can, it's good to ask yourself a couple of questions: What do I get out of that? Why is that important to me?

Now that you have your list, put them in order of priority. Hopefully, you will have at least ten towards values, and five away

values (sometimes away values can be tricky to discover). Back to
your journal:

- Scan quickly through your list and put a mark against your top
  ten. Then scan the top ten and put a second mark against your
  top five. Now take that top five and label them A to E in rough
  order of priority.
- Starting with A, and taking B as a comparison, ask yourself which
  value you couldn't do without. If the answer is A, compare it with
  B, and so on. If you get through B to E, and A is still the one you
  couldn't do without, then that's your #1 value.
- Continue the process from B through to E until you've created
  a final order of priority for your top five, numbered one to five.
- Repeat this process for your away values.

How did you go? That can be a tricky exercise, so well done for having a go. Now you have your top five values and insight into why you do what you do. Before we go on, let's do a quick test to see if that list feels right. (Sometimes this exercise is better done a couple of days later, after your brain has stewed on it overnight. You can always add new insights and shift around the priorities; this list does not have to be carved in stone.) Ask yourself:

- How do I feel when I look at that list?
- Do they make me smile?
- Are any of the values should's rather than being true to me?
- Do I need to change the order?

How to use your values

This list of values is going to come in handy when you decide to make some decisions. You will use some of these values when creating your life-purpose statement. This statement will guide you and help you stay on your true path.

When you make your next decision, you'll create a vision of the result of that decision, and while looking at and feeling the result of that decision, you will ask yourself how this vision compares with your values. Does it make your values shine? Can you see and feel a conflict, a degree of awkwardness to the vision?

It's great to know that the decision you're about to make will cause you some value pain later on, or that feeling of joy and fulfillment are headed your way if you do make the decision.

This exercise, I believe, is one of the most valuable (pardon the pun) you can do. And once these values are articulated in a mission statement, you will have a guiding light for all future decisions.

24 Are Rules Ruling Your Happiness?

> **"If you obey all the rules you miss all the fun."**
> **KATHARINE HEPBURN**

What are your rules to be happy? Do you want to be happy in your marriage, business, health, friendships and money? Rules are things we make up over time, and sometimes they are unrealistic or there are too many. In this chapter, we talk about standards. I'm suggesting that you raise your standards, but get rid of some of your rules.

Where do rules come from? The same place everything we have in our heads comes from: we just make them up based on our life experiences, and often what we are told are the rules for happiness.

Here is an example of what the popular media portrays as a happy relationship. A man and woman go out. The man arrives at the woman's home dressed in a black tuxedo, driving a beautiful, clean, latest-model Porsche. He knocks on the door with a bunch of flowers in his hand. She opens the door dressed in a three-thousand-dollar Armani dress that drapes perfectly over her slender frame, but reveals just enough cleavage to catch his eye and interest. They smile at each other, both full of energy and vitality. Perfect skin, perfect smiles.

He escorts her to the car, of course opening the door for her. They drive off, laughing and smiling, and arrive at a five-hat restaurant. He finds a car park right out front. He saunters around to open her door, and takes her arm, leading her into the restaurant. They're escorted to the best table in the house, complete with white tablecloth, candle and crystal glasses. He orders the 1952 Borjeale. They smile and laugh, ordering the full degustation menu.

They finish the meal with a fine cognac, still laughing and smiling, but now with a I-want-you look on their faces. He pays the bill, leaving an appropriately large tip. Back in the car, he suggests she come back to his place for a nightcap. They arrive at a large gated mansion, where the gates swing open and the Porsche purrs up the gravel drive. They enter the house, and it's not long before they're in the bedroom making love for hours, again and again. There is no mess to be cleaned up, and her makeup and hair remain picture perfect.

The next scene is when he brings her breakfast in bed: freshly squeezed orange juice, eggs Benedict, pancakes and freshly brewed coffee. She sits up in bed, draped in his shirt from the night before, and they go back to laughing and smiling. They don't have a care in the world, just each other.

Sound familiar to you? Now, I don't know about you, but the last time I checked, my marriage didn't look exactly like that every day.

Some people believe that this scenario is required for their relationship to be a happy one. They have a checklist of rules that they run through at the end of every day to assess whether they should feel happy. They do this, not only for their relationship, but also health, money, career and any other aspect of their life. They find a lot of their rules for happiness in that aspect of their life remain unchecked, and hence they feel unhappy.

How about you? Where in your life do you have too many rules? The key to more happiness is to have fewer rules or expectations.

Expectations

I love this equation for happiness. It's simple, just like happiness can be if we choose:

$$Life = life\ expectations$$

There are obviously two sides to this equation, so if you want more consistent happiness in your life, you can do one of two things, or even both. You can change your life. That is, you can be clear about your purpose, make a plan, set some goals, change your behavior, and take action. Don't like your job because of your expectations? Change your job. Not happy with your relationship because of your expectations? Leave the relationship and find another. Not happy with your body because of your rules (expectations) for what it means to have a great body? Get to the gym, eat less, read better books, change your physique.

Or you can change your expectations or rules. The fewer rules or expectations, the better.

Don't like your job? Get fewer rules.

Do you get paid? Yes. Check happy.

Not happy with your relationship? Lower your expectations.

Does he or she love you? Yes. Check happy.

Not happy with your body. Can you walk? Can you eat? Can you play? Can you engage in conversation? Did you wake up today? Yes. Check happy.

I'm all for you improving your life, health, money, career, and relationships, but do it in alignment with your purpose, values, and standards. Where in your life have you got a lot of rules, too many expectations that are stopping you from experiencing greater health?

" Remembering that I'll be dead soon is the most important tool I've ever encountered to help me make the big choices in life. Because of almost everything—all external expectations, all pride, all fear of embarrassment or failure— these things just fall away in the face of death, leaving only what is truly important. "

STEVE JOBS

📖 JOURNAL TIME

Pick an area of your life that you are not happy with right now. Write a list of all the things you need to be happy. Don't hold back. Dig deep. List all of your criteria: the expectations and rules you need to be happy in this area of your life. Your goal should be to get at least twenty things down.

Now take a look at the list. What are your must-have rules? Pick ten from the list. These ten must have rules for you to be happy? Got them? Excellent.

Now here is the gold. If you could have only one to three rules (one is even better) to be happy in this aspect of your life, what would they be? Take those one to three rules and put them in the following sentence:

"For me to be happy in _____, at the end of the day I just need _____, (optional) _____, and _____."

Imagine if that was all you needed to be happy. Would life feel better? I suggest that you repeat that exercise for each aspect of your life.

Expectations don't just exist around part of your life, but also around time. If you set expectations for what you want to achieve in a day, you have a checklist to get completed by the end of the day to be happy. Now take those expectations and use one of my favorite words: intentions.

What if, instead of expectations for your life or day, you had intentions? This doesn't mean they're any weaker, or that you pursue them with any less vigor or effort. In fact, go all out with the intention of getting them done. But if life happens, as it sometimes it does, be okay with it. Don't let it ruin your day, and prevent your happiness.

Rules? Have fewer of them. Know that you can change your expectations to match your life, or swap them for intentions. Don't let past stories of how life has to be (rules) dictate your level of happiness.

25 What Are You Focused On?

> **It is during our darkest moments that we must focus to see the light.**
> **ARISTOTLE**

A couple of years ago, I was having my usual morning personal training session. My trainer, Matt, was a cancer survivor who didn't understand the concept of giving up. He had eliminated that from his mindset. He believed that once you start on something you can always finish it. It might be ugly, but you will finish it (he ran a marathon on crutches).

This particular morning had had me on a machine called the "dreadmill" (like a treadmill but with a fixed a ten-degree incline). We had all had a go at fixing it, but Matt liked that it was broken and permanently in an inclined state. Matt's training method incorporated a hard-out run, for five minutes, on the dreadmill. At the end of an already intense training session. Five minutes might not seem like much, but a 110-percent effort on a ten-degree was hardcore.

I started off, and I was smashing it. At about the three-minute mark, Matt looked at me and said, "You're looking a bit pale, mate. Are you all right?" I thought I was fine, but then I did an internal body scan to see if there was anything amiss, and that's when it all started to unfold.

I truly believe that we all have the potential to be anything we want. It's all there inside us. And I also believe the world has the potential to give us everything we need, to be anything we want. It all depends on where we put our focus.

Imagine you're in a warehouse. Inside the warehouse is everything. Everything. Every single possibility. And inside the warehouse, all the lights are off. Someone hands you a torch, and wherever you shine the light, whatever you see, is what you think the warehouse is full of. You might see a pile of cardboard boxes in a corner, so that's what you think the warehouse is filled with. You shine the torch in another corner, on some silver drums. So you think the warehouse is full of silver drums.

But the warehouse is full of *everything*. Someone turns on the lights and you see that it contains cardboard boxes, silver drums, old cars, machinery, explosive substances, gas cylinders, batteries, oil, grease, fuel, plants, firewood, food, animal carcasses, chemicals, garbage... But it's also got a beautifully restored 1968 Ferrari Dino, a helicopter, antique furniture, a suitcase full of cash, a 500-year-old Ming vase, a treadmill... Every single thing you could ever want is in that warehouse. But when you first shone the torch, you saw only what you were focused on.

Wherever you put your focus is what you think life is about. But life is about what you focus on *plus* what you focus on *plus* what you focus on *plus* what you focus on...

Back to the dreadmill, and my scan of my body looking for the reason why I was "looking a little pale." Then I found it. The voice in head was saying: *I think I've stopped sweating. I think I'm feeling a little cold. I think I'm a little nauseous.*

At that point, Matt brought over the vomit bucket. All good gyms have one of these. When you train intensely, lactate builds up in the blood, causing nausea and sometimes vomiting. So now my focus was on all the things that could be wrong with me, and I had a vomit bucket to look at. Within twenty seconds of feeling fine and smashing it, I was dry-retching into the bucket.

And now I'll come to the point of this story. Matt told me later that at no point during the training did I look pale. It was just his way of having fun. But his comment had caused a shift in my focus to what could be wrong with me, and ended with my run on the dreadmill.

Be careful of where you put your attention, and who listen to. Where your attention goes, your life flows.

Would life change for you if you believed you had the potential to be anything? Think of potential as being like an acorn. An acorn is a small, hard seed. It carries within it the potential to become a magnificent, beautiful oak tree. All the seed needs is focused stimulation. Just like the acorn, you carry the potential to be more than what you are. Your life depends on where you choose to put your focus, and whether you take action.

One of the great skills of a CEO is an ability to focus their attention. To notice what is working and what isn't. To see the potential in team members, products and customers. To have the ability to help their teams adjust their focus so they can also see the potential.

Being your life CEO means that it's your responsibility to determine where you put your focus, and to be aware that what you see is often not all there is to see. If you don't like what you see, shift your focus.

26 The Triune of Tone

> " We live in deeds, not years; in thoughts,
> not breaths; in feelings, not in figures
> on a dial. We should count time by heart
> throbs. He most lives who thinks most,
> feels the noblest, acts the best. "
>
> **ARISTOTLE**

This chapter is all about state control. No, not the North Korean kind. Your ability to control your mental state: how you feel, your mood, your character or ethos. If you believe that you can be one hundred percent response-able for your life, you recognize that your feelings are also your responsibility.

Sometimes when I ask a client to tell me who they think they need to be, they will say, "I "just need to be myself." I reply: "You are always yourself."

All your emotions, feelings, tone (state), and resulting actions are always you.

✏ JOURNAL TIME

This is a quick little exercise, but it's worth doing. Write a list of all the emotions, feelings, moods, character traits, and states you've experienced in the last week. The ones that you liked and the ones you didn't like. Make a list of all those that you want more of, and a list of all those that you would like less of. Every single tone: joy, happiness, sadness, fear, anger, pain, wonderment, excitement, passion...

These emotions are what determine your actions. There's a reason why you have these emotions, and why they develop into feelings. Importantly, there is a difference between emotions, feelings, and your tone (state). In this chapter I will focus on tone, character or state, and how you chose to create it.

One of my most intense experiences was when my amazing mum passed away. I remember the call from the nurse at the palliative-care hospital. I remember hanging up the phone and within seconds experiencing a deep feeling of loss, of being left alone, of no longer having the one person that would always love me unconditionally. I burst into uncontrollable, primal sobs that lasted on and off for the rest of the night.

This feeling still comes up when I think of my mum. Even as I write this paragraph, I relive those feelings and tears well up in my eyes. The difference between this feeling and tone is that when I finish writing about my mum and move on to writing other things, that feeling will go and my underlying tone will remain upbeat.

How does that work? How is it that we can be feeling great, and then something changes in our environment and suddenly we feel angry, or upset, or sad, or any one of a hundred other emotions. Not just for a few minutes but sometimes for hours. We're at work, and we're feeling tired and miserable, but a friend calls and invites us to the opening of a new cocktail bar. Suddenly we're full of beans and smiles.

Every single feeling we have is driven by, or drives, something we do.

If I ask someone what they want, the conversation could go like this:

Them: "I want a new car. A Porsche."

Me: "Why do you want a Porsche?"

Them: "You know, because they look great."

Me: "Why is that important to you?"

Them: "Well, it's just the whole look. A Porsche looks good, and I'll feel good when I'm in it."

Me: "Why? Why would you feel good?"

Them: "Because it goes fast. It'll give me a thrill, a pump. I'll be excited. I'll feel proud."

It's not that he wants the Porsche. He wants the feelings and tone the Porsche will give him. Thrills, the feeling of speed, the feeling of pride. These are the reasons he wants that thing.

Everything is driven by feeling. Imagine how cool it would be if you could switch on that feeling whenever you wanted. Rather than needing to go out and buy a Porsche, you could switch on the feeling of being thrilled. Switch on the thrill, pump, and pride. Switch on the feeling of excitement.

There's a reason why you can be doing sadness in one moment and happiness in another. This is what I call the "triune of tone."

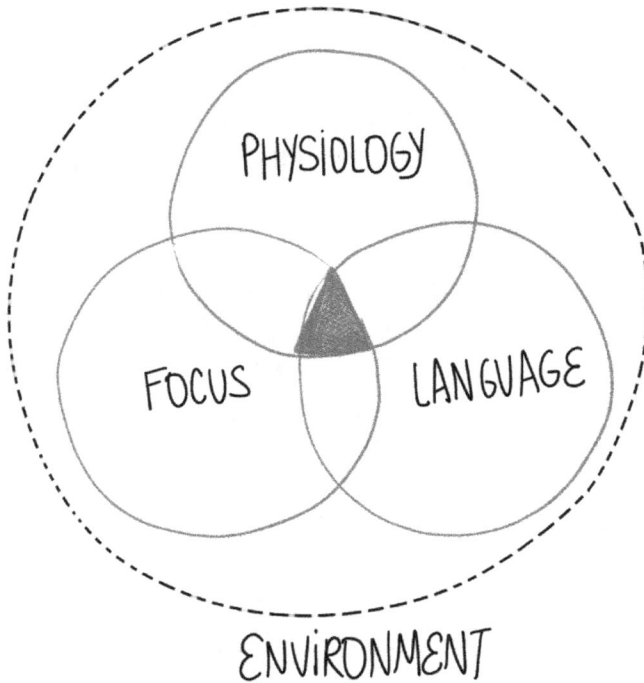

Your tone or state is determined by three factors, and each of these is completely under your conscious control. If you choose to control all three, you can retrigger, or activate any feeling and set your tone once again.

The first part of the triune is that what you do with your body. This determines how you feel.

Physiology

When I talk about physiology, I mean the body and its various components, mechanical, physical, and biochemical. All of your body's systems interact and influence each other. For instance, physiology can have an effect on your mental functions and psychology. Sometimes referred to as "embodied cognition," this is the theory that many features of cognition, human or otherwise, are shaped by aspects of the entire organism.

Imagine for a moment someone who is doing depression. What is their physiology like? Picture them doing massive depression. They are incredibly unhappy. Really, really sad. Imagine what they look like? Are they standing? Are they sitting? What does their face look like? How do they talk, read, move?

Now, I picture a slumped person, hunched over, looking down. There's no smile on their face. In fact, they're probably frowning. They look tired. They've moving slowly, breathing slowly. When they talk, their words are slow and unenthusiastic. They're probably sitting down because studies show that smiling and posture have an effect on emotions and tone.

Smiling: A clinical trial in 2012 involved the use of Botox and frown muscles. Botox, which makes the muscles relax, was injected just once into a specific part of the face—the frown area—in fifteen patients, and another fifteen were injected with a placebo of saline (saltwater).

Amazing improvements in state or tone were achieved in the first group after just one injection. Six weeks after a single treatment, the rating scales for depression in the Botox recipients were reduced, on average, by 47.1 percent. The placebo-treated group experienced only a 9.2 percent reduction in the measurement of their depression.

If you can't frown, you're happier and less depressed. How you hold yourself, your physiology, your posture, makes a huge difference to how you feel.

In another study, Matt Hertenstein and collaborators at DePauw University, Indiana analyzed hundreds of graduates (average age forty-six) and looked at the yearbook photos of the graduates. The researchers measured the intensity of the smiles in the photos and asked the subjects if they had ever been divorced. According to Hertenstein, "The top 10 percent of smilers had a divorce rate of about 1 in 20, whereas if you were a bottom 10 percent smiler, your chance of divorce was five times more likely!"

A study in 2001 went back thirty years and examined the photos of women students in an old yearbook to see if the amount of "positive emotion" shown measured success and wellbeing throughout their lives. By measuring the students' smiles, researchers were able to predict how fulfilling and long-lasting their marriages would be, how well they would score on standardized tests of wellbeing, and how inspiring they would be to others. The bigger the smile, the more fulfilling the life, and the greater the wellbeing.

Lastly, in a 1988 study, one group of participants was instructed to hold a pencil between their teeth, which forced them to smile, while rating how funny they found a mix of cartoons. The other group of participants was instructed to do the same while holding the pencil in their lips, which resulted in no smile and a frown. Researchers hypothesized that the group with the forced smiles would rate the cartoons funnier than the other group. Guess what? They were right. Smiling helps you to fund stuff funnier.

Posture: How do you hold yourself? Another study looked at the generation of positive and negative thoughts in either an upright or slumped position. Twenty-four participants, who had no clinical depression or anxiety, completed a questionnaire. Muscle tension, heart rate, and respiratory rate were assessed in either upright or slumped posture, and either positive or negative thought generation.

At the end of the study, participants rated which thought was easiest to generate in the two postures. Significantly more participants (22), or 92 percent, said it was easier to generate thoughts quickly, and general positive thoughts, in an upright position.

We know that slumped posture is a diagnostic feature of depression. In a 2016 study aimed at investigating whether changing posture could reduce negative effects and fatigue in people with mild to moderate depression undergoing a stressful task. Sixty-one community participants who showed mild to moderate depression were split into two groups, one to sit with their usual posture, and the other with an upright posture. Participants were then asked to complete a spoken stress test. Changes in effect and fatigue were assessed, as well as the words spoken by the participants.

Upright posture had a positive effect on emotion and fatigue compared to usual posture. The upright group also spoke significantly more words than the usual-posture group, with lower negative effects and lower anxiety across both groups. This study suggests that adopting an upright posture may increase positive effects, reduce fatigue, and decrease self-focus in people with mild to moderate depression.

An experiment in 2015 aimed to investigate whether an upright posture could influence the heart's responses to a mentally stressful task, compared to a slumped seated posture. Seventy-four participants were randomly assigned to either a slumped or upright posture. The participants completed a reading task, a spoken stress test, and were assessed for mood, self-esteem, and perceived threat. Blood pressure and heart rate were measured continuously.

The upright participants reported higher self-esteem, more arousal, better mood, and lower fear compared to slumped participants. Speech analysis showed slumped participants used more negative-emotion words, more sadness words, and fewer positive-emotion words and total words. Upright participants had higher pulse pressure during and after the stressor.

The study concluded that adopting an upright seated posture in the face of stress could maintain self-esteem, reduce negative mood, and increase positive mood compared to a slumped posture. The researchers believed that sitting upright may be a simple behavioral strategy to help build resilience to stress and that this is consistent with embodied cognition theories claiming muscular and autonomic states influence emotional responding.

Another great study in 2016 looked at physical activity performed in three different ways: as one bout in the morning; as microbouts spread out across the day; and as a day spent sitting. The study compared the effects of the three different forms of physical activity on mood, energy levels, and cognitive function. It was found that in addition to the beneficial impact of physical activity on levels of energy and vigor, spreading out physical activity throughout the day improved mood, decreased feelings of fatigue, and affected appetite. Introducing short bouts of activity during the workday of sedentary office workers is a promising approach to improving overall wellbeing at work without negatively impacting cognitive performance.

Lots of studies indicate that a stooped posture may activate negative mood, but does a stooped posture influence recovery from a pre-existing negative mood? An experiment involved 229 participants who were randomly assigned to receive either a negative or a neutral mood induction (made to feel bad), after which they were instructed to take either a stooped, straight, or control posture while writing down their thoughts.

Stooped posture (compared to straight or control posture) led to less mood recovery in the negative-mood condition, and more negative mood in the neutral-mood condition. Furthermore, stooped posture led to more negative thoughts overall compared to straight or control postures.

In a second experiment, 122 participants underwent a negative-mood induction, after which half received instructions to help change their mood, and half received no instructions. Again, stooped (compared to straight) position led to less mood recovery. Notably, this was independent of regulation instruction.

Movement

Now let's look at movement and mood, tone or state. Two experiments in a simple study in 2009 looked at the walking-style patterns associated with sadness and depression. In the experiment, the walking patterns of fourteen inpatients suffering from major depression were compared with those of never-depressed participants.

Walking-style patterns associated with sadness and depression are characterized by reduced walking speed, arm swing, and vertical head movements. Moreover, depressed and sad walkers display larger lateral swaying movements of the upper body, and a more slumped posture. The results of the study indicated that a specific walking style characterizes individuals in a depressed mood.

A 2013 study tested whether exercise reduces the adverse effects of sad-mood inductions in individuals who have recovered from depression. Forty-one women recovered from major depression, and forty healthy control women were randomly assigned either exercise for fifteen minutes, or quiet rest.

Afterward, participants were exposed to two sad-mood inductions and reported their levels of affect throughout the study. Recovered depressed participants who had not exercised exhibited higher negative effects after the second sad-mood induction. In contrast, both recovered depressed participants who had engaged in acute exercise, and healthy control participants showed no increase in negative effects in response to the repeated sad mood induction. Participants who exercised also reported higher positive effects after the exercise bout. Exercise and movement help you manage your mood or tone.

Body chemistry

What you eat has an impact on your mental state. The research is massive on this issue. If you want to improve your ability to control your state, tone or mood, be careful about what you put in your mouth. It will affect your physiology, which will affect your mood.

Your brain is always working, and to work it needs fuel, nutrients, and water. That "fuel" comes from the foods you eat, and better-quality fuel produces better brain performance, just like premium fuel versus standard fuel in your car. Eating premium foods that contain lots of vitamins, minerals, and antioxidants support the brain and protect it from the "waste" (free radicals) produced when the brain uses oxygen, which can harm your cells. What you eat impacts the structure and function of your brain and, ultimately, your state or tone.

Diets high in refined sugars are harmful to the brain. They give you that rollercoaster of energy, and they also stimulate inflammation. Various studies have found a correlation between a diet high in refined sugars and impaired brain function, and a worsening of mood.

Serotonin is a neurotransmitter that helps control sleep and appetite, facilitate moods, and inhibit pain. Up to 95 percent of your serotonin is produced in your gastrointestinal tract, plus your gut is full of nerve endings. How well these gut neurons work, and how well serotonin is produced, is governed by the ratio of good bacteria in the gut versus bad. If you feed the bad bacteria more than the good, you will be in trouble.

In fact, studies have shown that when people take probiotics, their anxiety, stress, and mindset all improve. Other studies have shown that a typical Western diet increases the risk of depression up to 35 percent compared to a Mediterranean diet. Scientists' explanation for this difference is because Mediterranean diets tend to be high in vegetables, fruits, fish and other seafood, and contain small quantities only of lean meats and dairy. They are also free of refined foods and sugars.

Here is some research to back it up. This cool research revealed that poor eating was more consistently associated with negative moods than positive moods, and with moods across a two-day span rather than a one-day span, as typically studied in past research. The more calories, saturated fat, and sodium consumed by the students, the more likely there were to report negative moods two days later. The results suggest that foods come first, then mood.

Ever been told by your parents to eat your vegetables? This study revealed that on days when young adults experienced greater positive mindset, they also reported eating more servings of fruit and vegetables. They also had a better and more positive mindset the next day. Meaningful changes in mindset were observed with the daily consumption of seven to eight servings of fruit or vegetables.

Another study looked at the association between eating a Mediterranean diet and the risk of stroke, depression, mental impairment, and Parkinson's disease. They found that a strict Mediterranean diet was consistently associated with reduced risk of stroke, depression, mental impairment, and Alzheimer's disease.

What are you in the mood for, the chicken or the egg? Another study studied whether moods influence our preference for particular foods. The results from four experiments showed that a positive mood causes you to think big picture, and put more importance on long-term goals such as health, leading to a greater inclination for healthy foods over indulgent foods. The results also showed that a negative mood causes you to be short-sighted, and to put greater importance on more immediate, tangible things such as mood management, leading to a greater preference for indulgent foods over healthy foods.

This interesting study is important because it looked at the effects of diet in the modeling and socialization period of (5–18 years for this particular study). They wanted to see if an association exists between diet quality and patterns, and mental health in children and adolescents. They found evidence of a significant connection between unhealthy diets and poorer mental health in both groups.

They also saw a stable tendency for the relationship between good-quality diet and better mental health. They concluded: "Their findings highlight the potential importance of the relationship between dietary patterns or quality and mental health early in the lifespan."

We know that your physiology, in particular how you hold yourself, makes a massive difference to your state, including whether you're smiling or not. Emotion is created by motion. What you do with your body determines your emotional state. Look after your physiology, and all your body's postures. Move, breath and eat well.

Focus

As discussed earlier, in any given moment you can choose your focus. No matter what's happening around you, you can choose what to put your focus on. If it's an overcast day, do you feel miserable or happy? Are you miserable because its dark and cold, or happy because the rain will be good for the garden, and you can light the fire and sit in front of it with a glass of red?

In any moment, you can focus on someone you don't like, or someone you love, someone who loves you. Think about that person, the person you love. The person you know who loves you. How do you feel?

What you focus on determines your feelings.

Language

Also discussed previously are language patterns and the power of questions. I can't highlight enough the power contained in the words you use, and the questions you ask yourself. Try to ask yourself better questions. Many people ask questions like, "Why can't I?" or "Why does this always happen to me?"

The statement "I think you're a little mistaken" is very different from "What you're saying is wrong" or "You're lying." Each of those sentences has a different feeling, a different emotion, but the words are basically saying the same thing. *Mistaken. Wrong. Lying.* Kind of the same thing, but each has different emotional intensity.

The questions you ask yourself can determine how you feel. Instead of saying, "Why can't I do this," you could say, "How could I do this?" That will create a different feeling within you. What you say to yourself on a daily basis, the questions that you ask yourself on a daily basis, have a huge influence on your tone on a day-to-day basis.

In the triune of tone, all things interact with each other. A ripper little study from 2004, titled "Why the sunny side is up: an association between effect and vertical position," discovered how posture (position) and language interact to affect mood. The study found that words or sentences that were linked by location (position relative to the reader) and emotion (feeling up or down) might have sensitive but far-reaching effects on the appraisal of the words.

In three studies, participants appraised words presented on a computer. In the first study, the evaluation of positive words was faster when words were on the up position rather than the down. The evaluation of negative words was faster when words were in the down position rather than the up. This means that positive words were easier to read when presented to the reader in the up position, and negative words were easier to read when in the down position.

The second study found that positive appraisals activated higher areas of the visual space in the brain, and negative evaluations activated lower areas of visual space in the brain.

Both studies suggest that mood, tone, and state are definitely affected by language and position.

Quick recap: the triad. The ways that you can determine how you feel. First, what you do with your body, posture, and body motion determines your emotional state. Second, what you choose to focus on has a huge influence on what you're feeling. Third, the questions you ask yourself have a huge influence on how you feel.

So take care of this. Look after your body, look after how much and how often you move. Look after your focus, and examine what you say to yourself, your story. That can make a huge difference to your emotions and feelings.

Feelings

A few examples of the things that clients often say to me: *They made me feel this way. Whenever I see them, I feel this way. What they said made me feel angry. What they said made me feel sad.*

Other people don't make you feel a certain way; *you* choose how you feel. Other people don't make you sad, *you* choose to be sad. Or angry. Or frustrated. As we discussed earlier, you have complete control of your feelings. How you feel is determined by your physiology—how you hold yourself, your posture. It's determined by what you focus on. And it's determined by what you say to yourself. You're responsible for all of it. No one else.

What about the environment? It's true that the environment can have an influence on your state, but again only the meaning you put onto it. This can become a powerful tool in controlling your state. Certain environments can help you move, focus, and create the self-talk (language) that influences your tone.

There is a huge amount of research on this topic in a variety of disciplines, but none so much as the workplace. The research clearly shows that employee wellbeing is strongly linked to employee productivity and performance, and even a minor shift in wellbeing can have a massive impact, with one of the main factors of wellbeing being the physical workspace.

Workers who enjoy the environments they are a part of will be more engaged, productive, happy, and healthy. A few of the more recent studies, such as Gensler's Workplace Index, the Leesman Index, Steelcase, and many more, have investigated the association between physical space and business performance, productivity. What workers feel is important. They all found a clear link between physical environment and performance.

Personally, I think of my work environment as a sanctuary. It's neat, organized, with my desk surrounded by inspirational pictures, my success library full of books, and some comfy chairs to sit in and reflect. When I get up in the morning, I can step into this space and instantly adopt the state or tone of inspired productivity. The meaning and associations I've put into that environment help me be who I need to be. I've anchored a certain state or tone to it.

Anchoring your state to things can be helpful in activating that state or tone in the future. Anchors are stimuli or environments that stimulate your state or tone. A good example is Pavlov's experiment with dogs. Pavlov sounded a bell each time the animals were given food, and they salivated when they saw the food. After repetitions of linking the bell with the food, the bell alone provoked salivation.

My daughter Eden recently told me of her memory of me getting up on Sunday morning and baking bread in my dressing gown with *Grand*

Designs on the TV in the background. She said every time she hears the Grand Designs theme song, it brings back warm, safe, comfy home feelings.

We are affected by anchors because of where they send our focus and language, and sometimes our physiology. They are often created unintentionally as we move through life, or they can be created by choice. Sportspeople use anchors all the time. Boxers have their pump-up theme songs, teams have their chants, and of course famous tennis players like Nadal pick their undies out of their bum, wipe their nose and fix their hair before each serve as a way of triggering their best state.

Further discussion about anchors is beyond the scope of this book, but know that environment can dictate performance, but only to the extent of the meaning you have chosen to link to that environment.

The triad of controlling your emotions is like a muscle. The more you work this triad, the more you practice, the more you train, the stronger, the faster, the more powerful you're going to be at changing your emotions in an instant. Practice the triad. Catch yourself out. Maintain awareness of your emotional state.

Check in with yourself. Are you feeling sad? Check your posture. Check what you're focusing on. Check the questions you're asking yourself. And then can change your emotional state.

Being your life CEO means that you're taking response-ability for the culture and tone of your life. As you have learned, you can be response-able. This is very freeing—to know that it's your choice to determine your state.

27 We All Have Needs

> ❝From each according to his abilities,
> to each according to his needs.❞
> **KARL MARX**

Needs are not the same as wants. They're needs—core human needs. Too many people are drowning, on a day-to-day basis, in their needs. What do I mean by that? Imagine you're a surf lifesaver. If someone is drowning, you won't just dive straight into the water and swim up to the drowning person. You'll swim in behind them, put your arm around them, and only then bring them to safety. Why do you do this? Because the drowning person won't think twice about sacrificing you to meet their need for oxygen. They might be someone of impeccable character, but they will drop their standards and values, forget about the importance of human life (yours), to survive.

If you're drowning from your needs, you will sacrifice your values and standards to get your needs met.

> ❝If who I am, is what I have, and what
> I have is lost, then who am I.❞
> **ANONYMOUS**

I'm sure you have moments, as we all do, when you look back and think of something you did or said that was not the real you. When you know you're better than that. Whatever you did or said was not in alignment with our values or standards. The reason that happened, the reason you said or did what you did, was that your needs were not getting met. You were drowning in your needs, and at the time you found a way to get your needs met.

The six core human needs are just like oxygen for the body. They were first explained to me by one of my mentors, someone who has been pivotal in my coaching life, the great man Anthony Robbins. He first introduced the needs over ten years ago, in 2006, at a TED conference in Monterey, California. His talk was titled, "Why We Do the Things We Do."

Happiness and fulfillment come when we get all our needs met in a resourceful way, when we're on purpose, living our values, maintaining our standards, and experiencing all our six needs being met. That's when we start living a life that is the real us, where our values and our standards show through.

The six core needs can be broken into two parts: needs of personality, and needs of purpose.

Needs of personality

The four needs of personality, and their order of importance, will determine your day-to-day behavior and play out in your life's missions. They will express themselves in your relationships, health, money, and career. They are:

1. Certainty (home)
2. Uncertainty (adventure)

3. Significance (stand out)
4. Connection (fit in)

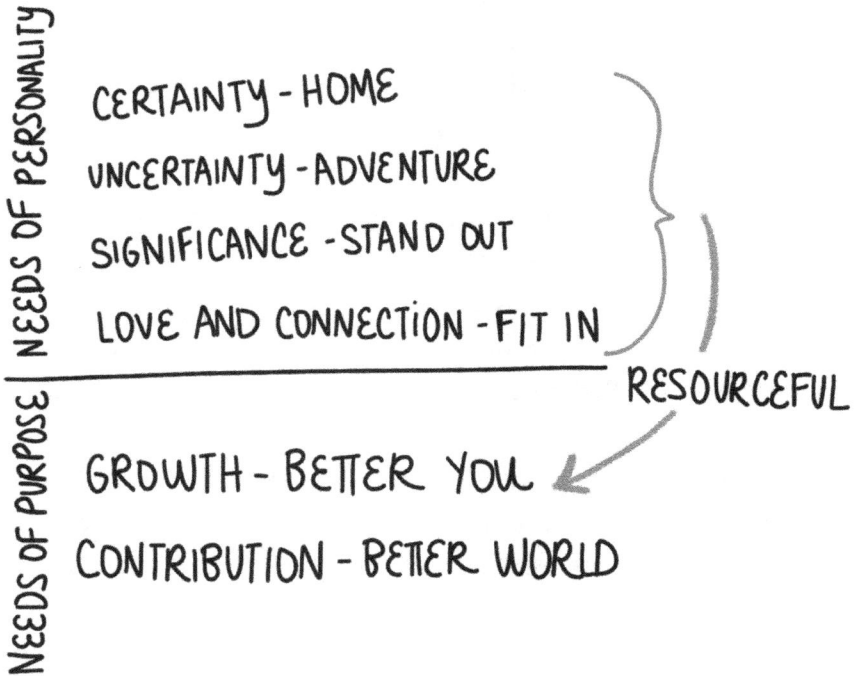

NEEDS OF PERSONALITY

CERTAINTY - HOME

UNCERTAINTY - ADVENTURE

SIGNIFICANCE - STAND OUT

LOVE AND CONNECTION - FIT IN

})

RESOURCEFUL

NEEDS OF PURPOSE

GROWTH - BETTER YOU ←

CONTRIBUTION - BETTER WORLD

These four needs can be grouped into two pairs of opposites to create your unique balance: certainty and uncertainty are opposites; significance and connection are opposites. They are each other's yin and yang.

Certainty: The first need of personality is certainty. This is the need for safety, survival, and security. For many, this is all about the known—predictable routines and rituals in life. It's about staying in control and avoiding pain, but also experiencing pleasure. I think of it as the need for home.

There's a saying: "It's great to get away, but it's good to get home." Home is a place of certainty. There's adventure when you go away on holiday, but eventually you want to come home to a place of certainty. You drive up the driveway, unlock the door, walk in, and there's your favorite chair. There's your kitchen, your favorite mug, and the tea or coffee you like. Even the shower in your bathroom knows how to get the water temperature just right.

Many of us have a high need for certainty, comfort, and security. A place to call home.

This need can be met in an unresourceful way, a way that might feel good at the time, but is not necessarily good for us and usually not good for the people around us. Or this need can be met in a resourceful way. This is where we see the difference in people's lives. Whether or not we feel fulfilled when this need is met depends on the way in which we do it.

First I'll discuss the ways people can have this need met in an unresourceful way. Sometimes people do it through food, because food gives them certainty. It creates a connection with certainty, otherwise known as comfort eating.

When I arrive at my practice in the morning, I perform a beautiful ballet that I have down to a fine art. I turn on the lights; turn on the background music; turn on the lobby TV, muted; turn on the coffee machine; turn on the coaching-room lights. Then back to the coffee machine, and I pour that first cup of coffee.

I don't need the coffee because I'm thirsty, or for the buzz of caffeine. I have the coffee because it gives me comfort. My coaching clients are often full of surprises, and the coffee meets my need for certainty, or the known, before I tackle the day.

Is this unresourceful? If I was drinking coffee to excess, or was unable to start the day without it, then probably.

Is the world a better place because of it? No. It's just a neutral way to get my need for certainty met each morning.

190

Routines are a way for us to feel in control of our world. We all have obligations. We have to do this, go there, then do this, then go there, and so on. Some people over-organize their lives as a way of feeling in control.

I would consider it unresourceful if the only way you could get certainty was through routine. I have a language distinction in this area (remember, language is important), and the distinction is this: I believe that routines are habits that are not always beneficial; and rituals are habits that are beneficial, and create a more resourceful you.

I will give an example of a routine: You can't wait for the evening to come. You put on the six-thirty news because you always put on the six-thirty news. First they do breaking news, then general news, then the fun story, then sport, then the weather. Then at seven-thirty it's *Big Brother*. Then at eight-thirty it's *The Biggest Loser*.

And now here is an example of a ritual: You can't wait for tomorrow. You always get up at five-thirty, put on your sports gear and head out the door for a five-kilometer run, then come home, have a shower, and get dressed for the day at seven A.M.

Some, unresourcefully of course, have their need for certainty met through the control of others. They want to control the people around them, because this gives them a sense of certainty and control in their own lives.

People will sometimes have their need for certainty met unresourcefully, by staying in relationships that are unhealthy. We've all wondered why a certain couple is still in a relationship when we know it's not a great one. They stick it out because it's something they know. Better the devil you know than the devil you don't.

Sometimes people have their need for certainty met by giving themselves a label: *I'm a procrastinator.* Now they've got a label, they have certainty about whom they are. Of course, it's possible to create a label for yourself that's positive. For instance: *I'm predictable. I'm a place of security. I'm a place of safety.*

The best way of creating certainty is to have the certainty of self. To know that who you are is a place that's safe. It's a place of certainty. That's important, because if the only way your need for certainty is being met is a place outside of you—food, watching TV, the control of others, your relationship—that can lead to uncertainy. Sometimes those things in life can change. They can disappear, and when they disappear, you have nothing left. You have no level of certainty.

If you have certainty of self, it doesn't matter if things around you change. It doesn't matter if your environment changes. You'll always have this place to go to, where you know there is safety and security. How do you create that certainty of self? Through being consistent. By doing what you say you're going to do, you will learn about the importance of trust and how to use your willpower.

The catch, of course, as you can imagine, if we have way too much certainty. If we get our need completely chock-a-block met. In fact, over-met, eventually, what happens? We get bored. We get unhappy because there's no growth. If you stay in a place of knowledge and a place of certainty, there's no growth. So, this leads us to the second core need, which is, of course, the need for uncertainty.

Uncertainty: The need for variety, adventure, the unknown, challenges, novelty, stimulation, surprise, and the new is the spice of life. As you move from a place of certainty to a place of uncertainty, that's when you grow. Growth occurs when you spend some time in uncertainty. In fact, it has been said that the quality of your life is equal to the amount of uncertainty you can live with. The more uncertainty you can live with, the more surprise and adventure that you can live with, and the greater the quality of your life.

> **" Without the element of uncertainty, the bringing off of even, the greatest business triumph would be dull, routine, and eminently unsatisfying. "**
>
> **J. PAUL GETTY**

A good example of this is a recent client of mine. He had worked hard all his working life in a sales job that was constantly changing. He had done all the things that many of us do. He had saved his money, put some into superannuation, paid off his mortgage, all so that when he retired he would be certain to have security. His wife had convinced him to retire. Everyone said it was time to slow down, take it easy, relax. So he retired. He sat at home in the recliner, reading his paper, taking it easy. He was living the dream.

Except that he wasn't. He became incredibly bored, and the reason he was being coached was because he had recently been diagnosed with depression.

If we're not green and growing, we're ripe and rotting. We grow from challenges. We grow from variety. We've all heard stories about people who retire and then, within weeks, days, months, or years they're dead. They've died of boredom. Our need for variety is that important.

We can have this need for uncertainty and variety met in resourceful or unresourceful ways. In the movie *The Wolf of Wall Street*, the main character has a high need for uncertainty. If you've seen the movie, you'll know that his need is met through drugs, alcohol, promiscuity, and taking high risks with his and other people's money. He is constantly totally out of control because he has a massive need for uncertainty.

Self-sabotage is another way to meet this need for uncertainty. If life is too predictable, we'll often throw something into the mix to mess it up, create some drama. Watching our favorite show on TV us some certainty, but constantly changing channels gives us a sense of variety. As simple as that may sound, I know what my wife would say: "Simple is right."

This is where we see kids doing crazy stuff. We talk about teenagers going off the rails, but sometimes we put them on the rails too much. We create too much certainty in their lives. Too much security. Too much predictability. Particularly in high school. Off to school in the morning, back from school in the afternoon, snack time, study time, dinner, bed. As parents, we want to protect our children from anything that distract them, anything uncertain.

Two nights a week I do sports training, and I also attend a Saturday-morning sports competition. This predictability, this routine, that our children are subjected to, particularly in some of our private schools, can, I believe, create too much certainty.

Uncertainty and certainty need to be in balance. It's understandable if young people, finding themselves with three or fours hours on a Saturday morning of freedom, want to fill those hours with as much uncertainty as they can to balance out the excess certainty. Sometimes they'll do it an unresourceful way. They might do drugs, drink alcohol, or act out risky behaviors like train surfing, jumping in a car and driving too fast, simply because they don't have enough adventure and challenge.

I believe it's important that we parents don't hold our children's leashes too tightly. That we give them some slack. That we give them the opportunity to create some variety in their day. Otherwise they'll go and find a way to get that need met unresourcefully.

Of course, a resourceful way to get this need for uncertainty met is to embrace adventure. Embrace the challenge. Embrace the play that comes with it. Look for ways to be creative. Look for ways to do different, to do change. To do some things that might not feel good but are good for us.

These two needs—certainty and uncertainty—might seem like opposites, and they are. However, one cannot do without the other. This is the paradox of these two core needs. Each of us has a need for both, but the one we prefer will determine our personality and our behavior.

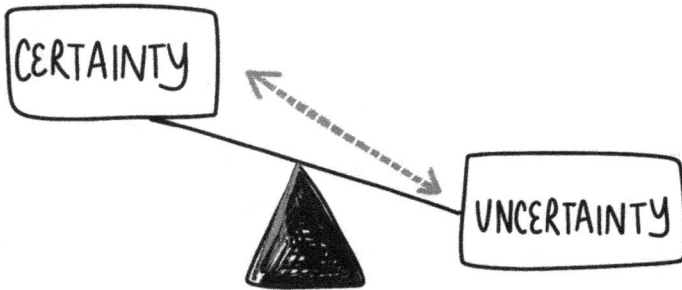

📖 JOURNAL TIME

Look at those two core needs—certainty and uncertainty—and feel them in your body and mind for just a minute. Now ask yourself these questions:

- Which do you think you need more of right now, today, this week?
- Which seems the more attractive to you, the one you are most attracted to experiencing in your life?

The answers to these questions are great things to know about yourself. The key to these core needs is being able to recognize how you can balance these needs in your life, and knowing when the balance is off. Take the time to look at why the balance is off and what you can do to bring it back into alignment.

JOURNAL TIME

Do you feel like your first two core needs could do with balancing? If so, what could you do to bring them back into balance? Write a list of things you could do to balance them.

If you get too much of one or the other—certainty or uncertainty—you might find ways to get them balanced in an unresourceful way, sometimes by sacrificing one of your values or standards.

This situation can also produce symptoms. If you have too much certainty—everything is the same, life is predictable, nothing changes—how do you feel? Bored. And if you keep going until you're super-bored, what is that symptom called? Depression. Many people are depressed because they have too much certainty in their lives.

If you have too much uncertainty—too many challenges and chaos—how do you feel? Overwhelmed. And if you keep going and get overwhelmed, what is that symptom called? Anxiety. Anxiety is a reflection of too much uncertainty and not enough certainty.

When it comes to certainty and moving into uncertainty, again it helps to have the certainty of self, because that fear is going to come up. Importantly, the antidote for dealing with fear as you move into uncertainty is gratitude. Gratitude for what you're certain of. Gratitude for what's in your life that you know. The stuff that's predictable. The more you have gratitude for certainty, and the more you have gratitude for the stuff that you have, the better you will deal with the stuff that you don't have: the uncertainty.

Significance: The third need of personality is the need for significance, the need to stand out. Now, this is a ripper. Sometimes we might look at the word significance negatively, but this is a cool need. It's a need that we all have. It's the need to be an individual, to stand out, to feel important, wanted, worthy, validated. The emphasis here is on being different. I often find this need being met in unresourceful ways.

> " When we talk about having a life of significance and meaning, it's not about fame or money or resources. It's about people and lives and hearts. That's my biggest passion in life. "
> **TIM TEBOW**

In Australia, we have the expression "the tall-poppy syndrome." The tall-poppy syndrome is about getting our individual need for significance met. It's about belittling others. Putting other people down. It's a very unresourceful way of meeting this need for significance. The more you put someone down, the higher you go relatively.

In the extreme, this need gets met with violence. If someone pulls a gun or a knife on you in the street, you're going to feel pretty insignificant compared to them, the person holding the gun or knife. They, on the other hand, are going to feel awfully significant, unfortunately. This is the behavior of the bully. Bullies aren't bad people; they are just people who have a low quality, an unresourceful way of meeting their need for significance. This is also the explanation for bullying in schools.

Bullying often occurs because of two core needs being met unresourcefully. The first is a need for control; when people bully, they start to control their environment. The second is a need for significance. Bullies raise themselves up and put other people down.

Sometimes, unfortunately, the bullying starts because the need for control and significance is not being met at home. People might have had significance taken from them (sometimes at home) so they have learned this strategy to compensate.

Belittling, bullying, or taking significance from someone else is one of the worst of all the unresourceful ways to get a need met.

A few years ago, I bought a cool red Alfa Romeo. It was a used car that I got for just $14,000. I know some might question the reliability of this car, but I never had an ounce of trouble with it. It was a great-looking car, a bit like a Ferrari but different. It was that great Alfa red, with lots of chrome and sexy alloy wheels. I picked it up early in the morning and couldn't wait to get it home to give it the big clean and polish. I spent the rest of the day getting into every nook and cranny, scrubbing, washing and polishing it to within an inch of its life. It looked amazing.

Just as I finished, a friend and his wife arrived for dinner. My friend was impressed. He couldn't believe that I'd paid only $14,000 for the car. He was full of praise as he admired my amazing-looking care. In doing so, he helped me meet my need for significance.

Then his wife walked into the garage. She looked at the car, walked up to it and pointed out a scratch. She didn't make one comment about the rest of the car, just that it had a scratch. It was a not-so-subtle attempt to take significance from me. (I now call this couple the" scratch people." Do you have any scratch people in your life?)

The other way we meet our need for significance is, of course, by playing the victim. *You think your life is screwed? Wait until you hear about my life. My life's way worse than yours.* This is not getting significance by doing something cool. This is getting significance by being super-uncool by telling people how uncool your life is.

Sometimes people will do it through drama: *Wait till you hear what happened to me!* Or through gossip, which is a kind of drama—not their own drama but someone else's: *Wait till you hear what happened to Phil. Let me tell you about him.* They think that by gossiping about others, creating drama about others, they're going to get significance. Well, they do, unfortunately, but I can tell you it's certainly not resourceful. It's not good for them or others, but it meets the need.

People sometimes get significance through being dramatic about illness: *You've no idea how sick I am.* You might say to someone, "I twisted my ankle the other day." Quick as a wick, they will say, "Wait until I tell you about *my* ankle. I've twisted it, like, twenty-five times. The left one, I've done it seventeen times. Plus I've dislocated my hip six times." People like to brag about how sick they are.

Then there is my favorite, what I call the "super-wanker." They are all, look at me! They are flash—they flash their clothes, money, choice of partner, home, opinions, status.

A famous entrepreneur, let's call him Gary, loved to show everyone his flashy cars and flashy homes. He was always in the media; excitement and drama followed him everywhere. He wore clothes that were seriously out there, and always had a partner who, for a short time, would become his wife after he proposed in a very public place in front of cameras. His life was all capital letters: *LOOK AT ME!*

Super-wankers are often found in high places because of their need for significance. We know when we've been in the presence of a super-wanker, drama queen or bull because we feel worse for it. You know the people I mean. You've finished the conversation, you're walking away, and you're wondering why you feel so bad. What happened to the good feeling you had before. This kind of behavior, of getting the need for significance met in an unresourceful way, is a real turn-off for other people.

It is simple to have this need met in a resourceful way. Just become a master in some field of endeavor. Become a master of knowledge, or skill.

Go back to school and increase your knowledge. Get a degree, or diploma, or some other certificate that makes it clear you stand out in some way. Or get a skill that is recognized: plumber, coach, hairdresser, and so on.

Achieving your goals is a great way to get the need met. When I watched the Winter Olympics I was awed by some of the incredible feats demonstrated by the skiers and skaters. These athletes get medals; they get recognition and significance, and they deserve it. They've trained hard for it. They're standing out. They're achieving goals.

Sometimes this need is met by collecting toys: the cool car, the cool watch, the cool clothing. We style ourselves in a certain way, sometimes eccentrically. People will dress a little weird, and this meets their need for significance. Others sculpt their bodies. Still others train at the gym, not necessarily to be healthy but to create an image that gives them significance. None of this is bad or good; it just meets that need for significance.

The ultimate way to meet the need for significance is to give it to others. Yes, you read that correctly. The more you give this need to others, the more you get. A great example of this is Mother Theresa and the work she did in the streets, giving significance to the poor. The filthy and unkempt. She gave massive significance to these people, and as a result she got massive significance in return. Mother Theresa is a great example of giving significance and, as a result, getting back massive amounts of it.

Is there somewhere in your life where you could do better at this? I have a simple strategy for this, as I like to keep my high need for significance in check. I actively seek out opportunities to find the great in people. The things that people do, or have; the way they behave; the things they achieve. It's important to do this authentically and genuinely. I find it's always possible to see something great in someone if you look hard enough.

No need to get out your journal, just go out into the world today and start giving significance. Who could you call, send a message to, or make a comment about on Facebook right now? Go and do it. Give yourself a dose of significance and help someone else get their need for significance met at the same time.

Love and connection: The fourth need of personality is for love and connection—the need to fit in. Unlike significance, where the emphasis is on being different, with love and connection the emphasis is on being the same. This is about the tribe and having a sense of belonging. We want communication, approval, attachment, and to fit in with others. This is about family and relationships.

> " Being deeply loved by someone
> gives you strength while loving someone
> deeply gives you courage. "
> **LAO TZU**

This need can also be met in an unresourceful or resourceful way. Unresourcefully, sometimes this need is met by becoming sick or injured, and creating drama around our illness to gain attention and connection. By creating drama with our health, money, career, or relationships, we hope someone will come to rescue us. When they do, we will feel connected.

Weirdly, creating an argument with someone you care about meets this need. And it can also be met through violence. If someone pulls a gun on you, you feeling connected to that person at that moment. At that moment, it's all about you and them.

The opposite of the person looking for drama is the rescuer. Rescuing is the common behavior of someone who is getting this need met unresourcefully. These people are always on the lookout for others who in trouble. You know the type. They're always asking if you're okay. They take in homeless dogs and cats. They put up their hands for the working bee, they help out in the school canteen, and they're the first to offer to drive your kids to the next sports day. They spend their days looking for ways to rescue people. They might get their connection, but they also end up exhausted.

Gangs often meet all four personality needs that have been covered so far. Gangs meet the need for certainty. There's a predictability to gangs; gang life often includes rituals and routines. And there's also uncertainty in some of the behaviors and things they do. The need for significance is met through gang colors, loud motorbikes, the jacket and emblem, and the various ranks within the gang. As for love and connection, I don't know about the love bit, but there's certainly connection in gangs. This tribal mentality that comes with gangs means you belong, it's your family.

The need for love and connection can be met resourcefully through belonging to a club, community group like Rotary and Lions, and sporting clubs. This need for connection gets met beautifully in clubs, and it's good for you and others.

This need can also be met, beautifully, through intimacy. Nothing creates a greater connection than sexual intimacy.

And there's spirituality, of course: the connection with God or something else that's bigger than us. It's an incredibly resourceful way of getting that need for love and connection met. A walk in a forest is a way of connecting with nature itself. Pets, which give lots of love and connection, meet this need well and truly.

Love and connection are about sharing. This need is all about support. Again, the more love and connection you give, the more love and connection you'll receive.

When it comes to relationships, by the way, there is a balancing act that's needed between significance, and love and connection. At the beginning of a relationship, it's all about significance. It's about standing out, when that raw connection occurs. Over time, individuality starts to fade and the couple becomes more connected, more in love, more the same, more feeling like they are family and belong.

As the relationship continues, one or the other person may start to want their identity back. They start wanting to feel different, validated, to stand out. Sometimes that need is met in an unresourceful way. If balance can be maintained between identity, and love and belonging, a relationship can be a great place to be.

When you move from significance to love and connection, you need two things. Whenever you go for more love and connection, you need to realize there may be some fear around that. Firstly, the way to overcome that fear is to have the certainty of self. Know that you're solid. Know that you're reliable. Secondly, you must have courage (the word "courage" comes from the Latin *cor*; the heart).

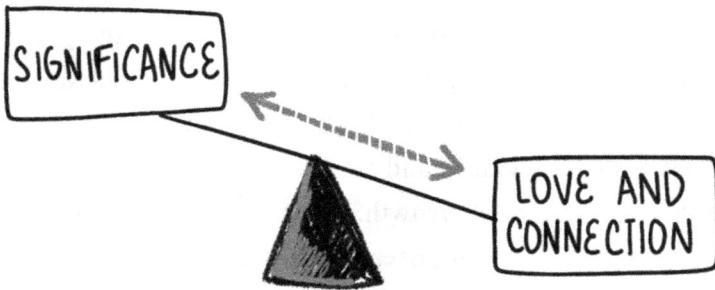

So, to go from a place of significance, where it's all about you, to a place of connection, where it's about others and relationships, you need to come from a place of courage. From a place in the heart. From a place of vulnerability. To have more love and connection, you need to have vulnerability. You need to be willing to be vulnerable, willing to come from the heart.

Who in your life could you show some vulnerability to? Who could you show your heart? Who could take a chance with, and with courage tell them how you feel about them.

If these four needs of personality are met in a high-quality and resourceful way, the needs of purpose will also be met.

Needs of purpose

The next two needs are often referred to as the needs of spirit, but I prefer to think of them as the needs of purpose. They are central to the life purpose of you as a human, and often show up in purpose statements. They are:

1. Growth (becoming your best)
2. Contribution (making the world better)

The needs of purpose are only met when you meet the four needs of personality in a healthy, resourceful, and high-quality way. That means that the need is met, and by meeting the need, it is truly good for you, for the people around you, and for the greater good of the planet.

In the process of meeting the need, it might feel good, or even a little uncomfortable, but in the end, by getting the need met you stay in alignment with your values and standards.

Growth: The fifth need, growth, means a better you. The need for growth is about life with a purpose, and that includes a better you. This is about cultivating your life, and developing yourself emotionally, intellectually, and spiritually. It's about being green and growing, versus ripe and rotting.

> " Growth is painful. Change is painful.
> But, nothing is as painful as staying
> stuck where you do not belong. "
> **N. R. NARAYANA MURTHY**

Contribution: Our sixth need, and the second need of purpose, is the need for a better world. This means contributing beyond yourself. It's about service to others. Caring. Sharing what you have. Extending who you are. Leaving a legacy. It means a life bigger than you. To have a life bigger than you, you must fulfill this need for contribution.

When you cease to make a contribution, you begin to die.
ELEANOR ROOSEVELT

Recap of the six needs

Six core needs. Depending on how we get those first four needs met (needs of personality), that will influence whether we experience growth or contribution, and fulfillment. For example, if the need for certainty is achieved by controlling others, or uncertainty by risky behavior, or significance by belittling others, or love and contribution by creating drama, the needs of growth and contribution, and purpose won't be met.

Any great CEO knows how to help their team; knowing how to help the team have their needs met is important if the CEO wants to keep them. They also know how to do it in a way that's great for the ethos of the company. The CEO makes sure the needs are met in a resourceful way.

Let's have some fun with this. I might ask a group: "Who gets fulfillment from cleaning house? Who gets their needs met from cleaning house? Who loves cleaning their house? Who hates cleaning their house?"

I might get a whole show of hands from people who love cleaning their house, and a whole show of hands of people who hate it. Now, who loves or hates it depends on whether their needs (or values) are being met, and being met in a resourceful way.

I say to people who hate cleaning their house, "On a scale of one to ten, where one means the need is only just being met, and ten means it's being met in a massively resourceful way, how certain do you feel when you clean the house?"

A typical answer often goes like this: *Man, cleaning the house? Are you kidding me? It's boring. There's mess everywhere. The need for certainty and cleaning the house? No way.*

So then I ask about the need for uncertainty.

Are you kidding me? Again, it's so boring. Who wants to clean house? It's just dull, same old, same old. Picking up stuff that's here. Picking up stuff that's there. No way. No.

I ask about the need for significance.

No one cares. No one ever notices when I clean the house. Significance? Who cares about people who clean houses? No way. No. Need for significance not met.

Love and connection?

Zero. Cleaning the house? It's a job I have to do by myself. There's no connection. I just wander around the house picking up people's stuff. Boring. No one cares. There's no love and connection.

Of course, coming to the task of cleaning the house with that sort of attitude towards the four needs of personality is certainly not going to lead to a feeling of growth or contribution.

Now I ask someone who loves cleaning houses, who feels fulfilled by it, about their six core needs, specifically the need for certainty, and whether they're being met. Their reply could sound something like this: *Certainty? Cleaning the house? That's my place of control. That's a place where I can go where I know what I'm doing. I have a ritual. I have a routine that I follow. I start in the fridge. Then I do the sink. Then I vacuum the floors. Then I mop the floors. Then I go into the bathrooms.*

For these people, jumping into routine and ritual gives them an absolute place of certainty: *Yeah, a hundred percent.*

What about uncertainty?

Have you got kids? They put stuff everywhere. Every time I come home, I go into my routine of cleaning the house, and who knows what I'm going to find. The need for uncertainty? Absolutely. Seven out of ten.

What about the need for significance?

Have you seen my house when it's clean? It's like something out of a magazine. In fact, I'm going to call Vogue magazine when we've finished this chat. I'm going to tell them to come and take some photographs. You should see my house when it's clean. Unbelievable. Significance? I feel fantastic when the house is cleaned. Yeah. Ten out of ten.

What about love and connection?

Love and connection? This is my special time. When I'm cleaning the house, I go into this almost meditative state. I think about family. I think about relationships. I think about my attachment to others. I connect almost at a level of prayer. I have moments of gratitude. I absolutely feel love and connection. Nine out of ten when it comes to love and connection.

With that last answer, if someone feels that way about cleaning a house, their need for certainty, uncertainty, significance, love, and connection is being met. They feel great. They feel like they're growing and contributing. They have fulfillment.

You see? You can organize your game. You can organize the game of life to get your needs met. You've just got to change the way you think about it.

The trick is that if you're going to live at choice, and live at cause; if you're going to accept that you're one hundred percent responsible for your life, it's your duty to get your needs met. *Your* duty. Not someone else's.

Imagine that you do everything in your life in a resourceful way that creates fulfillment. You've found a way to be fulfilled doing the things you love and the things don't love. If you could do those tasks in such a ways that the six core needs were being met in a sustainable and resourceful way, your life would be amazing.

JOURNAL TIME
LifeCEO.com/RESOURCES

Open to a blank page in your journal. Down the left-hand side of the page, write the six core needs. Leave a gap after each one. Next to each one, put a number from zero to ten. The number is a reflection of how you feel about that core need.

Now pick something you love to do. It could be going for a run. It could be cleaning the house. It could be heading out for coffee with a friend. Write this at the top, then rate how each of the needs feels about that activity.

Next to that, make another column and write down an activity you don't like doing. You don't feel fulfilled by it. Write a list. Starting with certainty, write down a number from zero to ten indicating how you feel that need is getting met.

You can see that there's a difference between the things you love to do and the things you hate doing. You can see that you're not going to feel fulfilled doing the stuff you hate doing. Well, here's the cool thing. You can choose to change the meaning you assign to things and have your needs met.

In the last column in this journal exercise, across from certainty, uncertainty, significance, love and connection, etc., answer this question: What could you now think about this activity (i.e. what meaning could you put to it) in order to have all your needs met by doing that activity?

It's a great question. It's going to change the way you feel about doing that task and the level of fulfillment you get from it. Imagine that all the things you did in the past that you didn't want to do now met your needs and you felt good doing them. How fulfilling your life would be. How *outstanding* your life would be.

	GOING FOR A RUN	DOING THE DISHES	
CERTAINTY	9	3	The dishes are always there and by doing them I would always have a clean knife and fork to use.
UNCERTAINTY	8	2	There are always a mix of dirty dishes. sometimes a lot sometimes just a few, I could see how quick I could do it each day.
SIGNIFICANCE	7	2	Knowing I have done the dishes would make me feel good about me, and people would probably comment how good a job I'm doing.
LOVE AND CONNECTION	8	4	It would give me time in the kitchen to chat with my family at the end of the day.
GROWTH	9	1	Finding a better way to life my life by finding the powerful ways to get the boring stuff done.
CONTRIBUTION	8	5	It free's my wife up to relax and spend time doing important things that grow our family.

You might be in a relationship with your employer, or your employees, or your spouse, boyfriend, girlfriend. You might be in a relationship with your job. If two of the six core needs are getting met, you'll feel a connection with that person. If you're getting four of the six core needs met, you're going to feel a bond. If six of those core needs are being met in a sustainable and resourceful way, you will never want to leave that relationship. If you're getting six out of six of those core needs met in your career, you will never want to leave. That's very cool.

The more things or vehicles in your life that meet your needs in a high-quality way, the better your life and the world will be. It's your choice.

28 Four Zones of Behavior

"I'm always inspired by people who choose to do what is right, not what is easy."
SHERRI SAUM

The invitation read: *Bucks' party. All food and drink laid on, just turn up looking sharp and have a good time.* The first voice in my head said: *That'll be nice. A few drinks, say hello and go home early so I can be productive the next day.* The second voice said: *Woo-hoo, party time.* On the day I received the invitation, I listened to voice number one. Unfortunately, on the night of the party, I listened to voice number two.

We've discussed what it means to get our needs met in an unresourceful way. It might feel good, but it's not necessarily good for you. That comes from the four zones of behavior, which is best described by looking at the diagram below, showing the four zones in a grid.

In the top left quadrant is Zone I, the first zone of behavior. This is the zone where it feels good—to do this activity, to do this action, to think this way. It feels good, and it's good for you and others. It's good for the greater good. That's a great place to be—where it feels good.

PLEASURE

ZONE I

DO WHAT FEELS GOOD
AND
IS GOOD FOR YOU
IS GOOD FOR OTHERS
IS GOOD FOR THE GOOD OF THE PLANET

ZONE III   CHILD

DO WHAT FEELS GOOD
AND
IS NOT GOOD FOR YOU
IS GOOD FOR OTHERS
IS GOOD FOR THE GOOD OF THE PLANET

FEAR

ZONE II

DO WHAT DOESN'T FEELS GOOD
(AT THE TIME)
AND
IS GOOD FOR YOU
IS GOOD FOR OTHERS
IS GOOD FOR THE GOOD OF THE PLANET

GROW

ZONE IV

DO WHAT DOESN'T FEELS GOOD
AND
IS NOT GOOD FOR YOU   PAIN
IS NOT GOOD FOR OTHERS
IS NOT GOOD FOR THE GOOD OF THE PLANET

ADULT

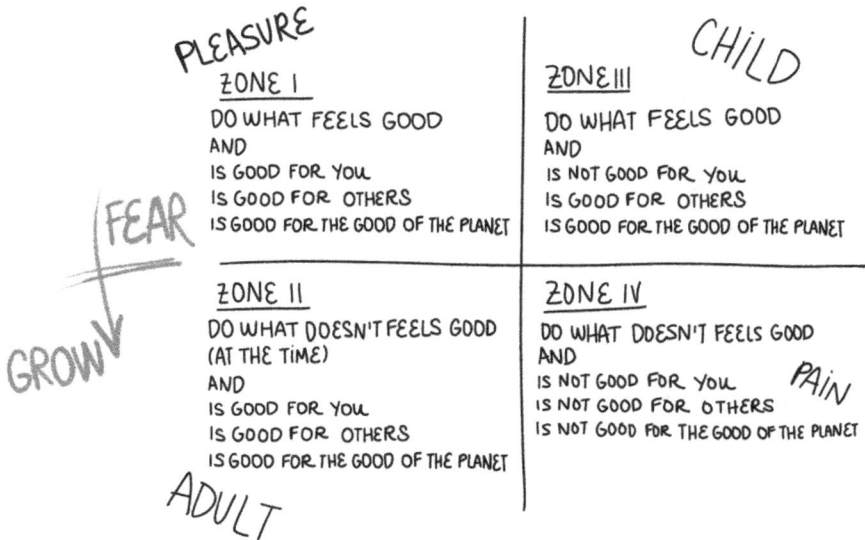

It could be reading the paper, catching up with friends, going out for breakfast, taking in a movie, or going for a walk. It's not an activity or behavior that is life changing, but it's still good. This is the place of certainty, the comfort zone.

Below that is Zone II, the second zone of behavior. This is where it doesn't feel good (at the time), but it's good for you, for others, for the greater good. It may not always feel good to step out of your comfort zone. It might feel awkward, it might be uncomfortable because there's usually some fear around it, but it's good for you. It's the place where you grow. This is called being an adult. It's what adults are supposed to do (but often don't).

It could be reading a challenging book (like this one). A book that stretches your thinking asks you to answer questions you haven't considered before. It could be going for that run when you'd rather sit on the couch with a block of chocolate. It could be making that call to a friend you haven't spoken to in a while because of a falling out. It could be writing another chapter in your book on a Sunday morning instead of reading the paper, with a second cup of coffee and a croissant.

It could have been me at that bucks' party, recognizing that I'd had enough food and drink, and deciding to go home at a reasonable time. Sadly, it wasn't me.

Top-right in the grid is Zone III, the third zone of behavior. This is where it feels good, but it's not good for you. It's not good for others. It's not good for the greater good. This is the unresourceful way of getting your needs met.

It could be sitting on the couch watching TV every night with a glass of red wine and a box of chocolates. It could be sitting for hours every day looking at social media. It could be choosing to stay on at the party and keep drinking.

This is called being a child. Children only do what feels good and is good for them, or feels good and isn't good for them. If I showed a child an apple and a bag of lollies, asked them to tell me which of the two was good for them, they would say the apple. If I asked which one they wanted, they would say the lollies.

Being a child is doing only what feels good. This is why kids get weird as they transition into being adults (teenagers). It's the internal battle they experience moving from a mindset of only doing what feels good to doing what doesn't feel good but they do it anyway because they know it's good for them.

If we stay in Zone III, unfortunately we will end up in Zone IV. This is where it doesn't feel good. It's not good for you. It's not good for others. It's not good for the greater good. We don't want to spend any time in this zone.

PLEASURE

ZONE I

DO WHAT FEELS GOOD
AND
IS GOOD FOR YOU
IS GOOD FOR OTHERS
IS GOOD FOR THE GOOD OF THE PLANET

CHILD

ZONE III

DO WHAT FEELS GOOD
AND
IS GOOD FOR YOU
IS GOOD FOR OTHERS
IS GOOD FOR THE GOOD OF THE PLANET

ZONE II

DO WHAT DOESN'T FEELS GOOD
(AT THE TIME)
AND
IS GOOD FOR YOU
IS GOOD FOR OTHERS
IS GOOD FOR THE GOOD OF THE PLANET

ADULT

ZONE IV

DO WHAT DOESN'T FEELS GOOD
AND
IS NOT GOOD FOR YOU
IS NOT GOOD FOR OTHERS
IS NOT GOOD FOR THE GOOD OF THE PLANET

PAIN

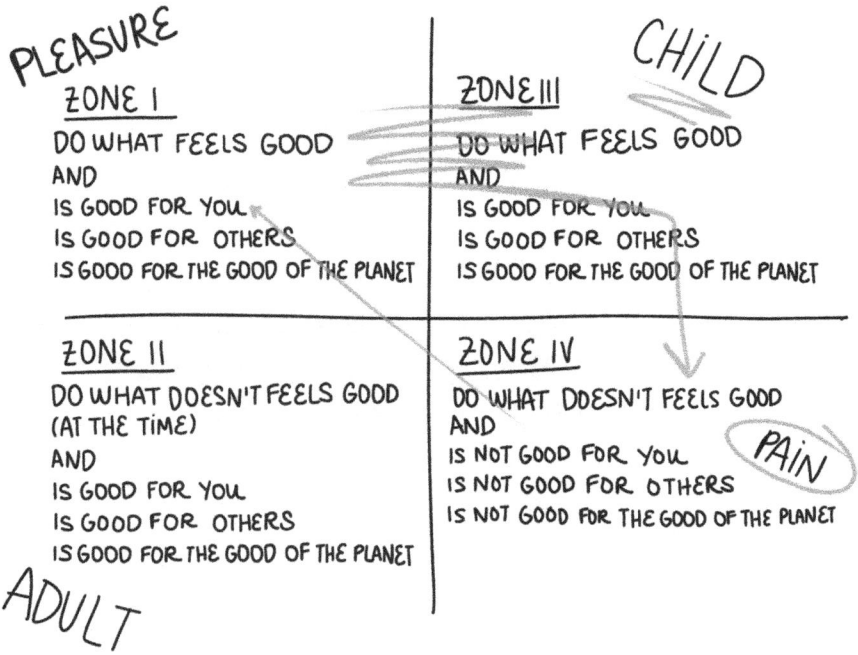

This is where I found myself after getting home at two A.M. on Sunday morning, having had one too many tequila slammers, and two too many vodka lime sodas, and three too many champagnes. The same morning of my daughter's fifteenth-birthday family breakfast. Ouch! I was in bad shape, and in Zone IV, the zone of pain. It's in the zone of pain that we often have those defining moments that cause a shift in our behavior, sometimes for good.

213

29 Fear

> " Nothing in life is to be feared, it is only to be understood. Now is the time to understand more, so that we may fear less. "
>
> **MARIE CURIE**

Many of the decisions that we make on a day-to-day basis are based on this next state that we can find ourselves in: a state of fear. This chapter is devoted to the big topic of making a shift in your mind to embracing fear. Embracing uncertainty. Embracing confusion. Embracing the unknown. It's such a huge concept, but I promise you that if you take some of the concepts covered in the next few pages and apply them in your life, you will break free.

We discussed earlier the feeling of being trapped, doing the same thing over and over again, when what you really want to do is something different. Trapped in your career. Trapped in health. Trapped in relationships. Or just trapped in life itself.

This leads to symptoms of procrastination and self-sabotage, and eventually feelings of low self-worth, low self-esteem, and low self-confidence. You come to the mistaken conclusion that something's wrong with you.

I can tell you that nothing is wrong with you, and there is a door to this cage, to this trap that you're in. All you need to do is reconnect with the real you. Embrace the fear of opening the gate and getting outside the cage, of no longer having that trapped feeling. You will get to the point where you're outside the cage and feeling more comfortable.

The trick is not just in getting outside the cage, because you could still be stuck in the zoo. The life beyond the zoo is where you're meant to be: out of the cage and in your life. Into the comfort zone. The life that is supercharged. The life that is switched on. In that life, you're out of the cage. You're beyond the zoo, and you're in the theme park of your life, the life that you envisioned for yourself. You're back to being connected with your sense of purpose, vision and mission. You wake up charged each morning, turned-on and ready to get into the day.

> ❝ It is not death that a man should fear, but he should fear never beginning to live. ❞
> **MARCUS AURELIUS**

Thousands of years ago, we were primitive beings with primitive brains. Our brains were hardwired for day-to-day living. When we headed down to the watering hole for a drink, we were on the lookout for predators. Imagine that you're down at that waterhole and out of the bushes jumps a sabre-tooth tiger.

Your primitive brain, that hardwired primitive brain, checks the three options available to you and chooses one of them.

Option A is the choice of flight: getting out of there as quickly as you can. As you run, adrenaline and cortisol are secreted in your body. Those chemicals feed the muscles. The raise your heart rate, shut down your digestive and reproductive systems, and your immune system, and all your energy is forced into an explosive flight from the sabre-tooth tiger.

What a fantastic thing. What a great response. And all coordinated subconsciously, before you can think consciously think about what to do.

Option B is to fight the tiger. If you choose that option, the same chemical release occurs. Adrenaline or cortisol is released into your body, and your heart starts to race, your muscles start to get stronger. Your immune, digestive, and reproductive systems shut down. Hopefully, after ten or fifteen minutes, you beat the tiger and survive.

The last option, option C, is to freeze and hope the tiger won't notice you if you keep completely still.

All three options produce the same chemical results in your body, and the response is hardwired. It doesn't go through the conscious part of your brain. You don't get to think about what you should do in that moment.

When you put your hand on a hot element on the stove, you reflexively pull away from the heat. You don't have to think about it. It's hardwired into your nervous system. The same thing happens when it comes to your body detecting fear. You will flee, you will fight, or you will freeze.

That was a terrific thing back when your life was in danger from sabre-tooth tigers. In the twenty-first century there are no sabre-tooth tigers, but the hardwiring still exists. The sabre-tooth tiger has been replaced by the massive prefrontal cortex, the huge frontal lobe at the front of the brain. This is what makes us what we are now, an intelligent, incredible animal that can think about the future. We can think about tomorrow, next week, next month, next year, five years and ten years from now. Now, instead of fearing sabre-tooth tigers, we fear the future. The catch is that when we fear the future, the same chemical reaction occurs in our bodies.

Imagine you're at a live event and a hundred people are listening to me talk about this concept of fear and how we embrace it. I say to everyone, including you, "In a minute I'm going to get you all to stand and tell me who you are, where you're from, and what your greatest fear is. And I'm going to start with..." And I point to you.

How would you feel?

When I do this with a live audience, I see people's faces change; I know they want to run from the room. Some even get angry. They start making excuses in their head, or looking for the nearest exit. *I just came here to listen. I didn't come here for this.*

And some people freeze. They shrink down into their seats, hoping I won't pick them. In the instant that I ask them to stand up, their hearts start to race. They worry about what people will think of them, or what they're going to say. They're experiencing the same chemical reaction that occurred hundreds of thousands of years ago, when we ran from sabre-tooth tigers.

In short-term stressful situations, stress can be beneficial to your health and help you perform better. It can help you cope with potentially serious situations. That's perfect for the fifteen minutes or so while you're fighting or running from the tiger, but in the world we now live in people don't have just fifteen minutes of stress. They have fifteen hours, fifteen days, or even fifteen weeks (if you're mentally adding *fifteen years*, then you definitely need to keep reading this chapter).

If the stress response doesn't stop firing, and the stress levels stay elevated far longer than is necessary for survival, to the point that they become chronic, our health can be seriously affected.

" Its not stress that kills us, it is our reaction to it. "
HANS SELYE

The effects of stress (fear)

Nerves and hormones: The brain and nervous system is in charge of the fight-or-flight, or stress, response. Deep in the brain, there is a special part called the hypothalamus, and it starts things off by telling the adrenal glands to release the stress hormones adrenaline and cortisol.

This has a cascade effect in the body. When we think the fear has gone, the hypothalamus normally tells the body to go back to normal. If the stressor doesn't go away, the reaction will remain (more about the symptoms of stress in a moment).

Heart and lungs: During the stress response, we breathe faster to quickly deliver oxygenated blood to the body. Under stress, the heart also pumps faster, and sends blood rushing to the parts of the body that need it the most for the flight response, such as the muscles, heart, and other important organs. Stress hormones cause some blood vessels to constrict, and divert more oxygen full blood to the muscles to give them more strength to take action.

But this also raises blood pressure. As a result, recurrent or chronic stress makes the heart labor too hard for too long. When blood pressure increases, so does the risk of experiencing a stroke or heart attack.

Digestion: Under stress, the liver creates extra blood sugar (glucose) for an increase in energy. During chronic stress, the body may not be able to keep up with this additional glucose flood, and may increase the risk of developing type 2 diabetes. This rush of the hormones cortisol and adrenalin can also upset the digestive system. This can lead to heartburn or acid reflux.

Stress can also affect the way food travels through the body, leading to diarrhea, constipation or bloating. There is a greater awareness now of the importance the gut microprobe (the balance between good and bad gut bacteria) plays in health. This too will be affected.

Muscles: In stressful situations, the muscles get tense and ready for action. They become primed for a quick response. They will turn off again if the response is not needed, but under continual stress the muscles may not get the chance to relax. Tense muscles cause headaches, back and shoulder pain, and body aches.

Reproduction: Stress is draining for both the body and mind. It's not unusual for the libido to drop under constant stress. This is a condition called pregnenolone steal. All the important sex hormones, and the stress hormones, are made from a single precursor hormone called pregnenolone. We only produce so much of it, and if the body allocates it to producing cortisol (stress hormone) there will not be enough left to produce testosterone and estrogen in the adrenal glands. High cortisol levels also cause a reduction in the signaling of the pituitary gland to stimulate the production of hormones in gonadal tissue (ovaries and testes).

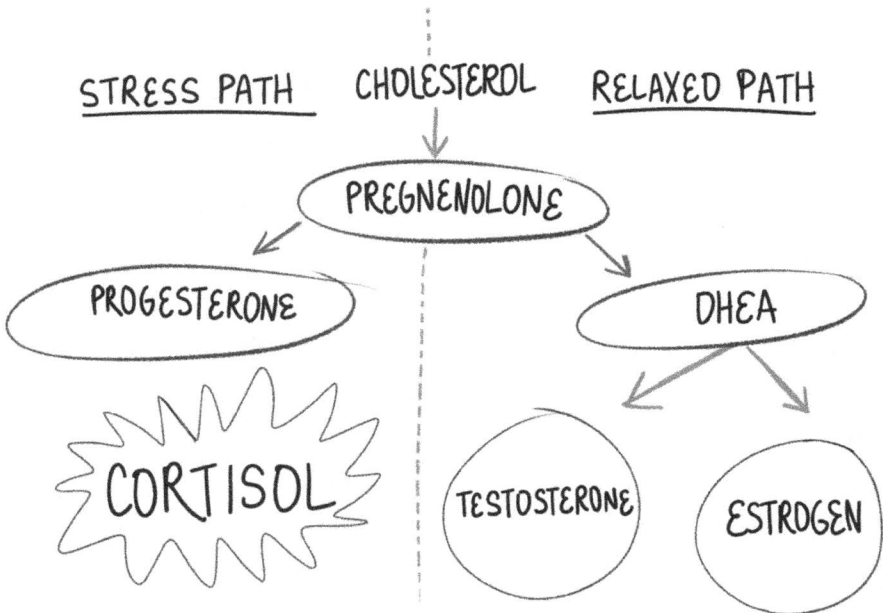

STRESS PATH   CHOLESTEROL   RELAXED PATH

PREGNENOLONE

PROGESTERONE   DHEA

CORTISOL   TESTOSTERONE   ESTROGEN

If stress continues for a long time, a man's testosterone levels can begin to decline. This can impede sperm production, and be the source erectile dysfunction or impotence. For women, stress can affect the menstrual cycle, with irregular, heavier, or more painful periods. Chronic stress can also increase the physical symptoms of menopause.

Immune system: Stress suppresses the immune system to help conserve energy for dealing with the danger. That's okay in the short term, but in the long term it weakens the immune system and reduces the body's response to foreign invaders. Chronic stress also drops the amount of a protein that is key to signaling other immune cells called lymphocytes. They kill attacking organisms that cause disease, and they identify harmful substances and help protect against them. Without their backup, the body is vulnerable to contracting acute illnesses and prolonged healing times.

People under chronic stress are also more vulnerable to viral infections like the flu and the common cold, as well as other diseases.

All of this is not a great advertisement for long-term stress, so it would be good to get a handle on it.

Remember that one of the six core needs we humans have is to grow and become better versions of ourselves. This means that we don't want to keep doing the same old things because that leads to us becoming stuck. The life where you're turned on—where you're constantly moving beyond the known, from the things you're certain of to the place of the unknown—is a life of growth. You're moving towards your goals. You're moving towards some kind of outcome. You're moving towards experiencing some kind of event.

Growth occurs when you move from the known into the unknown. It makes sense that you won't grow if you keep doing the same thing over and over again. Unfortunately, most people want to stay in the known.

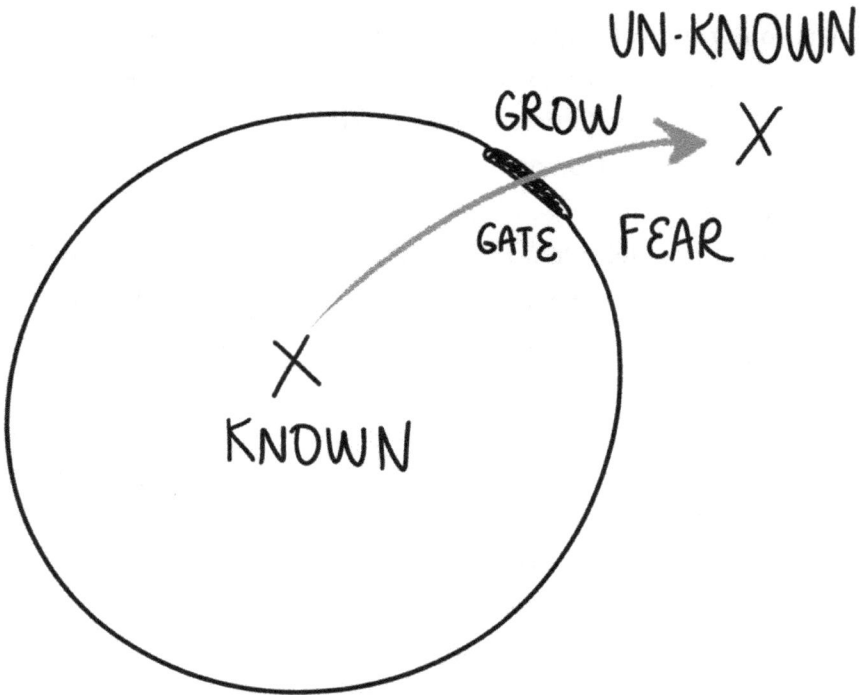

Often, my clients will tell me they need me to help them get more control. If they had more control, they say, and if they were a little more certain about what was going on, they would be much better.

The key to more growth and more certainty is to have more uncertainty, because every time you move into more uncertainty, the level of certainty you have grows. You grow from certain to known into the unknown, and you grow as a human.

There's a catch, though. Every time you open the gate and go from the known into the unknown, whether you like it or not you experience fear. Every single time. Every time you do something that's different or unusual, you experience fear.

Many clients come to me and say they're stressed. Stress is just another word for fear. If someone is feeling stressed, they're in fear.

221

When you grow, you experience fear. Every time you get to the gate, the door on the boundary of what you know, and you go to step into the unknown—every single time—you experience fear.

Do not ignore it. Do not pretend that the fear is not there. The key is to embrace it.

So many people, when they experience fear, do things to resist that fear. They resist experiencing it. Every single time they do that, the gate doesn't open. Every single time they do that, they don't move into the unknown, and they don't grow. The key is to embrace the fear.

In the coming pages I'll be giving you some key strategies—golden strategies—for how to embrace the fear that will allow you to open the gate and step on through. But first we should take a second to look at what people do when they don't embrace the fear.

Blame and excuses

One of the first things many people do is move to a place of blame and excuses. Instead of saying yes and stepping on through, they make excuses: *Oh, I can't, because of him. I can't because of that.* They go to what I call "living in effect." People who don't embrace fear, who do the blame and excuses thing, move into effect.

" A man can fail many times, but he isn't a failure until he begins to blame somebody else. "
JOHN BURROUGHS

📖 JOURNAL TIME

Write in your journal the words I'm about to give you. Write the words down one under the other, because I will give you the ultimate word at the end. Language is powerful, so watch yours. The way to watch it is to create an awareness of it. So split a blank page in half, and at the top of each column write *Cause* and *Effect*. Then fill in the columns with...

People who are in effect use words like *can't, should, hope, problem, have to*. People who are in *effect* believe they don't have any choice. That's why they're stuck. They go to step through the gate at the boundary of their known, and they experience fear. Instead of embracing it, they do blame and excuses and go into effect. They use the words *has to, should* and *can't* (which they vocalize or think in their heads) and believe they have no choice. So they remain stuck.

If they stay in effect for long enough, if they believe for long enough that they have no choice, eventually they become helpless. Instead of just being in the cage, they're in the back corner of the cage, rocking back and forth, waking every morning wondering what the world is going to throw at them.

That's not the life that you want. The way out of that life is to live at the cause.

If we look at the opposite of the word *effect*, we find the word *cause*. The opposite of *can't* is *won't*. Instead of saying *I can't come for dinner on Friday*, someone that lives in cause will say *I won't be able to come because we're having a family dinner*. Or *I won't be able to come because I'm working late*.

As soon as you say the word *can't*, you're insinuating that something outside of your control is going to stop you from attending or going. When you use the word *won't*, that word means that it's within your power and you are at choice. Being at choice is where you want to be. Being at choice is *cause*. Instead of saying *I should do that*, someone at cause will say *I could do that if I wanted to*.

Again, it's about choice. Instead of *I hope*, someone in cause will say *I wonder*. Compare *I hope it's good weather this weekend* with *I wonder if it's going to be good weather. If it's not, I wonder what else the weather is going to be like. If it's not fine weather, I wonder what else I could do*. This person is at choice.

Instead of *problem*, there's *possibility*. When you talk about growing from the known into the unknown, sometimes what's in the unknown is something you want. It might be a new job or a new a new relationship. It's something that you desire, an outcome that you want.

Sometimes, life being life, things will get thrown at you that you don't want. The loss of a loved one. The loss of a relationship. The loss of a job. The loss of money. Sometimes things happen, but if you always see them as problems, they will always be problems.

That's *effect* language. If you look at them as possibilities, that's a whole different thing. The fear will come up when you go from the known into the unknown for something you want, or you go from the known into the unknown for you don't want, but how you think about it makes a difference. It's whether you decide to be at cause or effect that will determine the outcome.

Instead of *problem* there's *possibility*. Instead of *have to* there's *want to* (*have to* is not empowering).

Sometimes when I coach parents, I'll make a suggestion for dealing with their problem or issue. Invariably, the reply follows a pattern.

"Oh, I can't do that," they'll say. "You don't understand."

And the will list all the reasons why they can't do what I have suggested. They have to finish work early to pick up the kids. They have to cook dinner. They have to make the kids' lunches. *Have to, have to, have to.* That parent feels helpless because their language throughout the day is based on *have to.*

If I challenge them on their language, and ask them if they really have to do something, they will invariably say, yes, they do have to.

Ben: "So, you're saying you don't want to pick up the kids?"

Parent: "No, I have to. You don't understand. I have to pick up the kids."

Ben: "So, you don't want to?"

Parent: "No, it's not that. I *have* to. I mean, they can't walk home by themselves. I have to pick them up."

Ben: "Are you saying you have to or you want to? Isn't it that you *want* to pick up the kids?"

Parent: "Well, of course I want to pick up the kids."

Ben: "Well, say *want* to instead of *have* to."

Parent: "Well, that's all right. But by the time I get home, then I have to cook dinner."

Ben: "Well, do you *have* to cook dinner or do you *want* to cook dinner?"

Parent: "Well, I have to. I can't let my kids go hungry."

Ben: "Well, you could. Do you want them to go hungry?"

Parent: "Well, no. Of course, I don't."

Ben: "So, you want them to be fed?"

Parent: "Yeah. Well, of course, I do."

Ben: "So you don't *have* to cook dinner. You *want* to cook dinner."

And that's when they get it.

Have to means that you have no choice and you *have* to do it. But you *do* have a choice. The truth is, you *want* to do it. You don't have to. The opposite of no choice is choice. The opposite of helplessness is one hundred percent response-ablity for your life.

One hundred percent response-able

This is a big one. In fact, it's a huge one. People who live at cause take one hundred percent responsibility for their lives. They believe they are responsible (response-able) for everything that happens.

Let's look at that word for a minute: *response-able*. It's almost two words. You can choose your response to any circumstance. If someone says something to you, if something happens to you, if someone bumps your car, you can always choose your response. That's living at cause. If you live at effect, every time something happens to you and you believe it's not your fault you'll place blame and make excuses.

When you live at cause, when you believe you are at choice, it feels incredibly powerful. That's how you feel the power—by living at cause. If you stay in effect, you will always feel like nothing is your choice and you are helpless in determining your future.

You can find your way out of living a stuck life, trapped in the cage. You can find your way out of living a life that's merely comfortable to living a life in your theme park, where every day you wake up turned on. The way out of that life is to live a life where you're at choice, where you take one hundred percent responsibility. It's an exciting place to be.

It's important to make the distinction between a hundred percent response-able and fault. The word "fault" comes from the Old French *faute*, meaning "opening, gap; failure, flaw, blemish; lack, deficiency."

one hundred percent response-ability = to respond
fault = to have a shortcoming or deficiency

Whenever fear occurs, you have options. The first option is to avoid embracing it and instead place blame and make excuses—to be in effect, in other words. To use words like *can't*, *should*, *have to*, *problem* and *I've got no choice in the whole thing*. The other option is to be a hundred percent responsible and be at cause—to say that you do have a choice.

❝ One's philosophy is not best expressed in words; it is expressed in the choices one makes... and the choices we make are ultimately our responsibility. ❞
ELEANOR ROOSEVELT

What are you afraid of?

I'm going to give you a couple of questions to answer. Again, this will require a pen and paper. It's a cool exercise that will help you understand what, under the surface, is your fear. What is lurking underneath the surface that has stopped you from leading the life, and making the choices, you really want to make?

"My wife was afraid of the dark... then she saw me naked, and now she's afraid of the light."
RODNEY DANGERFIELD

First I'll explain some of the emotions and feelings that come up when people experience fear. When people do blame and excuses, when they go into effect, these are some of the emotions that they experience: anger, impatience, exhaustion, feeling of self-righteousness, feeling of being misunderstood, being paranoid, feeling paralyzed, feeling shame, feeling guilty, defeated, feelings of being out of control or confused, feeling overwhelmed, feeling victimized. They get into the language in their head, or verbally, that are all effect words with emotions that we associate with fear.

What are you afraid of? When you go through the gate—when you go to go from the known into the unknown, when you make a call to start a relationship, when you go into the boss's office to have the conversation, when you're sitting at home and want to tell your partner how you feel about them—what comes up that stops you from having that extraordinary relationship, that extraordinary career, that extraordinary level of health and vitality?

JOURNAL TIME
LifeCEO.com/RESOURCES

Please do this exercise; it's a game changer.

The question is: *What are you afraid of?* When you know what you're most afraid of, you're better prepared to create a proactive choice and response rather than just a knee-jerk reaction. Rather than just going into blame and excuses, you can make a proactive choice and response.

Now write down a few words (you will be choosing from these words very soon): selfish, stupid, weak, incompetent, ordinary, loser, fake, lazy, invisible, rejected. You get the idea. Add any others that occur to you.

Now look at those words and get a feeling for which ones you get the most intense reaction from, especially when you think of putting them into the following sentence:

"If someone I love, respect and admire thought that I was _____, I'd be devastated."

What's your word? If you were to fill in that gap, what would be the word? A few possibilities: *If someone I love, respect and admire thought I was weak, I'd be devastated. If someone I love, respect and admire thought I was a fake, I'd be devastated.*

Look at your list of words and see what fits. How did you go? It's interesting, isn't it? What's even more interesting is looking at how you might respond.

So what do you do to avoid the feeling of fear? Many people disguise their problems as a way of avoiding their worst fears about themselves. I'm going to ask you to write down the following list of words and phrases, and then to pick your top three words. Then I'll follow with another question.

People pleaser	Make excuses
Isolate myself	Stay online for hours
Blame other	Give up
Compromise	Do drugs
Shop	Put myself down
Get negative and skeptical	Beat myself up verbally
Sleep too much	Hurt someone

Take stuff personally	Act irresponsibly
Over apologize	Do perfectionism
Get manipulative	Complain
Watch TV	Daydream
Pretend I'm stupid	Joke around
Procrastinate	Clean
Drink	Get angry

Now here's the question: "When I want to avoid the thought that I am _____ [whatever it was for you in the previous exercise], I do the following: _____, _____, _____.

Possible responses: *When I want to avoid the thought that I am weak, I give up. When I want to avoid the thought that I am weak, I try to be a perfectionist. When I want to avoid the thought that I am weak, I become negative and skeptical. When I want to avoid the thought that I am fake, I sleep too much.*

How did you go? Makes a lot of sense, doesn't it? When you look at some of the things that you do, some of the actions you take, you'll realize that some of the things that keep you in that stuck, trapped state are often driven by the fear you have of yourself.

Last year I was feeling a bit stuck. During breakfast, my wife could see I was in a stuck state, and she said, "Why don't you write out a to-do list for today? Get yourself unstuck. Take some action on some things."

When I started writing my to-do list, she said she would help me with accountability. She would give me a call at eleven o'clock and see how I was doing.

Off I went into my study. I churned through the list, ticking off a wide range of things. It was just going along beautifully until I got to the next item on the list. I had to make a call. I beg your pardon, I didn't *have* to make a call, I *wanted* to make a call. I was feeling well and truly in effect there.

As I prepared to make the call, the fear started to build. Then a random thought entered my head: *Look at that wax that got on the carpet from last week. I wonder how you get wax out of carpet.*

So instead of making the call I searched online to find out how to get wax out of carpet. I grabbed a tea towel. I got out the iron, and then discovered that the cord was too short for the iron to reach the wax. I found an extension cord, plugged in the iron, and soon I was busy ironing out the wax.

The call was still on my to-do list.

Then the phone rang. I looked at my watch and it was eleven o'clock. Of course, who was going to call me at eleven o'clock but my beautiful wife? When she asked how my to-do list was going, I told her it was all good, really great.

"What are you doing now?" she said.

"Um, getting the wax out of the carpet."

"I don't remember that being on your to-do list."

Well, of course, it wasn't. That was me doing procrastination. Instead of me embracing the fear, I decided that the better option was to procrastinate by taking wax out of the carpet.

It's amazing how easy it is to stay trapped, to stay stuck. If you don't want to do that anymore, how do you stop? What's the strategy?

Instead of going into effect, instead of doing blame and excuses, and saying you have no choice, you must embrace the fear.

The three keys to growth and fulfillment

Grace: The first key is to be of grace. What do I mean by that? Some do grace at the dinner table. Grace is about giving thanks. When it comes to embracing fear, grace is about giving thanks and saying yes. Saying yes to the challenge. Saying yes to the opportunity. Saying yes, and going for the outcome that you want.

> ❝ **I think I run my strongest when I run with joy, with gratitude, with focus, with grace.** ❞
> **KRISTIN ARMSTRONG**

Many of us get to the gate of opportunity, where the next step is from the known into the unknown, and say: *No. I don't want to know about it. No. Forget it. I'm going to put it to the back of my mind. I'm going to pretend it's not happening. I'm going to pretend...*

There is no *no*. The only way through to the other side is to say yes. Say yes to the challenge. Say yes to the potential. To step through that gate with *yes* is to be in grace. It's so important to say yes when you see a challenge, and you look at potential.

Of course, the old saying, "Say yes and work out how," is all about having grace. Say yes and work out how as you step through. As you open the gate and step through, trust that the *how* will come to you.

Gratitude: The second key to embracing fear is gratitude. When you get to the gate of opportunity and the fear starts to build, turn around. Before you step into the unknown, look behind you at what you have. Look at what you're grateful for. Look at the relationships that you have or have had in the past. Look at the career opportunities that you have and have had. Look at the experiences you've had. Look at your life and what you have now. Look at what you're grateful for before you head through the gate.

> ❝ Develop an attitude of gratitude, and give thanks for everything that happens to you, knowing that every step forward is a step toward achieving something bigger and better than your current situation. ❞
> **BRIAN TRACY**

When I think of gratitude, I picture the space shuttle taking off with massive billowing clouds of smoke and fire as it leaves the launch pad, heading into the unknown. Think of gratitude as your launch pad as you move forward into the unknown. Gratitude is the thing you put your metaphorical foot against as you drive through the gate and into your own unknown.

Courage: The third key is courage. Not the kind of courage needed to jump out of a plane or drive a fast car around a racetrack. I'm talking about *real* courage.

You word "courage" comes from the Old French *courage*, meaning "heart, innermost feelings; temper." The key is in the first part of the word: *cour-* meaning "come from the heart." This means being willing to experience (and share) your innermost feelings. Courage is a doing word, an action word. You don't do courage sitting in your chair.

As you step through the gate with grace and gratitude, you're showing that you're willing to be exposed. You're willing to be seen for who you truly are. Vulnerability is not a weakness; it is true power. Facing a challenge with grace and gratitude, and courage and vulnerability is how you embrace fear.

> ❝ The secret to happiness is freedom...
> And the secret to freedom is courage. ❞
> **THUCYDIDES**

A client I will call Susie had a fear of not being lovable, so she sabotaged her relationships before they got too serious. She didn't want to find out if she was lovable or not. She didn't want to challenge her fear. Before each boyfriend could dump her, she always found a way of sabotaging the relationship and ending it herself. This had been her strategy for some years.

She came to me wanting her current relationship to be different. We talked about fear. She told me the relationship was starting to be a little too good, and she was looking for a way to finish it before her fear of not being lovable surfaced. She was starting to dream up reasons why it wasn't going to work; her boyfriend had been sick this week and hadn't contacted her, a clear indication, in her view, that the relationship was over.

Our conversation went something like this.

"Have you called him this week?" I asked.

"No, what if he doesn't want to speak to me or be my boyfriend anymore?"

"Why don't you give him a call and tell him how you truly feel about him?"

Many people, when it comes to relationships, don't have the courage to be vulnerable enough to tell their partner, honestly, what they think of them. How much they truly love and respect them. They're not willing to share from the heart.

"I'm not going to call him," Susie said.

"Susie, it would be better if you put yourself on the line and told him how much you care about him instead of waiting for *him* to put himself on the line."

Susie said she would do it, but not while I was in the room. So I left and came back a few minutes later. Susie told me it went well. But then she said that boyfriend hadn't answered his phone.

"I know, I know," she said, "you're going to tell me I should've left a message. But I didn't."

The point of this story is not that Susie didn't leave a message. It was about the courage and willingness to be vulnerable she showed in making the call in the first place. She was willing to make the call and have the conversation.

To sum up: Grace means being willing to say yes to the opportunity to move forward. Gratitude means taking a moment to look back at what you have, at what you're grateful for. Courage means being willing to be vulnerable, to let people see the real you.

Bonus Branson questions

To be honest, I don't know where I heard that these were Sir Richard Branson's questions for moving forward out of the known into the unknown, but I can imagine him asking them. So go for it and ask yourself these questions:

- *What's the worst thing that could happen if I did this thing? If I faced this challenge, if I stepped through this gate, what is the worst thing that could happen?* Remember, this is the *worst* thing.
- *The worst thing has happened, and can I handle it?* That's another very powerful question. Probably, 99.9 percent of the time the worst thing would not be death, which is cool because that would definitely be tricky to handle. But if you answer no, maybe you shouldn't do it. But think again. You probably could do it. Take action with courage.

" My attitude has always been, if you fall flat on your face, at least you're moving forward. All you have to do is get back up and try again. "

RICHARD BRANSON

It's great once you get in

One Christmas, my family and I were staying at my in-laws' in Mordialloc. Their house is just back from the beach. You go through a little laneway, and there you are on the sand. It had been a typical Victorian Christmas: cold. Then suddenly we had a glorious sunny day. I was twenty meters from the beach. I had to go for a swim and make the most of the beautiful day. At the water's edge, I put my foot in to test the water. It was cold! So there I was, on the water's edge doing a kind of water dance, with one foot in and one foot out. Should I go in or not?

I was procrastinating. I had visions of the closing scenes from the movie *Titanic*. Instead of saying yes, having gratitude, taking action, and asking myself what was the worst thing that could happened and could I handle it, I had started to move into effect.

I told myself I couldn't go in, but I should. I had to go and pick up the kids. If I went for a swim, I would be wet. By the time I got home and dried off, I would have missed picking up the kids. I was making excuses. I started to blame my having to pick up the kids for not being able to go for a swim.

Before I knew it, I was putting my clothes back on and walking home. All the way, I was saying to myself: *I should've gone in. I could've done it. Loser. It would've been great in the water. It would've been beautiful, refreshing.*

This type of thing can happen when you go from the known to the unknown. If you do it often enough, eventually you'll start wearing a deep trench into this cycle of fear. The trench will eventually get so deep that you can't see out, and you'll be well and truly stuck. Then you'll find yourself sitting in a corner, feeling helpless.

About a week later there was another beautiful sunny day. This was it. I was going back down to the beach and this time I would have a swim. It got to the water's edge, stripped off, and did it again. I made the same mistake. I put my foot in first to test the water. It was still cold. I started to do the dance again.

Then I heard a scream behind me and the thud of feet on the sand. My brother Jim was running down the beach, stripping off his clothes as he ran. He hit the water at full speed and dived under. He came up with a big stupid grin on his face.

"Come on," he yelled to me. "It's great once you get in."

That's the thing with fear. It disappears the instant you're on the other side. As soon as you're into the unknown, the fear goes. It's only when you're at the boundary that you feel the fear.

A great mate of mine, Ryan, says he knows he's doing the right thing when he has "nervous excitement." Nervous excitement = joy. I love that. This is when you're nervous about what's about to happen, but excited at the same time. You don't get that if you stay in your comfort zone. This is when you grow.

Excitement without nervousness is merely novelty. Novelty is going to the movies or a party, having a few drinks, eating out, buying a new outfit, and playing Xbox. These things may be exciting at the time, but there's no growth, no joy, because there is no accompanying nervousness. Novelty is what keeps us in the trapped or tepid life. Life might be good, but there's no joy, no racing of the heart.

If you're going through hell, keep going.
WINSTON CHURCHILL

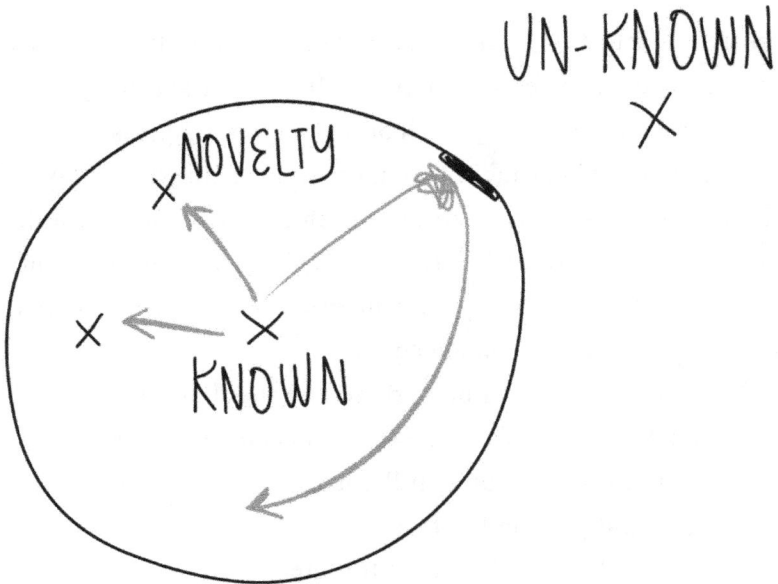

As we've discussed, the key to having more certainty in your life is to have more uncertainty by embracing fear. This is not something that is necessarily going to come to you straightaway. It's a muscle that will take practice to strengthen. Practice on little things like going for a swim in cold water. Practice on big things like relationships and career choices.

I truly believe that if you embrace fear, it will take you from a trapped life, beyond the tapered life, to the turned-on life. It's simple: embrace fear.

I truly wish you all the best in your journey forward into more uncertainty, into getting more of what you want in life. Live life, perform at your best, and be well.

30 Caterpillar to Butterfly

> **❝** There is nothing in a caterpillar that tells you it's going to be a butterfly. **❞**
> **R. BUCKMINSTER FULLER**

W hy do some adults behave like children and always take the easy road by not doing things that seem hard but will be good for them? How can you as a parent help your child turn into an adult? (Remember, parents, you are raising adults, not children.)

I think the answer can be found by looking at the caterpillar and the butterfly. A caterpillar is not the prettiest thing in the world. It has all those legs, a squishy body, a funny-looking head, and a strange-looking beak. It crawls around on a constant search for something to eat. Then one day it disappears and goes into a cocoon.

The caterpillar begins to lose its legs and grow wings. But the biggest shift it undergoes is not physical but mental: a change in mindset. It stops thinking about crawling around eating leaves, and starts to think about flying around sniffing flowers. This process has to be challenging. The creature has a new body, a new chemistry, and a new mindset.

What happens is that the caterpillar loses its whole body by emitting enzymes to dissolve all of its tissues and effectively digesting itself.

If you were to cut open a cocoon during that process, caterpillar soup would ooze out.

Special cells called imaginal discs, which the caterpillar has carried since it hatched from the egg, survive the process. When all the tissues except for the imaginal discs have been digested, these discs use the protein-rich caterpillar soup to fuel the fast cell division essential to form the wings, antennae, legs, eyes, genitals, and all the other structures of an adult butterfly.

The caterpillar and the butterfly are the same species, but totally different creatures.

It's the same with a child and an adult. They are the same species, but totally different creatures. The child and the adult have different bodies and different chemistry. Their metabolism, hormone system, immune system, and nervous system are all different. They have different body parts, especially in the area of reproductive systems. They have different bone structure and tissues.

Like the caterpillar, the child has a different mindset to the adult. And just like the butterfly, the child contains all the special cells needed to transition into an adult.

As we've already discussed, children will do something because it feels good. Adults will do something that may not feel good at the time, but they know will be good for them in the long term.

BUTTERFLY X

ADULT

COCOON STAGE

DO WHAT DOESN'T FEEL
GOOD, BUT IS GOOD FOR
YOU AND OTHERS

LEARN TO MAKE DECISION

CATERPILLAR

TEENAGER

X CHILD

DO WHAT FEELS GOOD
(FULLSTOP)

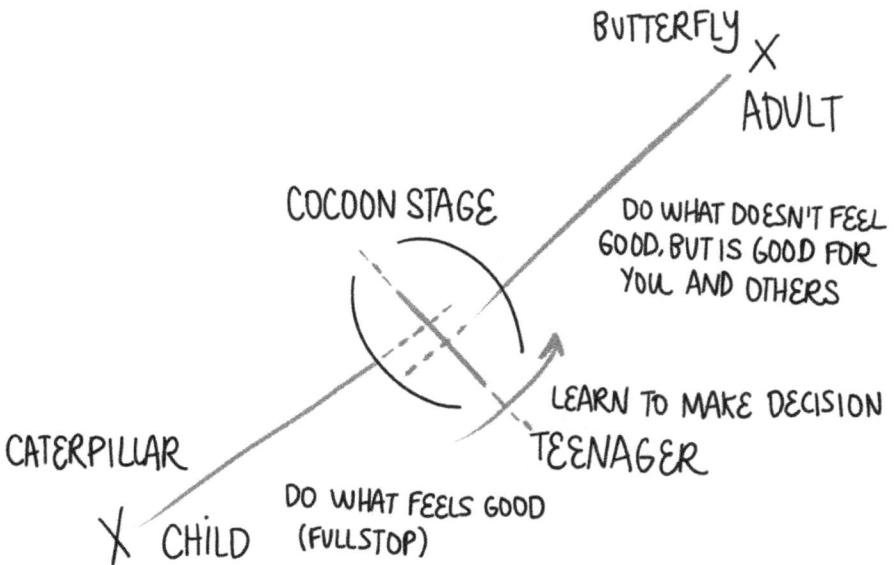

What stops a child from turning into an adult in mind and body? I believe it's because they are not given the opportunity to make the transition while in the cocoon (teenage) stage of their development. Unlike the caterpillar, which disappears into a cocoon while it undergoes its transformation (metamorphosis), as parents we get to see the transformation. We get to see the awkward, painful, confusing, and often frightening transition as the child battles with the change in body, chemistry, and mind.

This is why teenagers go into fear, often blaming the world for their troubles (especially their parents), making excuses, getting angry and frustrated, procrastinating, and lacking motivation.

We watch this awkward transition and try to make it more comfortable for them. Big mistake. This is the time for our children to start making some decisions that don't feel good, but are good for them. Decisions like going to bed early, doing their homework, tidying their rooms, eating healthy food, exercising, helping out around the house, or putting out the rubbish without having to be told five times. As our children start to move into teenage years, we need to allow them to make decisions. By making decisions, and facing the consequences—sometimes good, sometimes not good—they are able to make the transition in their minds, as well as the inevitable transition in their bodies.

When Bella, my eldest daughter, was in year eleven she was taking biology, a year-twelve subject. Midway through the year, my wife arranged for Bella to attend a special lecture in the city to review her biology. I agreed to drive her there. It was a Saturday morning, and I came into the kitchen to find Bella getting breakfast. To my surprise, she told me she didn't really want to go. When I asked her why not, she said, "I can't be bothered." To which I replied, "Well, don't go then."

This was the risky bit for me. I wanted her to go, but I had to let her make the decision.

"Mum will make me go," she said.

"Don't worry about Mum," I said, "I'll handle her. Look, it's no big deal for me if you don't want to go. In fact, it suits me. I'm not that keen to drive into the city, and I wanted to wash the car today anyway. I'm going to make myself a coffee. When I've finished it, let me know what you've decided.

Ten minutes later Bella had decided she wanted to go after all. When I picked her up later that day, she told me the lecture had been great.

So here is the magic. Who gets the credit for Bella going and having a good time? Bella does. She decided to go, so she gets all the credit. If I had made her go, I would have gotten the credit. Bella made a decision that didn't feel good at the time, but was good for her. She gets all the credit for that decision, so her self-esteem and self-worth goes up. She has moved one step closer to becoming an adult.

We have to allow our teenagers to make their own decisions, build their own self-worth, and let them to take responsibility for their own lives so they can become responsible adults.

I believe that our children are not our responsibility. Instead, I believe we have a duty of care to raise them into adults: to provide shelter, food, and education. If we want (it's a choice) we can love them, care for them, and be an example for them. We can be their champions in tough times, encourage them to be their best, ask them to raise their standards, and to be a soft landing place when they fall. The more responsibility we give our children, the quicker and deeper they move into being adults.

I know it's not easy. In fact, it can be extremely hard sometimes. I know I fail at it all the time. I step in and make decisions for them, I stop them from experiencing the wrong choice (whatever that is), I make sure they do what *I* think is right.

It's important, as your life CEO, to empower the people around you by giving them responsibility for their own lives. Not only is it good for them, it's amazing for you.

JOURNAL TIME

If you have children, either under or over eighteen, where could you give them choices? Is there any area where you could take a step back? Let them succeed and get credit for the success, but also let them fail and get credit for that as well. Write down three ways you could let go of control. Ideally, the choices you give them will not affect your life and standards.

You could give your children the choice of leaving their clothes all over the house, and making a mess. But you could also add a fair and reasonable consequence if they do.

31 Your Dashboard

> **" Feedback is the breakfast of champions. "**
> **KEN BLANCHARD**

I write this chapter, Audi has just released its new dashboard called "the virtual cockpit." It replaces the traditional tachometer and speedometer dials with a screen that gives feedback on everything: speed, tachometer, temperature, fuel, and navigation. In fact, pretty much anything you would ever want to know about your Audi is now right in front of you.

Why would anyone need all that information? Well, it helps the driver keep heading in the right direction (satnav), and it also monitors the car's behavior. It tells the driver when they're revving too much or going too fast, the engine is overheating, or the car is low on fuel. Everything is monitored so the driver has a safe journey, and gets to where they're going in the most efficient way.

Wouldn't it be great if we had a dashboard like that? It would help keep us on track, and as effective and efficient as possible. Well, you can. You just have to make one up, and then check it regularly to see if you're on track and behaving the way you need—or want—to be.

If you were to create a dashboard that monitored your behavior, what key aspects of your behavior would you choose? I'm going to suggest you choose the following three to start with.

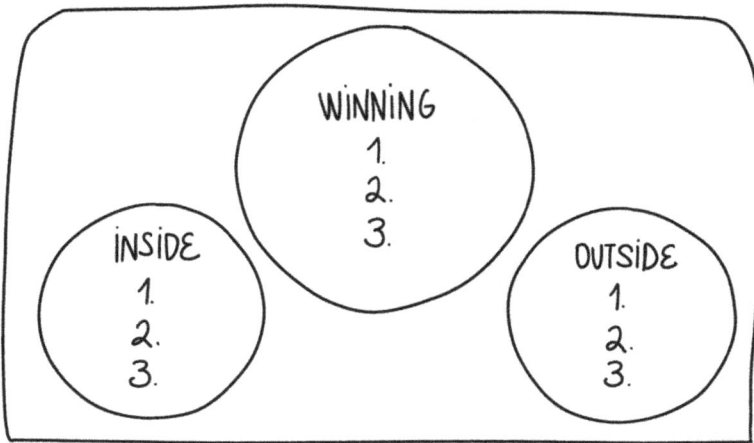

First, which behaviors would you choose, from all your behaviors, to create the most success in your life? In the past, which behaviors have led you to victory? That is who do you need to be to be the most productive, to achieve the best performance, and to profit as a result.

Second, who do you need to be there for you when no one else is around? Who do you need to be on the inside? Which character traits, behaviors, tones are best for you?

Third, who you do I need to be for others? What behavior produces the best results when you're with others? What tone allows you to connect, influence, interact, impact, and help others?

You will have discovered these character traits if you've done the previous exercises in this book, but this is an opportunity for you to simplify everything—values, life purpose, missions, beliefs, rules, state, needs, and fear—into just three aspects of your life, and to focus on just three behaviors in each.

To give you an idea of how this might look, I will share mine as an example:

- For success: creativity, hard work, compress 4 quality
- For me: solid, energized, bold
- For others: respectful, inspirational, cheeky

245

I keep these nine words on my dash all the time. When I'm out and about, even just shopping at the local supermarket, I glance at the dashboard in my mind and look at the "for others" dial. I check to see that I'm being respectful, inspirational and cheeky.

JOURNAL TIME

Draw a dash with three circles and fill them with the top three states, character, or tone that you turn on and monitor as you drive down the freeway of life.

Part 6

STEP 4

PRODUCTIVITY: WHERE THE RUBBER MEETS THE ROAD

32 Make the Decision

To decide means to cut off, to shift from where you are to somewhere else. It means to leave something behind, and to end up somewhere else. Making a decision is the most powerful thing you can do. The catch is that it involves action.

Years ago, a book (and documentary) was released called *The Secret*. Many people who read the book thought that success was a mindset thing only. Mindset is important. In fact, eighty percent of this book has been devoted to helping you work your mindset; however, mindset does not change your world, or the world around you.

Many who watched or read *The Secret* thought all they had to do was find themselves a comfortable chair, close their eyes, and imagine the new house or car, the relationship, money or health. But it doesn't work like that. You have to move, make a call, get in your car, work, and sweat for something to change, including your life. (And I promise you that if you reach this point in *this* book without taking action, nothing will change.)

When you make a decision, take immediate action, start the ball rolling. Do something that causes the world to be different.

Different in your mind is not enough; the decision must be followed by action.

If you have built the mindset that supports you losing weight and getting healthy, that's great, but you must take action. For instance, shopping for better food, eating less, exercising more, hanging out with healthy people.

If you have built the mindset that supports you creating more financial health, that's great, but you must take action. For instance, opening a savings account, getting a job, putting money in the bank, spending less.

If you have built the mindset that supports you improving your relationship or marriage, that's great, but you must take action. For instance, booking a date night, buying flowers, cooking a romantic dinner, making love, or telling someone you love them.

In my experience, there are four things that people who succeed at decision-making do; four things that help them to be productive, follow through, and experience profit in their lives:

1. They make the decision for themselves. They connect the decision with their life purpose and related mission. They link the decision and the success of that decision directly to their sense of identity. Who they are is that decision. If they don't follow through, that reflects on them; that's putting some skin in the game. They go public and say, "I am the result I get. I am responsible for the outcome. I am the CEO."

2. They make the decision about others. They look at their decision and, again, by connecting it with life purpose, which almost always contains something about making the world a better place. This links the decision to producing a result that will make a difference to the world in some way. They say, "I am the CEO who is responsible for fulfilling my purpose and positively impacting the world around me."

3. They get immersed in this next thing in their mission. They go deep about the thing they have decided to do. (My wife often calls me "the fad man" because whenever I pursue a new interest, I invest a lot of time, money, energy and sanity. I buy the books, watch the videos, attend the course, acquire the equipment, and change my screensaver to an image of the new interest.) You can believe that any CEO who takes over leadership in a new company will become immersed in everything to do with that company.

4. They get it scheduled with a clear, well-defined goal. There is massive power in a well-defined goal. It has a clear outcome you can be one hundred percent responsible for. It's connected with purpose and mission, and it's kind so it's good for you and others. Importantly, it has a completion date. All successful people attach deadlines to their decisions. Even a CEO of a company must report to a board and shareholders at the end of the financial year.

Productivity is about making decisions and giving it your all. *Go!*

33 Checking In

> ❝I think it's very important to have a feedback loop, where you're constantly thinking about what you've done and how you could be doing it better. I think that's the single best piece of advice: constantly think about how you could be doing things better and questioning yourself.❞
> **ELON MUSK**

Last year I decided to take up triathlons. I had no bike, struggled to run due to my smashed-up foot, and couldn't swim more than a few lengths of my pool, but I thought triathlons would fulfill a number of my missions, including my tribe, sharpen the saw, and fun.

Once I had made the decision, I became consumed by it and set some goals. I booked booking and paid for my first official event in three months' time. I filled the house with *Triathlete* magazines, researched gear online, bought wetsuits, borrowed bikes, and watched YouTube clips.

One of my greatest challenges was going to be swimming fifteen hundred meters in open water when the furthest I'd ever sum was twenty laps of the local pool (about five hundred meters).

In my research on ocean swimming, I came across a technique called "total immersion swimming," developed by coach Terry Laughlin (sadly, Terry died recently from prostate cancer). I watched the online videos, practiced the strokes in the pool, did a few laps, started to feel confident. It was time to hit the big pool: Frankston Beach. With my new wetsuit on, my triathlete goggles, and triathlete watch (did I mention I am a fad man?), I was ready.

Frankston Beach has markers 250 meters offshore to warn boats of the five-knot speed zone. I decided on swimming to one of those and back my target, a total of a thousand meters. Off I went, feeling good. It felt easy, and I was covering the distance. I could see the sandy bottom pass under me as I swam along. After a while, I thought I'd pop my head up to see how much further I had to go to reach the marker. To my horror, I found I hadn't been swimming along the shoreline but directly out into the ocean.

My mistake was in assuming that my efforts were getting me where I wanted to go. Without regularly checking in, getting feedback, and using that feedback to alter my course, I was about to drop off the edge of the earth.

The moral of the story is to check in regularly once you've begun to take action. Always check behavior first. Check in with your dashboard. Are you being who you need to be for you, other people, and victory? Check in to see if your actions are the right ones. Are there things in your life that might be getting you off course?

If you check in and everything seems to be going to plan, don't change a thing. Keep going and check in again later. If you're getting to where you want to go, stop everything, beat yourself up, and give in (just kidding).

What has got you off course? What is preventing your progress? Is it behavior? If so, reconnect with your mission, change your state, and get your tone and character right again. Is it action? Are you doing the wrong thing?

Are you spending time not being productive? That's something I learned from the total-immersion swimming technique. Efficiency when swimming is vital, and that comes from technique. Is your strategy or technique wrong?

This cycle of action/check in, action/check in, action/check in should continue until you get the result you're looking for. At no point do you throw the failure card; at all times hold the responsibility card. Take responsibility for where you are. Adapt, change, modify, commit to excellence, and keep moving.

No CEO would plot through the year without getting regular departmental reports on how the company is traveling. These regular reports are what allow the CEO to shift tactics to deal with change, or errors in calculation. A great CEO doesn't get paralyzed by poor feedback, or stop pushing for growth because of good feedback. They simply focus, and make another decision.

Being your life CEO is no different. Use feedback to drive you forward, remain flexible, and stay inspired by the feedback you seek.

34 Commitment to Excellence

> **❝** Excellence is an art won by training and habituation. We do not act rightly because we have virtue or excellence, but we rather have those because we have acted rightly. We are what we repeatedly do. Excellence, then, is not an act but a habit. **❞**
>
> **ARISTOTLE**

When I think of commitment to excellence, the word *arete* comes to mind (if you recall, it means "the attainment of excellence in life"). As Aristotle noted in the quote above, it's through our actions that we attain excellence. When I think of commitment to excellence, I think of three key aspects, all of which require some discomfort to perform:

1. Education: Do you seek to be educated? What are you reading? Are you reading books like *Fifty Shades of Grey*? If they spice up your relationship in the bedroom, do you become a better person because of it? Or are you reading books like *Good to Great*, a book about bringing out excellence by Jim Collins? Which magazines do you read? *Who* magazine, with its celebrity gossip?

What are you listening to? For instance, podcast interviews with people who are making the world a better place. Are you finding out why and how they do it, what kind of people they are, the strategies that use to achieve fulfillment in life?

Are you attending seminars that stretch your mind? Or are they seminars that are a little painful, and annoy you just a little? Do you have a headache from the battles raging in your mind throughout the day?

What are you watching on TV? Are you educating yourself on a daily basis with things new and different? Things that challenge you, give you new perspectives on the world and how it works, that open up options and choices you may not have considered before?

2. Experience: Do you go out into the world and experience what you have learned? It's worth repeating: knowledge is not power, action is. I love a quote from the movie *Batman*: "It's not who I am underneath, but what I do that defines me." Are you doing it? Are you performing?

3. Engagement: Whom are you hanging out with? It has often been said that if we take the average income of our five closest friends, that income will be ours. If we take average quality of their relationships, that quality will be ours. If we take the average standard of their health, that level of health will be ours. Perhaps it's time for you to get some better friends.

On that last point, I was interested to find out if this was true, so I had a look at the research and here is what I found: a happy mate equals a happy life. One study looked to see if happiness can spread from person to person, and whether pockets of happiness form within our social networks. The research showed there were definitely groups of happy and unhappy people observable in the community, and the relationship between people's happiness extends up to three degrees of separation (for example, to the friends of one's friends' friends).

People who are surrounded by many happy people, especially those who are central in the network, are more likely to become happy in the future. The happiness results from the spread of happiness and is not just a tendency for people to associate with others similar to themselves. A friend who lives within a couple of kilometers, and who becomes happy, increases the probability that their friends will be happy by 25 percent. Even next-door neighbors of a happy person have a 38 percent increased chance of being happy.

If you hang out with happy people, you're more likely to be happy.

Now for the not-so-good news about friends. Another study I found looked at obesity to see if it can be spread from person to person. They used longitudinal statistical models to examine whether weight gain in one person was associated with weight gain in their friends, siblings, spouse, and neighbors.

They found that a person's chances of becoming obese increased by 57 percent if they had a friend who became obese. Among pairs of adult siblings, if one sibling became obese, the chance that the other would also become obese increased by 40 percent. If one spouse became obese, the likelihood that the other spouse would become obese increased by 37 percent.

The who-you-hang-out-with effect appears to be relevant to the biological and behavioral traits of obesity, and obesity appears to spread through a person's social ties.

Like to have a drink with your mates? Another study explored whether behavior related to alcohol consumption spreads from person to person with social networks of friends, co-workers, siblings, spouses, and neighbors. The participants were asked to record alcohol consumption (average number of drinks per week over the previous year, and number of days drinking within the previous week), and social-network ties.

They found that changes in the alcohol consumption of a person's social network had a statistically significant effect on that person's own subsequent alcohol consumption. The behaviors of immediate neighbors and co-workers were not affected, but the behavior of relatives and friends was.

What about your smoking buddies? Another study wanted to know if smokers hung out with smokers, and if quitters hung out with quitters. There were clear groups of smokers and nonsmokers present in the community. Despite the decrease in smoking in the overall population, the size of the clusters of smokers remained the same across time, suggesting that whole groups of people were quitting in concert. Smokers were also progressively found on the periphery of the social network.

Smoking cessation by a spouse was found to decrease a person's chances of smoking by 67 percent. Smoking cessation by a sibling decreased the chances by 25 percent, and smoking cessation by a friend decreased the chances by 36 percent. Among persons working in small firms, smoking cessation by a coworker decreased the chances by 34 percent. I love this bit: friends with more education influenced one another more than those with less education.

Moral of the story: if you want to stop smoking, hang out with other people who are also giving up.

Do you have any friends who are getting divorced? Yet another study explored how social networks influence divorce, and vice versa, by looking at the data from the long-running Framingham Heart Study. The results suggest that divorce can spread among friends. Clusters of divorces extend to two degrees of separation in the network. Popular people are less likely to get divorced; divorcées have denser social networks, and they are much more likely to remarry other divorcées.

Intriguingly, the presence of children does not influence the probability of divorce, but each child reduces the chance of being influenced by friends who get divorced.

Overall, the results suggest that attending to the health of our friends' marriages may serve to support and enhance the durability of our own relationship.

I'm not saying that you should go out today and dump your friends. I wonder, though, if you could choose to surround yourself with, for want of a better word, "better" people. Is it time to find some friends with *arete*?

"He that lieth down with dogs shall rise up with fleas."
SENECA

JOURNAL TIME
LifeCEO.com/RESOURCES

Take a moment to write down the names of all your friends, relatives, co-workers and neighbors, anyone you come into contact with more than twice a year. Everybody.

On a scale of 1–10, rate each friend on their personal excellence. Are they an example of how you want to live your life? Are they an example of someone who has a great career or relationship? Are they in better health? (Ten out of ten.) Or are they a poor example, and your association with them could possibly be holding you back from achieving your best? (One out of ten.)

I'm not suggesting you stop loving those whom you rated poorly, but I am saying it might be time to create some distance between these people, and perhaps increase your proximity to those who are an example of excellence. As the CEO of your life, you must surround yourself with people who lift you up.

A company CEO running a multimillion-dollar business doesn't seek advice from the local milk bar on how to run their company. They seek out multibillion-dollar company CEOs because that is the direction they are taking the company, not in the direction of the milk bar.

35 Plans B, C, D, and E

> " It's not only moving that creates new starting points. Sometimes all it takes is a subtle shift in perspective, an opening of the mind, an intentional pause and reset, or a new route to start to see new options and new possibilities. "
>
> **KRISTIN ARMSTRONG**

Life happens. My dad always quoted the famous line by Robert Burns: "The best-laid plans of mice and men often go awry." Sometimes we can get hung up on a certain plan as a way to achieve our mission. If we take a closer look at that mission, we might find that there are other ways to get it completed.

A client of mine, Kathy, wanted to get pregnant (plan A). She and her husband had tried the traditional way (sex), and they had tried IVF multiple times. Nothing had worked. They were stuck mentally. They both felt like life was being done to them.

When I started coaching Kathy, we spent some time looking at life purpose and missions, making sure that all the missions were aligned to create the best chance for the family mission to be fulfilled.

Next, Kathy spent some time checking in on behaviors, state, and strategy. These were not good. She was not behaving in a way that would allow her body to get pregnant. She was attempting to get pregnant in her work state, dressed in her corporate clothes, with a clipboard crowded with agenda items and a checklist under her arm. Instead, she should have been in a lovemaking state, naked, with music and candles.

Remember, state determines performance. Kathy had no chance.

Next she looked at strategy and became committed to excellence. She did more research on pregnancy, actioned that research, and hung out with people who were in love, making love, and getting pregnant.

Next we talked about plans B, C and D. This involved her looking at her family mission and asking how else she could fulfill it. As we discussed earlier, some things you cannot be a hundred percent responsible for. Kathy could only be responsible for Kathy. There were things in nature outside of her control, like getting pregnant. However, there were things within her control that could maximize her chances of getting pregnant.

What Kathy discovered about her family mission was that its fulfillment wasn't dependent on her having a biological child, or being the one who got pregnant. This opened up options: a) conceive a biological child naturally, b) get pregnant with IVF, c) use a surrogate for pregnancy, d) adopt, or e) foster.

Creating choices didn't take away Kathy's determination and intentions for plan A, but it did free her to feel less trapped, and to know that she had a choice.

Take a look at some of your missions and intentions. How else could you fulfill them?

📖 JOURNAL TIME

Where in life are you feeling a little stuck? Where do you feel you have no choice? Take a look at the mission in that aspect of your life (plan A). How else could you fulfill it? What are your plans B, C, D and E?

36 Book It In

**" There cannot be a crisis next week.
My schedule is already full. "**
HENRY KISSINGER

Sometimes I'm asked: Is there any room for downtime? Does life always have to be about achievement? Is it okay to just sit and watch TV or mess around? Am I a loser if I go out on the town, and drink and eat too much and then sleep in? Does everything have to be about making the world and myself a better place?

The answer is no. The problem comes when we use TV, the Internet, gaming, food, drink, and sleeping in as a distraction from doing the stuff that really matters. This is lazytown. Why do we sometimes find ourselves here? You've worked out what's important. You know your purpose, have a plan, have sorted out who you need to be, and might even have started doing some stuff.

But sometimes life happens, and you go back to old habits (yes, you will still be human even though you have a clear sense of purpose). There are times when you do this as part of a strategy to be unproductive. Maybe you do it randomly, whenever the going gets tough. These distractions found in lazytown become a way not to grow.

The hunger I experienced in writing this book was amazing. Every time a topic became too hard, I would suddenly feel an urgent need to eat. I put on four kilograms, despite exercising more and eating my regular healthy meals.) I went onto scheduled eating, so that by the time the book was finished I was back to my fighting weight.

What is scheduled eating? It means eating to a schedule, with scheduled food. It takes the emotion out of the equation. It means taking the act of eating and putting it in a box marked *Not Urgent But Important.*

Create a schedule

Dwight Eisenhower was a very productive man. What he achieved in his lifetime was amazing. Before becoming president, he was a five-star general in the United States Army, and served as the supreme commander of the Allied forces in Europe during World War II. He became the thirty-fourth president of the United States, serving two terms from 1953 to 1961. While in office, he launched NASA, and the Internet (DARPA), and developed the Atomic Energy Act. Eisenhower was also the first supreme commander of NATO.

> " What is important is seldom urgent, and what is urgent is seldom important. "
> **DWIGHT EISENHOWER**

Somehow Eisenhower found the time to pursue hobbies like golfing and oil painting. He had an amazing ability to maintain his efficiency, not just for short periods but also for most of his life (he died at seventy-eight). His greatest productivity strategy is known as "the Eisenhower box," and it's a great way to think about how you spend your time. It's simply four boxes that you can choose to spend your time in. Yes, you choose.

1. You can do things that are urgent and important.
2. You can do things that are not urgent and important.
3. You can do things that are urgent and not important.
4. You can do things that are not urgent and not important.

You don't have to be a rocket surgeon or brain scientist to work out where not to spend your time. Do not spend time in the not-urgent-and-not-important box. This is the distraction box. This is the box you go to when you want to escape life. Spending time in this box feels unfulfilling and robs you of self-worth. Of course it's okay to watch TV and chill out with a glass of wine. But ask yourself if this activity (or similar) is a distraction from life. Is it not important and not urgent? Or is it important? If you're doing it for reasons that lead you to become a better version of yourself and help create a better world, then I say it's schedulable. Schedule it for when you feel in an empowered state. This will stop it becoming a distraction and taking you away from life to becoming something that is a part of your life.

In my family, Friday treat night is scheduled on everyone's calendar. That's when we have pizza, fish and chips, or barbecue for dinner, and my wife and I have a glass of wine. As a family, we watch a movie, play cards or just sit in front of the fire. It's time in, not time out.

265

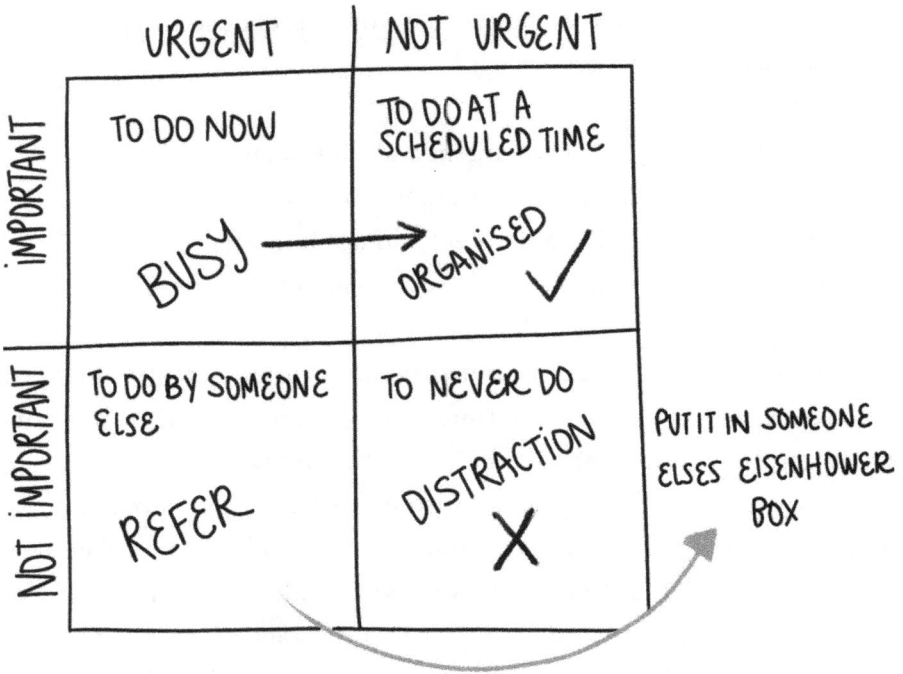

You also want to spend less time in the not-important-and-urgent box. This is a great box to delegate to someone else.

For me, the key to the Eisenhower box is moving as much of my life as I can from the urgent-and-important box to the not-urgent-and-important box. Get scheduled and organized, and create structure around your life. All high performers—people who follow through on their plans—have a structure to their work. They schedule as much of their life as possible, which helps remove the random chance of succeeding as well as the distractions.

By using the important-but-not-urgent box more often, you'll find there are fewer urgent tasks in your life. Life will feel smoother, quieter, more fulfilling, and you will achieve more. You'll be less busy and rushed. By scheduling time for family, exercise, and nutrition, you create time to focus on one task, rather than trying to fit things in between doing other tasks. By focusing on one task, you will become more efficient.

It might see crazy to have to book in time for relationships, health, or even time alone, but in a busy world it's to get caught up in busywork rather than your life's work.

Switching

There's a lot of evidence showing that multitasking is not efficient. Working on a project while answering emails and responding to text messages is inefficient. Multitasking doesn't work. When you think you're multitasking, you're really just switching rapidly between single tasks.

MULTI-TASKING
BOOK WRITING | SWITCH | EMAIL | SWITCH | BOOK WRITING | SWITCH | TEXT | SWITCH | BOOK WRITING

SINGLE-TASKING / MORE PRODUCTIVITY
BOOK WRITING | BOOK WRITING | BOOK WRITING | SWITCH | EMAIL | SWITCH | TEXT

STUFF ON YOUR MIND iE. NOT SCHEDULED
HANGING WITH FAMILY | SWITCH | THINK BUSINESS | SWITCH | HANGING WITH FAMILY | SWITCH | THINK BUSINESS | SWITCH | HANGING

WORK AND FAMILY SCHEDULED MORE FULLFILMENT
THINK BUSINESS | THINK BUSINESS | SWITCH | HANGING WITH FAMILY

Multitasking affects fulfillment as well as productivity. Studies show that when you're distracted, thinking about something that might happen, or about something that might need to be done, it affects your relationship to the primary task. Not only will this affect your own fulfillment, but also the fulfillment of the people around you.

One study looked at students attempting to multitask while studying, and its effect on their grade-point average (GPA). The students were searching for online content not related to courses, using Facebook, emailing, talking on their phones, texting while doing schoolwork. Analyses revealed that using Facebook and texting while doing schoolwork reduced their overall college GPA. They concluded that if students used Facebook or texted while trying to complete schoolwork, it could alter their processing of information and impede deeper learning.

Another study compared heavy media multitaskers to light media multitaskers, monitoring their cognitive control and ability to process information. They found, when deliberately distracting the subjects, that heavy media multitaskers were, on average, 77 milliseconds slower than their light media multitasker equivalents at recognizing changes in patterns.

In a longer-term memory test that asked the subjects to recall elements from the previous experiments, the high media multitaskers more often incorrectly identified the elements. When distracted, high media multitaskers were 426 milliseconds slower than their equivalents to switch to new activities, and 259 milliseconds slower to engage in a new section of the same activity.

The researchers concluded that heavy media multitaskers are more easily distracted by the multiple streams of media they consume, or, alternatively, that those who infrequently multitask are more effective at allocating their attention despite distractions."

Another study looked the relationship between the presence of cellphones and the quality of real-life-person social interactions. In a naturalistic field experiment, a hundred dads were randomly assigned to discuss either a casual or a meaningful topic together. The study found that conversations in the absence of a cellphone were rated as significantly superior to with those conducted in the presence of a cellphone. In fact, people who had conversations without a cellphone reported higher levels of empathetic conversations.

Participants chatting in the presence of a cellphone who were friendly with each other (had a close relationship) reported lower levels of empathy compared with dads who were less friendly.

Just because you know the person well (a family member), it doesn't reduce the need to be focused and present, without distraction.

> " Your conscious brain cannot multitask.
> If I'm speaking to you and checking my
> I-Phone at the same time, I'm doing neither.
> This is why our society is frazzled; this
> misconception that we can consciously do
> more than one thing at a time effectively. "
> **DEEPAK CHOPRA**

Rituals

We have already discussed the importance of rituals. To recap, the more you schedule your life, and add a ritual or routine to your schedule, the more certainty you will have, and the more uncertainty you will be able to handle.

I think of rituals and routines as sacred, unlike habits, which have a negative vibe. Bad habits include smoking, sleeping in, and picking your nose.

I like to think of rituals as planned, scheduled, repetitive behaviors that are sacred. In my experience, all successful people have rituals in their life. As we have discussed, many sports people have a ritual that they use as an anchor to fire off a certain desired state.

" There is a comfort in rituals, and rituals provide a framework for stability when you are trying to find answers. "
DEBORAH NORVILLE

When creating a schedule for your life, I suggest you look for opportunities to create repetition in your week, a routine. It's in routine or discipline that you will find freedom.

" In discipline, we find freedom. "
JOCKO WILLINK

One of the most powerful times in the day to have a ritual is in the morning. How do you start your day? Do you hit the snooze button a few times before getting up, the get up and wonder what to do first? Is every morning based on the randomness of how you feel? Do your mornings look like they come out of a morning generator? If so, you're wasting precious energy, time, and resources. More than that, you're letting the world dictate your day, rather than making sure you are the master of your day.

I strongly suggest that you create a sacred ritual to your mornings. The discipline required to stick to a routine will build your self-confidence, and the routine will build control and certainty into the start of your day. Over time, this routine will become a ritual. It will become something that you schedule your life around.

Starting your day with a ritual prevents you waking overwhelmed by the day ahead. Here is my morning ritual:

5:30 A.M.: Wake (I set an alarm, and although I'm sometimes already awake I wait until 5:30 to get up. I also get up immediately without hitting the snooze button. This is the most important thing you can do to start your day empowered)

5:31 A.M.: Toilet

5:33 A.M.: Dress in gym gear (black under-armour shorts, T-shirt, socks and runners. All my gear is laid out in my wardrobe the night before)

5:35 A.M.: Make morning Berocca

5:36 A.M.: Head into my study

5:40 A.M.: Drink Berocca, and review overnight emails and Facebook (review only, don't respond. I'm just checking to see if there is anything that might alter my schedule for the day)

5:50 A.M.: Drive to personal-training studio

6:00 A.M.: Train for thirty minutes HIIT

6:35 A.M.: Drive home

6:45 A.M.: Have cup of tea with my wife, catch up with kids

7:15 A.M.: Shower, dress (in clothing that I've anchored to who I need to be for the day)

7:45 A.M.: Ready to tackle the day's scheduled missions and their plans

I stick to this ritual Monday to Friday, and ninety percent of the weekends. I sometimes alter it depending on the missions I have planned for the weekend.

I'm not saying that you, too, need to get up early, or exercise, or drink tea. I am strongly encouraging you to create a ritual with what you do in the first hour of the day. Make the day yours. Own it. Start it on your terms. You'll find this process much easier once you're clear on your life purpose and missions.

With clear plans and goals in place, and a commitment to excellence (immersed in what you're pursuing at the moment), you'll find yourself feeling like you're being *pulled* out of bed. You'll wake before the alarm you enter the day with determination rather than dread.

It's time for you to decide what's important, schedule it and create rituals within the schedule.

JOURNAL TIME

LifeCEO.com/RESOURCES

If you have never done this exercise, I have to tell you it's one of the best ways to feel empowered. Get yourself a weekly calendar, or simply draw this up in your journal. You'll need seven columns, one for each day of the week. Down the left-hand side, write the time, starting at five A.M. (or your wakeup time) in thirty-minute increments up to eleven P.M. (or your bedtime).

I use this method to do my rough draft, and then I use an electronic calendar to play with it and tidy up the schedule. It also allows me to schedule things that may take only five minutes to complete.

Now start by putting in the big things. What are the most important and largest consumers of time? Be realistic about the amount of time you allocate, but also look for ways to compress the time.

Now add the smaller things (not as important and less time). Make sure you schedule time for the things that feel good and are good for you (chilling in front of the TV, gardening, reading the paper on Sunday morning).

Keep going until the entire calendar is full, with no empty spaces. You might even schedule a time when nothing is on, when you can do some of the more urgent and important things.

You have now set the intention for how your week (life) will look.

37 Be in Charge of Your Inbox

> ❝This is a ruthless world, and one must be ruthless to cope with it.❞
> **CHARLIE CHAPLIN**

These days these is less and less snail mail, and many of us are finding our computer inboxes filling up with emails. Over time, this can become overwhelming and create a little stickiness.

Do you dread going into your study or office because you know your in-tray will be full? Is your email inbox full of emails? Are some of them emails you haven't even got around to reading yet? Some will be important, and will help you achieve what you really want in life. Some will be distractions only. They might have interesting subject lines promising you something important. It doesn't matter. Don't go there.

I have a solution for dealing with email that I've been using for years. It's helped me keep paper in-tray empty, and my email inbox beautifully clear. It's called the TRAF technique. The TRAF technique is simple and powerful, but you have to be disciplined to use it.

T = Trash: It's time to throw out some stuff. When you open your paper mail, be ruthless. Look at the envelope. If it looks like junk, mass mail, ask yourself if your time would be best utilized opening it and reading it, or throwing it away. I'm suggesting you go with the big T. Trash it. Throw it in the bin.

If you do open the mail, again, be ruthless. Look at it and ask yourself if you really need to do anything with it, or can you just throw it away? Trash it. Throw it out.

R = Refer: The second thing you have to ask yourself when you open that mail is if you need to refer it onto somebody else. This is especially important when dealing with emails. When you open your email, have a quick scan and ask yourself if this is something for you to do, or for someone else to do. Even if you could respond to it quickly, if it's not for you to do, forward it. Refer it to someone else.

A + Action: Is the email you've opened something you need to action? If so, don't trash it. Don't refer it. Once you've decided that it's for you, ask yourself if you can handle it within the next two minutes. If the answer is yes, action it immediately. Type a reply, attach a file if you need to, and hit the send button. Get rid of it from your system.

If you think it will take longer than two minutes, leave it in your inbox to action when you have that administrative time scheduled in your calendar.

F = File: You might open an email and decide that you don't want to trash it. You want to keep it. It's something important. You don't want to refer it on. There's no action be taken. It's something you want to store for another day. Move it from your inbox into the relevant email folders.

It's the same thing with paper. You might open a letter and know there's nothing you need to action immediately. Maybe it's a bank statement, something like that. Punch some holes in it, and put it in a folder or filing cabinet. File it away.

A quick recap: T= trash, R = refer, A = action, and F = file, in that order. If you apply this system, and are ruthless with it, and stay disciplined, it will work. That sometimes means you're going to have to hit the trash button, but that's okay. Sometimes you have to be ruthless. If you apply this system, I promise you that your inbox will remain empty. Your in-tray will remain empty. It will be a pleasure to come into your study or office and open your email. You will have created more space in your head and desk for more productive and creative endeavors.

Part 7

STEP 5

PROFIT: REPORT BACK ON YOUR RESULTS

38 Was It Profitable?

"Once I've decided to do something, I do usually try to carry it through to fruition."
SIR EDMUND HILLARY

Now that you are clear on purpose, and are making plans, managing your state, and taking action, what is the result? Have your actions borne fruit?

I love the word *fruition*; it's so sweet sounding. It comes from early Latin and means an "act of enjoying."

Any company must be profitable. It must, after allocation of assets, make a profit. Even not-for-profit companies and charities make a profit, even if they then give it away. There must be some gain for all company's efforts.

The largest charity in the US raised $3.8 billion in 2016, and after deploying $500 million in assets, gave away, through charitable services, $3.3 billion. The company mission: "United Way fights for the health, education, and financial stability of every person in every community."

No fruit

Now its time to take stock and review your results. Do you feel more fulfilled? Are you happy with the results? If you got what you wanted and don't feel fulfilled, or the results are not what you wanted, ask yourself a few questions:

- Was what I pursued in alignment with my life purpose and mission, or was it a *should*?
- Did I have well-formed plans that were in alignment, with clearly identifiable steps? Did I have clear, well-defined goals that I could be responsible for?
- Did I manage my personality? Did I keep my awareness with who I needed to be for myself, others and for success?
- Did I take action, consistently? Did I immerse myself in achieving the outcome?

Most commonly, I find that poor results are based on one or more of these questions coming back with a negative answer. If that happens to you, that's okay, throw a pity party if you want to. Do it well, set a deadline to stop the carry-on, and then find out what went wrong. Remember that the definition of insanity is doing the same thing over and over again and expecting a different result. Take responsibility for the outcome; don't look for blame or fault.

Find out where you went wrong, and rectify it. Start taking action straightaway; don't sit back paralyzed by the feedback. That's where being stuck starts, where ego rears its head and does engages you in the I-told-you-so conversation.

> ❝ There is no better than adversity. Every defeat, every heartbreak, every loss, contains its own seed, its own lesson on how to improve your performance the next time. ❞
>
> **MALCOLM X**

Put the poor result in perspective. What did you learn along the way? Where did you hold back? Who could you have called? What email didn't you send? In what situation were you not the best version of you? If you didn't get what you want, what did you get? What was the benefit of the journey? In what way are you better? How is the world around you better?

Quality questions will not only sort out your state (remember, language is important), but they will also help you find the answers to solving how you can do it differently next time.

The full fruit salad

But if it did go as planned, and after all that effort you got the result you wanted, take a moment and celebrate. Don't skip the opportunity to tip the win into our bank account. Don't let it slip through your fingers without feeling the full weight and value of it. Take a moment to see, hear, and feel the moment.

> ❝ The more you praise and celebrate your life, the more there is in life to celebrate. ❞
> **OPRAH WINFREY**

When someone wins an event at the Olympics, they don't just get a pat on the back, a "well done" and a "see you in four years." No way. The games stop, there is silence, the national anthem is played, the winner gets to stand high on the podium, a medal is placed around their neck, their hand is shaken, the world applauds, they have their picture taken, and they appear in newspapers around the world.

Imagine taking that approach to your wins in the future. Stop, put on your theme song, dance, clap, scream with joy, and pump the air. Be in the moment. Add this success to your memory. Take credit for it.

So often I find my high-achieving clients take responsibility (sometimes blame or fault) for things that don't work, but are too quick to skip over or not take any responsibility at all for things that do work. I suggest you create a ritual to celebrate your wins and successes. This will help you anchor the experience to access again when life gets tough, at times when you're questioning your abilities. It will burn the experience into your mind, which will be important when you need to look for things to be grateful about.

39 Gratitude

"Gratitude unlocks the fullness of life. It turns what we have into enough, and more. It turns denial into acceptance, chaos to order, and confusion to clarity. It can turn a meal into a feast, a house into a home, a stranger into a friend."

MELODY BEATTIE

No personal-development book would be complete without a chapter on gratitude. I have also discussed its importance in the chapter on fear. Now is also a great moment to spend some time filling up this account, creating language around the images, sounds, and feelings that have come from making it to the finish of your current journey.

What were the lessons? What did you learn about yourself and the world? What are you grateful for? Who are you grateful for, or to?

JOURNAL TIME

This exercise is easy and fun. Write a list of all the things, people, experiences, events, and emotions you're grateful for as a result of the journey in getting the outcome, as well as the outcome itself.

You may choose to do this in a special section of your journal so you can add to it later, when you find more to be grateful for.

This will become a place to go to when you find yourself stuck, and you will if you're constantly seeking growth. Remember, you are human.

" Feeling gratitude and not expressing it is like wrapping a present and not giving it. "
WILLIAM ARTHUR WARD

Who helped out along the way? Who could you share your gratitude with? I encourage you to reach out to those who supported and championed you during the journey. Who gave you a leg up? Who dared to challenge you when you needed it? Who championed you, mentored you, or believed in you? Who said you can do it?

Send them a card, email, or text. Better still, give them a call and express your gratitude verbally. It's yet another opportunity to grow. You're worth it, and so are they.

As your life CEO, the buck stops with you. Give gratitude for the work you and others have done. Take note of where you have battled tough times and won, or lost but gave your best. The more you look inwards to fill you cup of gratitude, the better. Make a habit of being grateful.

" When it comes to life the critical thing is whether you take things for granted or take them with gratitude. "
GILBERT K. CHESTERTON

40 What's Next?

Successful people maintain a positive focus in life no matter what is going on around them. They stay focused on their past successes rather than their past failures, and on the next action steps they need to take to get them closer to the fulfillment of their goals rather than all the other distractions that life presents to them.

JACK CANFIELD

Now you have looked at your profit, and what you have learned during the journey, including celebrating the outcome. You have topped up your gratitude bank account and shown others your gratitude. You have taken a moment. What's next?

What's next is the next step. Your life purpose is not a destination; it's a direction. All you have done is reach a destination. What's the next destination? Take a look at your life-purpose statement and your mission statements. What is the next thing that could help fulfill both purpose and mission? And which mission needs some attention right now?

Take a moment to reflect on that mission, and ask yourself what you could do to become a better version of you in this mission, and make the world (others) better as a result of pursuing it.

Create a goal, check in with who you need to be, and take action. Simple.

Here's the thing: life is unpredictable. Despite all your best plans, and your best efforts and intentions, sometimes things don't turn out how you hoped. This book is less about getting what you want than becoming who you want to be on the journey to getting what you want.

Afterword

This book is the result of my lifelong desire to help people be their best. Many of the original concepts, and the structure, chapter layout and stories did not make it into the final draft. And while this book is the best that I can write at this precise time, it's not exactly the book I had planned to write. Here's the thing: life is unpredictable. Despite our best plans, efforts and intentions, things don't always turn out the way we intend.

Sometimes they turn out better.

Through writing this book, I became a better dad and a better business owner. I became healthier, met new people and had some incredible conversations and, importantly, tried on whole new levels of courage, consistency, discipline, and focus. I realized that, for me, writing a book was about more than just getting published; it was about the experiences and character I had and developed along the way.

I hope that through reading this book, you will become less about getting what you want and more about becoming who you want to be on the journey to getting what you want.

Do what matters. Unleash your greatness. Be amazing. Go out into the world and flourish.

Make it count.

References

Chapter 10

"Purpose in life predicts allostatic load ten years later." J Psychosom Res. 2015 November; 79(5): 451–4t7. doi:10.1016/j.jpsychores.2015.09.013.

Midlife in the U.S., http://www.midus.wisc.edu/),

"Purpose in life predicts better emotional recovery from negative stimuli." Stacey M. Schaefer 1, 2, 3*, Jennifer Morozink Boylan 4, Carien M. van Reekum 6, Regina C. Lapate1, 2, 3, Catherine J. Norris 7, Carol D. Ryff1 5, Richard J. Davidson 1, 2, 3.

Bond, Malcolm & T. Feather, N. (1988). "Some correlates of structure and purpose in the use of time." *Journal of Personality and Social Psychology*, 55. 321–329. 10.1037/0022–3514.55.2.321.

Hill, P. L., Turiano, N. A., Mroczek, D. K., & Burrow, A. L. (2016). "The value of a purposeful life: a sense of purpose predicts greater income and net worth." *Journal of Research in Personality*, 65, 38–42.

Psychosom Med. 2009 Jun;71(5):574-9. doi: 10.1097/PSY.0b013e3181a5a7c0. Epub 2009 May 4. "The purpose in life is associated with mortality among community-dwelling older persons." Boyle PA1, Barnes LL, Buchman AS, Bennett DA.

Chapter 13

Apple releases updated diversity report, "A Lot More Work."

The Cook Doctrine at Apple/Fortune.

Chapter 19

Surprising to-do list facts(todolistblog.blogspot.com.au/p/surprising-to-do-list-facts).

Chapter 26

Journal of Psychiatric Research, volume 46, issue 5, May 2012, pages 574–581, "Facing depression with botulinum toxin: A randomized trial." AxelWollmer.

The Tell: The Little Clues That Reveal Big Truths about Who We Are, November 12, 2013, Matthew Hertenstein.

Harker, L., & Keltner, D. (2001). "Expressions of positive emotion in women's college yearbook pictures and their relationship to personality and life outcomes across adulthood." *Journal of Personality and Social Psychology*, 80(1), 112–124.

J Pers Soc Psychol. 1988 May;54(5):768–77. "Inhibiting and facilitating conditions of the human smile: a nonobtrusive test of the facial feedback hypothesis." Strack F1, Martin LL, Stepper S.

Appl Psychophysiol Biofeedback. 2004 Sep;29(3):189–95. "The effects of upright and slumped postures on the recall of positive and negative thoughts." Wilson VE1, Peper E.

J Behav Ther Exp Psychiatry. 2017 Mar; 54:143-149. doi: 10.1016/j.jbtep.2016.07.015. Epub 2016 Jul30. "Upright posture improves effect and fatigue in people with depressive symptoms." Wilkes C1, Kydd R1, Sagar M2, Broadbent E3.

Health Psychol. 2015 Jun;34(6):632-41. doi: 10.1037/hea0000146. Epub 2014 Sep 15. "Do slump and upright postures affect stress responses? A randomized trial." Nair S1, Sagar M2, Sollers J 3rd1, Consedine N1, Broadbent E1.

"Effect of frequent interruptions of prolonged sitting on self-perceived levels of energy, mood, food cravings and cognitive function." Int J Behav Nutr Phys Act. 2016 Nov 3;13(1):113. Bergouignan A1,2,3,4, Legget KT5, De Jong N6, Kealey E6, Nikolovski J7, Groppel JL8, Jordan C8, O'Day R9, Hill JO6,10, Bessesen DH6,10.

Cogn Emot. 2016 Sep 14:1-16. doi: 10.1080/02699931.2016.1225003. "Embodied mood regulation: the impact of body posture on mood recovery, negative thoughts, and mood-congruent recall." Veenstra L1, Schneider IK1, Koole SL1.

Psychosom Med. 2009 Jun;71(5):580–7. doi: 10.1097/ PSY.0b013e3181a2515c. Epub 2009 May 4. "An embodiment of sadness and depression: gait patterns associated with dysphoric mood." Michalak J1, Troje NF, Fischer J, Vollmar P, Heidenreich T, Schulte D.

J Abnorm Psychol. 2013 Feb;122(1):45-50. doi: 10.1037/a0029881. Epub 2012 Sep 17. "Acute exercise attenuates negative affect following repeated sad mood inductions in persons who have recovered from depression." Mata J1, Hogan CL, Joormann J, Waugh CE, Gotlib IH.

Appetite 2012 April; 771–775 Vol 58 Issue 2. "Which comes first in food—mood relationships, foods or moods?" Helen M.Hendy.

White, Bonnie A. Horwath, Caroline C. Conner, Tamlin S. "Many apples a day keep the blues away: daily experiences of negative and positive affect and food consumption in young adults." *British Journal of Health Psychology* 2013.

Ann Neurol. 2013 Oct;74(4):580-91. doi: 10.1002/ana.23944. Epub 2013 Sep 16. "Mediterranean diet, stroke, cognitive impairment, and depression: a meta-analysis." Psaltopoulou T1, Sergentanis TN, Panagiotakos DB, Sergentanis IN, Kosti R, Scarmeas N.

Meryl P. Gardner, Brian Wansink, Junyong Kim, Se-Bum Park. "Better moods for better eating? How mood influences food choice." *Journal of Consumer Psychology*, Volume 24, Issue 3, 2014, Pages 320–335, ISSN 1057–7408.

O'Neil, Adrienne et al. "Relationship between diet and mental health in children and adolescents: a systematic review." *American Journal of Public Health* 104.10 (2014): e31–e42. PMC. Web. 26 Sept. 2017.

Psychol Sci. 2004 Apr;15(4):243-7. "Why the sunny side is up: association between effect and vertical position." Meier BP1, Robinson MD.

Chapter 34

"Dynamic spread of happiness in a large social network: longitudinal analysis over 20 years in the Framingham Heart Study." BMJ 2008; 337 doi: https://doi.org/10.1136/bmj.a2338 (published05 December 2008). Cite this as BMJ 2008;337:a2338.

"The spread of obesity in a large social network over 32 years." Nicholas A. Christakis, M.D., Ph.D., M.P.H., and James H. Fowler, Ph.D. N Engl J Med 2007; 357:370-379July 26, 2007DOI: 10.1056/NEJMsa066082.

"The spread of alcohol consumption behavior in a large social network." *Annals of Internal Medicine.* J. Niels Rosenquist, MD, Ph.D.; Joanne Murabito, MD; James H. Fowler, Ph.D.; and Nicholas A. Christakis, MD, PhD.

"The collective dynamics of smoking in a large social network." Nicholas A. Christakis, M.D., Ph.D., M.P.H., and James H. Fowler, Ph.D. N Engl J Med 2008; 358:2249-2258May 22, 2008.

Breaking Up Is Hard to Do, Unless Everyone Else Is Doing It Too: Social Network Effects on Divorce in a Longitudinal Sample. Rose McDermott, James H. Fowler, Nicholas A. Christakis.

Chapter 36

Reynol Junco, Shelia R. Cotten, No A 4 U: "The relationship between multitasking and academic performance." *Computers & Education*, Volume 59, Issue 2, 2012, Pages 505-514, ISSN 0360-1315.

PNAS National Academy of Sciences. September 15, 2009 vol. 106 no. 37 15583–15587.

"The iPhone effect the quality of in-person social interactions in the presence of mobile devices." Shalini Misra, Lulu Cheng, Jamie Genevie. First published July 1, 2014, Sage Journals Research Article.

More Info

For more information about becoming your Life CEO including:

Activity Downloads
Bonus Chapters
Free Gifts

Go to
LifeCEO.com

www.ingramcontent.com/pod-product-compliance
Lightning Source LLC
Chambersburg PA
CBHW020829210326
41598CB00019B/1851